Chairn
Appet
Soups
Veget
Eggs,
Grillin
Fish &
Meat,
Desse

A Culinary View of the Commonwealth
Junior League of Richmond

Junior League of Richmond

The Junior League of Richmond was founded in 1929 by 59 energetic young women. It is a non-profit organization committed to improving the Richmond community through the effective action and leadership of trained volunteers. League members actively give of their talents and time to a wide variety of volunteer projects and non-profit groups throughout the Richmond area.

The desire to serve the needs of the community prompted the newly formed Richmond League in 1929 to offer its service to the area's Memorial Guidance Clinic. Out of this concern came the Therapeutic Workshop, the first of its kind in the country.

League members converted a garage into a workshop for woodcraft, and the Virginia Mechanics' Institute lent a room for woodwork. Art and music classes were conducted by the Junior League volunteers in an effort to provide constructive recreation for children. Because the development of the Therapeutic Workshop was a successful beginning, it has served as a model for the League's future efforts in the Richmond community.

For over 65 years, the Junior League of Richmond has contributed financial and volunteer support to a wide range of community projects including the Science Museum of Virginia, Women's Resource Center, Maymont, Parents Anonymous, Chesapeake Bay Foundation, Reception and Diagnostic Center for Children, Senior Center, Medical College of Virginia, and Family and Children's Services.

Most recently, the Richmond League has been the catalyst for foundation of an innovative parenting program in the inner-city community of Bainbridge that provides a preschool and daycare program for children and educational training for their parents. And, in partnership with the Literacy Council of Metropolitan Richmond, the League has raised the awareness of adult illiteracy in Richmond.

With the purchase of its current headquarters, the Mayo-Carter House, the League expanded its community support to include serving as a catalyst for the historic preservation of the 200 block of West Franklin Street in Richmond.

The house, one of the first to be renovated on the block, was designed in 1895 by the prominent New York architectural firm Carere and Hastings, and represents the Beaux Arts style that was popular at the turn of the century. This firm also designed the New York Public Library, and, in Richmond, The Jefferson Hotel and The Commonwealth Club.

The resources needed to support the League's community projects are raised through various channels including The Clothes Rack, a thrift shop founded in 1948 that offers Richmond residents quality used clothing and housewares at affordable prices, and an annual Book and Author Dinner that has been a Richmond tradition since 1945. In addition to **Virginia Fare**, the League markets another cookbook, **Virginia Seasons**, which offers new recipes from the Old Dominion.

The Junior League of Richmond's long history of service to the Richmond community serves as a blueprint for charting a future course. With a total membership of over 1,200, the League will continue to seek opportunities to commit its trained and dedicated volunteers to worthwhile community service.

Contents

Virginia Fare Menus

Cool Summer Entertaining at the Beach

Brie with Sun-Dried Tomato Topping
Tuna with Mustard Sauce
Lemon Rice
Spinach and Strawberry Crunch Salad
White Chocolate Russe with Raspberry-Strawberry Sauce

Holiday Cocktail Party in the Upper Valley

Cheese Pesto and Sun-Dried Tomato Mold
Pickled Oysters
Gingered Cream Cheese Grapes
Smoked Trout Pâté
Artichokes Florentine
Hot Crab Spread
Zesty Pork Pastries
Smithfield Ham with Chive Mustard Spread on Party Rolls
Lemon Coconut Squares
Miniature Chocolate Chip Macaroons
Champagne Punch

Virginia Fare Menus

New Year's Day Buffet in the Capital

Fresh Fruit Dip with Apple Wedges
Spinach Dip Olé with Fresh Cut Vegetables
Easy Garlic and Onion Bread Wedges
Mexican Cheesecake
Pork Tenderloin with Cinnamon and Rosy Relish on Buns
Vegetarian Chili
Praline Cheesecake
New Year's Day Punch

A Candlelight Dinner Party in Hot Springs

Dilled Shrimp
Fontina Herb Spread
White Onion Soup
Spinach Salad with Warm Champagne Dressing
Seafood Stuffed Beef Tenderloin
Browned Rice with Artichokes
Tipsy Carrots
Raspberries and Sour Cream

Dining with Wine

- **Pasta**

With red sauces	*Sauvignon Blanc*
	Merlot
With white sauces	*Chardonnay*

- **Beef**

Roast beef, steaks, hamburgers	*Cabernet Sauvignon*
	Merlot
	Pinot Noir
	Chambourcin

- **Lamb**

  Pinot Noir
  Merlot
  Cabernet Sauvignon

- **Pork**

Chops, roasts	*Riesling*
	Vidal Blanc
	Cabernet Sauvignon
Ham	*Gewurztraminer*
	Riesling

- **Poultry**

Chicken, Turkey	*Chardonnay*
	Sauvignon Blanc
	Seyval Blanc
	Vidal Blanc
	Pinot Noir

- **Seafood**

Shellfish with sauces	*Chardonnay*
	Vidal Blanc
Shellfish without sauces	*Seyval Blanc*
	Sauvignon Blanc

- **Fish**

  Seyval Blanc
  Chardonnay
  Sauvignon Blanc
  Vidal Blanc
  Riesling
  Gewurztraminer

- **Desserts**

  Gewurztraminer
  Riesling

An Herb Guide

	Basil	Oregano and Marjoram	Rosemary	Sage	Tarragon	Thyme
• **Beef**	Add basil to meatball recipes.	Marjoram may replace thyme in beef bourguign–onne.	Add to butter, salt and pepper and brush on steaks.	Add a pinch to steaks on grill.	Use fresh tarragon and chervil for bearnaise sauce.	Sprinkle lightly over a veal shoulder before roasting.
• **Pork**	Sprinkle lightly over pan-browned pork chops.	Add 2 tsp. oregano to pork goulash.	Rub on pork roast with garlic and sage.	Grind raw smoked ham, sage and favorite ingredients for ham loaf.	Mix small amount with gravy for sliced pork.	Rub leaves on ham before baking.
• **Lamb**	Rub on leg of lamb.	Marinate lamb chops in white wine, onion, bay leaf, pepper and marjoram.	Add to marinade for shish kabob.	Rub over stuffed shoulder of lamb.	Add a pinch to shep–herd's pie made with leftover lamb.	Good with leftover lamb in scotch broth.
• **Poultry**	Add with marjoram and thyme to chicken cacciatore.	Add small amount of marjoram to poultry stuffing.	Add some sprigs to pan after frying chicken. Good gravy.	Rub on chicken before baking.	Add to cold chicken salad.	Add to a wine-and-honey-based marinade for chicken.
• **Fish**	Puree 1 cup fresh leaves, cube butter, 3T clam juice. Use basil butter on salmon.	Add small amount to buttered bread crumbs for stuffed flounder.	Brush trout fillets with parsley and rosemary butter.	Sprinkle small amount over scallop and shrimp shish kebob.	Cold poached fish with green mayon-naise: Blend spinach, chives and tarragon with mayon-naise.	Marinate left-over broiled fish fillets 24 hrs. with thyme, onion, sliced lemon, olive oil. Serve cold.
• **Vegetables**	Add to ratatouille a few minutes before serving.	Mix either herb with butter and use sparingly with most vegetables.	Sprinkle on peas with butter.	Add a pinch to cold string bean salad with vinaigrette dressing.	Add a small amount to stuffed baked potatoes.	Add 2 tsp. to a pound of mixed vegetables with parsley, lemon, oregano, shallots, butter. Simmer.

Substitute dried herbs at rate of ⅓ to ½ amount of fresh herbs.

Chef's Chart

• Measurements

Pinch	=	less than ⅛ t.
1 t.	=	⅓ T.
1 T.	=	3 t.
2 T.	=	⅛ cup or 1 oz.
4 T.	=	¼ cup
5⅓ T.	=	⅓ cup
8 T.	=	½ cup
16 T.	=	1 cup
⅜ cup	=	5 T.
⅝ cup	=	10 T.

1 cup	=	½ pt. or 8 fl. oz.
2 cups	=	1 pint
2 pints	=	1 quart
4 quarts	=	1 gallon
8 quarts	=	1 peck
4 pecks	=	1 bushel
1 lb.	=	16 oz.
1 fl. oz.	=	2 T.
16 fl. oz.	=	1 pint
1 jigger	=	3 T.

• Substitutions

Baking powder, 1 teaspoon = ¼ t. soda plus ½ t. cream of tartar
Chocolate, 1 oz. or square = 3 T. cocoa plus 1½ t. fat
Cornstarch, 1 tablespoon = 2 T. flour
Cream, heavy, 1 cup = ¾ cup milk plus ⅓ cup fat (this will not whip)
Cream, light, 1 cup = ⅞ cup milk plus 3 T. fat
Garlic, 1 clove = ⅛ t. garlic powder or garlic salt
Herbs, fresh, 1 tablespoon = 1 t. dried herbs
Honey, 1 cup = ¾ cup sugar plus ¼ cup water
Ketchup, 1 cup = 1 cup tomato sauce plus ½ cup sugar and 2 T. vinegar
Lemon juice, 1 teaspoon = ½ t. vinegar
Milk, 1 cup = ½ cup evaporated milk plus ½ cup water
Mustard, dry, 1 teaspoon = 1 T. prepared mustard
Onion, ¼ cup chopped or 1 small = 1 tablespoon dried
Sour Cream, 1 cup = 1 cup evaporated milk plus 1 T. vinegar (let thicken)
Sugar, 1 cup = 1⅓ cups brown sugar, lightly packed
Sugar, 1 cup = 1 cup honey plus ¼ t. soda (reduce liquid in recipe by ¼ cup)
Tomato juice, 1 cup = ½ cup tomato sauce plus ½ cup water
Tomato paste, 1 tablespoon = 1 T. ketchup
Yogurt, 1 cup unflavored = 1 cup buttermilk

• Grilling Times

Chicken Breast	15 to 20 minutes total
Duck Breast	20 to 25 minutes total
Fish (1 inch thick)	7 to 10 minutes total
Flank steaks	5 to 15 minutes total
Hamburgers	8 to 15 minutes total
Lamb Chops (1 inch thick)	7 to 10 minutes per side
Pork Chops (1 inch thick)	7 to 10 minutes per side
Veal Chops (1 inch thick)	7 to 10 minutes per side
Ribs	26 to 60 minutes total
Steaks (1 inch thick)	6 to 16 minutes per side

Appetizers & Beverages

The Holy City

Richmonders used to say their city was founded, like Rome, on seven hills. Which seven hills provoked a running dispute. Even now someone will rear back and name his favorites - and wait to see who challenges the list. For its Roman hills and other reasons, older Virginians still sometimes refer to Richmond as the Holy City.

On one claim for the Richmond area, all agree: the superiority of the Hanover tomato to any other on Earth. Lauded by generations, it is mythic. There are those who assert that the apple of which Adam and Eve partook was really the love-apple, an early synonym for the tomato, and it was most certainly the progenitor of the Hanover.

And when you cup in your hands - you need both to hold it comfortably - a luscious Hanover, fresh picked from the fields, a deep rosy red from its long sojourn in the sun, and cut into it for a tomato sandwich, the thick red section at the center, dripping juices, laps over the slice of bread and you understand why our Grand Parents were willing to risk tasting it. And while you're making the sandwich, you might keep in mind that Richmond-based C.F. Sauer Company concocts two fine mayonnaises, Duke's and Sauer's. Hellmann's is excellent, too. Other consumers may opt for Kraft or what not; but, really, most any spread will do for a Hanover.

Edward Borchers, former director of an agricultural research station in Virginia Beach, says it's a pity Hanover farmers didn't copyright the name years ago the way Georgians did Vidalia onions.

Hanover's sandy, well-drained soil is a blessing, says former extension agent Ralph LaRue. Hanovers ripen early and reach Richmond's stores first. They become, for good reason, the standard for judging other varieties. Blindfolded, LaRue believes he could identify the Hanover.

Hanovers are grown on stakes. The plants have to be tied and suckered to remove bunches of shoots and foliage from between the branches. Free of cover, the tomatoes ripen fully in the sun; but, so exposed, they develop slight calluses around the stems. "The cracks don't do much for appearances, but they define the Hanover tomato. The slight blemish becomes its trademark," LaRue said. Oh excellent blemish that signifies perfection! It recalls poet Robert Herrick exclaiming: "A sweet disorder in the dress" and other slight untidiness "do more bewitch me, than when art is too precise in every part."

Requiring more nurturing by the farmer than other kinds of tomatoes, Hanover tomatoes cost more to grow than tomatoes that are unstaked or gassed into maturity or shipped while still green. The tardy arrival of less costly kinds tends to drive Hanovers off the market. But they linger in home gardens, and there is no friend like a friend who grows Hanovers.

As to those ubiquitous hills, in 1937 the City Council tried, in vain, to fix in the law these seven: Union, Church, Council Chamber, French Garden, Shockoe, Gamble's, and Navy. Advocates of a half dozen other hills, including Oregon, Libby, and Diamond, objected so the hills are still in limbo.

Richmond is the Capital of Virginia and was the Capital of the Confederacy. Earlier, it was home to Chief Justice John Marshall and heard Patrick Henry crying "Liberty or Death!" in St. John's. And what other state can claim a capitol designed by Thomas Jefferson?

As well as a tomato to match the Hanover?

-Guy Friddell

Oysters Rockefeller Dip

½ cup butter
1 cup finely chopped green
  onions
½ cup chopped lettuce
½ cup chopped green bell
  pepper
½ cup chopped celery
½ cup chopped fresh parsley
1 cup frozen spinach, thawed
  and squeezed dry
½ cup bread crumbs
1 pint oysters, drained and
  chopped
⅛ teaspoon minced garlic
¼ teaspoon salt
¼ teaspoon pepper
5-6 drops hot pepper sauce

- Melt butter in medium skillet; sauté onions, lettuce, green pepper, celery, parsley, and spinach for 5 minutes over medium heat.
- Add bread crumbs and oysters to vegetable mixture in skillet; simmer 3-5 minutes.
- Add garlic, salt, pepper, and hot pepper sauce; simmer 5 minutes longer.
- Serve in chafing dish with melba rounds.

Yield: 1 quart

Oysters, clams, and crabs are abundant in the waters of the Chesapeake Bay and its tributaries and in the shallow waters of the Eastern Shore. Virginia ranks third nationally in seafood production, following Alaska and Louisiana.

Hot Shrimp Dip

1½ cups cooked shrimp, cut
  into bite-size pieces
1 cup Parmesan cheese
1 cup mayonnaise
1 dash garlic salt
1 dash Worcestershire sauce
1 dash hot pepper sauce

- Preheat oven to 350°.
- Combine all ingredients. Spoon mixture into a small, lightly greased casserole dish.
- Bake for 20 minutes or until bubbly. Serve with crackers.

Yield: 6-8 servings

Substitute low-fat mayonnaise, if desired.

Easy and delicious! May be prepared ahead of time and refrigerated until ready to bake.

Spinach Dip Olé

1 (10 ounce) package frozen
   chopped spinach, thawed
   and squeezed dry
1 (16 ounce) jar salsa
   (medium or hot)
1 (4¼ ounce) can black olives,
   drained and sliced
1 (8 ounce) package cream
   cheese, cubed
2 cups grated Monterey Jack
   cheese
1 tablespoon red wine vinegar
Salt and pepper to taste

- Preheat oven to 400°.
- Combine all ingredients. Pour into a shallow baking dish.
- Bake for approximately 35 minutes until bubbly and top is brown. Serve with tortilla chips.

Yield: 8 servings

Sprinkle with fresh cilantro for added flavor.

Always a hit!

Light Spinach and Artichoke Dip

1 (10 ounce) package frozen
   spinach, thawed and
   squeezed dry
2 (14 ounce) cans artichoke
   hearts, drained
3 tablespoons low-fat
   mayonnaise
1½ tablespoons Dijon
   mustard
¾ cup grated Parmesan cheese
¼ cup chopped green onion
1 teaspoon minced garlic
½ teaspoon salt
⅛ teaspoon pepper
Extra Parmesan cheese

- Preheat oven to 350°. Spray a 1-quart casserole dish with non-stick vegetable spray.
- Place spinach, artichokes, mayonnaise, mustard, and Parmesan into food processor bowl; pulse several times until chunky (do not over-process). Stir in onion, garlic, salt, and pepper. Pour into casserole dish. Sprinkle with extra Parmesan cheese.
- Bake for 15-20 minutes or until top is golden and inside is heated through. Serve with shredded wheat crackers.

Yield: 6-8 servings

This dip can be made without spinach and still tastes great!

May be made ahead of time and refrigerated. Increase baking time to 25 minutes.

Fantastic...a real crowd pleaser!

16

Hot Crab Spread

12 ounces cream cheese
4½ tablespoons mayonnaise
3 tablespoons sherry
2 teaspoons Dijon mustard
½ teaspoon sugar
½ teaspoon salt
Juice of ½ lemon
1 pound cooked crabmeat

- Combine all ingredients except crabmeat in top of double boiler. Heat until mixture is smooth and creamy.
- Gently fold in crabmeat.
- Serve in a chafing dish with mild crackers, toast points, or in pastry shells.

Yield: 6-8 servings

Very easy...very elegant! A delicious addition to your next cocktail party.

Smoked Oyster Dip

1 (8 ounce) package cream cheese, softened
1 scant cup mayonnaise
4 dashes hot pepper sauce
1 tablespoon lemon juice
1 (4 ounce) can chopped black olives
1 (3.5 ounce) can smoked oysters, well drained (or rinsed) and chopped

- Combine cream cheese, mayonnaise, hot sauce, and lemon juice in a medium-sized mixing bowl. Stir until smooth.
- Fold in black olives and smoked oysters.
- Serve immediately or cover and refrigerate for later use.
- Serve with plain crackers, bread sticks, or raw vegetables.

Yield: 3 cups

• • •

Virginia is one of the four U.S. states designated as commonwealths. The other three are Kentucky, Massachusetts, and Pennsylvania.

Fresh Fruit Dip

1 (8 ounce) package cream
cheese, softened
1 (7 ounce) jar marshmallow
cream
1 teaspoon orange peel
1 pinch of ginger
½ teaspoon Triple Sec
Pineapple juice for desired
consistency

- Combine all ingredients.
- Chill before serving.
- Serve with fresh fruit pieces.

Yield: 2 cups

Crushed pineapple may be added for texture, if desired.

An unusual treat...a great sweet dip!

Very quick and easy. Preparation time: 10 minutes.

Texas Caviar

6 (16 ounce) cans black-eyed
peas, drained
2 cups diced green bell pepper
1½ cups diced jalapeño
peppers (wear rubber
gloves!)
1½ cups diced yellow onion
4 ounces diced pimientos,
drained
1 tablespoon finely minced
garlic
2 cups Italian salad dressing
Salt and hot pepper sauce to
taste

- Combine all ingredients; mix well. Marinate for a minimum of 3 days, preferably 7 days.
- Drain and serve with tortilla chips.

Yield: 3 quarts (recipe can be halved easily)

For added color, substitute 1 cup diced red bell pepper for 1 cup of the diced green bell pepper.

For a much milder version of this very spicy recipe, substitute three (4 ounce) cans chopped green chilies for the diced jalapeños.

This is an easy and inexpensive favorite that is very different from traditional salsa. This colorful appetizer will keep in the refrigerator for several weeks.

Great for a large crowd.

Shrimp Pinwheels

*1 15-inch Armenian cracker
   bread round*
*1 (3 ounce) package cream
   cheese with chives, softened*
½ teaspoon dried dill weed
*½ teaspoon prepared
   horseradish*
*1 (6 ounce) package frozen,
   peeled, cooked shrimp;
   thawed and drained*
*1 (2 ounce) jar sliced
   pimientos, drained*
Large romaine leaves
Cherry tomatoes, optional

- Soften cracker bread by dampening two large towels. Wring out towels so they are not too moist. Set towels aside. Moisten cracker bread on both sides under cold running water; place between damp towels. Cover with plastic wrap to prevent drying out. Let stand about one hour or until softened.
- Beat cream cheese, dill weed, and horseradish together in a small bowl until softened enough to spread.
- Finely chop the shrimp; stir into cheese mixture.
- Spread cheese mixture on cracker bread almost to the edges. Sprinkle with pimientos.
- Arrange romaine evenly over cheese mixture. Roll up tightly (like a jelly roll). Press to seal.
- Wrap in plastic wrap and chill for 2-24 hours.
- To serve, cut the rolls into ¾-inch thick slices. Arrange slices on a plate lined with romaine leaves. Garnish plate with cherry tomatoes, if desired.

Yield: 20 servings

Armenian cracker bread rounds can be found in international grocery stores.

Green Chili Wontons

1½ *pounds Monterey Jack*
cheese, grated
8 *ounces chopped green chilies*
4 *ounces chopped jalapeños,*
drained
1 *pound wonton skins*
Vegetable oil for frying

- Combine cheese and peppers. Mix well.
- Use a scant tablespoonful of filling in each wonton skin. Fold three corners of wonton skin into center. Place a small drop of water at fourth corner. Roll wonton skin toward fourth corner so that it looks like a miniature egg roll.
- Seal the wonton skin with water to be sure the wonton stays closed during frying.
- Place wontons in freezer while heating oil.
- Heat oil to 320°. Carefully place the wontons in hot oil. Deep-fry until light brown.
- Drain briefly and serve hot with guacamole and salsa.

Yield: 4½ dozen

The chili/cheese filling is great for quesadillas.

The secret is in not putting too much filling in the wontons. This causes the wonton skins to tear when rolling.

Guacamole

2 *moderately ripe avocados,*
peeled and pitted
1 *clove garlic, minced*
2 *tablespoons minced white*
onion
2 *ounces chopped green chilies*
2 *tablespoons lemon juice*
Salt and pepper to taste

- Put the avocados, garlic, onion, and green chilies in a mixing bowl. Combine with a fork until well mashed but lumpy.
- Season with lemon juice, salt, and pepper. Cover and refrigerate until ready to serve.
- Serve with tortilla chips.

Yield: 1 cup

Fontina Herb Bread

1 pound long loaf French or
  sourdough bread
10 ounces Fontina cheese,
  coarsely grated
¼ cup olive oil
3 tablespoons dry white wine
2 tablespoons chopped fresh
  basil
1 tablespoon chopped fresh
  chives
1 tablespoon chopped green
  onion
2 tablespoons chopped fresh
  parsley
2 large cloves garlic, minced
Salt and pepper to taste

- Preheat oven to 350°.
- Cut bread in half lengthwise. Remove enough bread from bottom half to create a ½-inch deep cavity.
- Mix cheese with remaining ingredients. Season with salt and pepper. Pack cheese mixture into cavity in bread. Replace top half of bread and press loaf together firmly. Wrap tightly in aluminum foil.
- Bake bread until heated through, about 30 minutes.
- Remove from oven, let stand 10 minutes.
- Remove foil. Cut bread crosswise into 1-inch wide diagonal slices and serve.

Yield: 12 servings

This appetizer can be made up to three hours ahead of time. Do not refrigerate, let stand at room temperature until time to bake.

Gingered Cream Cheese Grapes

2 (3 ounce) packages cream
  cheese, softened
2 tablespoons crystallized
  ginger, finely chopped
30 green seedless grapes
1 cup pecans; toasted lightly,
  completely cooled, and finely
  chopped

- Combine cream cheese and ginger in a small bowl.
- Place one teaspoon of mixture in the palm of your hand. Roll a grape in the mixture, covering well. Repeat until all grapes are covered with cream cheese mixture.
- Roll each covered grape in pecans and chill until firm.

Yield: 30 grapes

Delicious! Very easy and unusual.

Easy Garlic and Onion Bread Wedges

1 (16 ounce) baked cheese
  pizza crust
Olive oil
½ cup mayonnaise
¾ cup grated Parmesan cheese
½ cup chopped red onion
½ cup chopped fresh basil
4 large garlic cloves, minced
Salt and pepper to taste

- Preheat oven to 450°.
- Brush pizza crust lightly with olive oil.
- Combine remaining ingredients in a small bowl. Season to taste with salt and pepper. Spread mixture evenly over crust.
- Bake approximately 10 minutes or until crust is crisp and topping is thoroughly heated.

Yield: 12 servings

Top this outstanding white pizza with thin slices of Roma tomato and a generous sprinkling of chopped fresh oregano.

A committee favorite! This recipe brought raves from all.

Tomato and Goat Cheese Triangles

4 ounces goat cheese
1 (8 ounce) Boboli bread
2 large Roma tomatoes, sliced
¼ cup chopped fresh basil
Salt to taste

- Preheat oven to 350°.
- Spread goat cheese in an even layer over the Boboli.
- Cut Boboli into ten or twelve small pizza-slice triangles.
- Place one slice of tomato on each triangle. Sprinkle with basil and salt.
- Bake for approximately 10 minutes or until thoroughly warmed.

Yield: 6 appetizer servings

May substitute herb cheese for goat cheese.

Very easy and colorful! Great in summer when fresh tomatoes are abundant.

Frosted Pecans

1 egg white
¾ cup brown sugar
½ teaspoon vanilla extract
2 cups pecan halves

- Preheat oven to 250°.
- Beat egg white in a large bowl until soft peaks stand up.
- Add brown sugar and vanilla gradually; continue beating.
- Fold in pecans.
- Place well-coated pecans on a buttered cookie sheet.
- Bake for 30 minutes. Turn off oven, leaving the pecans in the oven to dry for an additional 30 minutes.

Yield: 2 cups

Quick and easy...preparation time: 15 minutes.

Mushroom Caps Stuffed with Crab Imperial

1 pound crabmeat
1 (2 ounce) jar sliced
*   pimientos*
2 teaspoons dry mustard
1 egg, beaten
4 tablespoons mayonnaise
Salt and pepper to taste
Paprika
24-36 large mushrooms,
*   cleaned and stemmed*

- Preheat oven to 350°.
- Combine crabmeat, pimientos, mustard, egg, mayonnaise, salt, and pepper; mix well. Spoon mixture into mushroom caps. Sprinkle with paprika.
- Bake 15 minutes. Serve hot.

Yield: 24 servings

Crabmeat stuffing may be used with croustades.

It is always best to use fresh crabmeat. When frozen, crabmeat becomes tough, watery, and less flavorful.

To clean fresh mushrooms, wipe them with a damp paper towel or quickly rinse them in a colander. Mushrooms should never be immersed in water.

Lump Crabmeat Orleans

½ cup mayonnaise
¼ cup sour cream
1 tablespoon lemon juice
1 teaspoon Creole mustard
1 pound lump crabmeat
Salt and pepper to taste
Capers for garnish

- Combine mayonnaise, sour cream, lemon juice, and mustard in a medium bowl. Chill.
- Gently fold in lump crabmeat. Season to taste with salt and pepper. Chill at least an hour before serving.
- Garnish with capers. Serve with crackers or homemade melba toast.

Yield: 6 appetizer servings

For a different twist, add a splash of sherry or several drops of hot pepper sauce to this recipe.

Pickled Oysters

1 quart fresh oysters
½ tablespoon salt
½ cup vinegar
½ tablespoon allspice
½ lemon, thinly sliced
Red pepper to taste

- In a medium pan, cook oysters in their own liquid and salt until edges curl. Do not overcook.
- Remove oysters with a strainer and lay on a sheet of ice. When thoroughly cold, place oysters in a jar.
- To the oyster liquid left in pan, add the vinegar and allspice. Simmer for a short time.
- Pour the hot vinegar mixture over oysters in jar. Add lemon slices and red pepper. Cover and place in refrigerator. Let oysters marinate at least overnight before serving.
- Serve as a finger food. No added condiment is necessary.

Yield: 1 quart

"A recipe that is perhaps as old as Virginia, if not older."

A favorite of food writer Betty Wrenn Day of the Gloucester-Mathews Gazette Journal in Gloucester, Virginia.

Dilled Shrimp

1½ cups mayonnaise
⅓ cup lemon juice
¼ cup sugar
½ cup sour cream
1 large red onion, thinly sliced
2 tablespoons dry dill
¼ teaspoon salt
2 pounds medium-sized
  shrimp, cooked and peeled

- Combine mayonnaise, lemon juice, sugar, sour cream, onion, dill, and salt in a large bowl. Stir in shrimp. Cover and refrigerate overnight.
- Stir and serve with wooden toothpicks.

Yield: 8 servings

Drain shrimp immediately after cooking to prevent curling and toughening.

Smoked Trout Pâté

2 smoked trout, skinned and
  boned (about one pound)
¾ cup mayonnaise
2 green onions, finely minced
1 tablespoon drained bottled
  capers
1 tablespoon Dijon mustard
2 teaspoons sweet paprika
Pepper to taste

- Blend trout, mayonnaise, green onions, capers, mustard, paprika, and pepper in a food processor until mixture is smooth.
- Transfer mixture to a small crock or individual ramekins and chill covered for 24 hours.
- Serve with toast points or crackers.

This recipe can be easily halved.

Yield: 2 cups

Has a mild, elegant flavor. It keeps well for several days refrigerated.

Ham and Cheese Rolls

1 stick butter, softened
2 teaspoons prepared mustard
2 tablespoons poppy seeds
2 teaspoons Worcestershire
  sauce
1 small onion, grated
1 package (20) party rolls
1/4 pound thinly sliced boiled
  ham
1 (4 ounce) package sliced
  Swiss cheese

- Preheat oven to 350°.
- Combine butter, mustard, poppy seeds, Worcestershire sauce, and onion.
- Open rolls and spread mixture on both sides of roll. Fill rolls with ham and cheese.
- Wrap in foil, place on a baking sheet, and heat until cheese melts, 10-15 minutes.

Yield: 20 rolls

May make ahead and freeze before baking. These are nice to have in your freezer for drop-in guests!

A favorite from **Virginia Seasons!**

Chive Mustard Spread

1/3 cup sugar
1/4 cup dry mustard
  (Coleman's brand for best
  results)
1 1/2 tablespoons all-purpose
  flour
1/4 teaspoon salt
3/4 cup milk
1/3 cup white vinegar
1 egg yolk
3 tablespoons minced fresh
  chives

- Combine sugar, mustard, flour, and salt in a small saucepan. Stir well, but do not heat.
- In a small bowl, combine milk, vinegar, and egg yolk. Beat well.
- Gradually stir milk mixture into mustard mixture over low heat; stirring constantly until thickened and bubbly. Remove from heat. Stir in chives.
- Cool completely. Store in the refrigerator.
- Serve as a spread for ham biscuits or with deli sandwiches.

Yield: 1 1/3 cups

Bite-Size Beef Wellingtons

4 green onions
12 ounces fresh mushrooms,
  halved if large
1½ sticks unsalted butter,
  melted and divided
Salt and freshly ground black
  pepper
10 thin sheets phyllo pastry,
  each 17"x12"
8 ounces fillet of beef,
  trimmed and cut into
  1½"x½"x½" pieces.

- Preheat oven to 375°.
- Using a food processor, finely chop green onions and mushrooms.
- Sauté the mixture in 4 tablespoons of butter over moderate heat until the mixture is dry, about 8 minutes. Season with salt and pepper; cool.
- Cut each phyllo sheet into four 17"x3" strips and cover with plastic wrap.
- Take one phyllo strip, brush with melted butter, and put a piece of beef and 1½ teaspoons of the mushroom mixture on one end of the strip approximately ½" from the end. Fold the ½ inch of phyllo over the filling and roll over several times. Fold in the sides and continue to roll and fold to the end. Place seam side down on a baking sheet and brush lightly with butter. Repeat with remaining strips. (The recipe may be made ahead up to this point and frozen, well wrapped, for two weeks. Bake frozen.)
- Bake the Wellingtons in the center of the preheated oven until golden brown, 10-12 minutes. Cool slightly.

Yield: 40

A classic made simple!

Escargot in Mushrooms

3 tablespoons minced parsley
3 tablespoons minced onion
3 cloves garlic, pressed
5 tablespoons butter
Salt and pepper to taste
2 dozen medium-sized fresh
  mushrooms
2 dozen snails
Fresh parsley for garnish

- Preheat oven to 400°.
- Combine parsley, onion, garlic, and butter in a large bowl. Add salt and pepper to taste.
- Remove stems from mushrooms and place a snail in each mushroom cap. Cover each snail with butter mixture.
- Place on baking sheet and bake for 10 minutes.

Yield: 24 caps or 6 servings

An elegant first course to any formal meal! Serve with cocktail forks. Garnish with fresh parsley.

Mini Cornmeal Muffins with Smoked Turkey and Chutney

1½ cups self-rising cornmeal
1 cup all-purpose flour
⅓ cup sugar
1 teaspoon salt
1½ cups milk
¾ cup butter, melted
2 eggs
½ pound smoked turkey,
  thinly sliced
½ cup chutney (suggest using
  Cranberry Chutney, page 66)

- Preheat oven to 400°.
- Mix cornmeal, flour, sugar, and salt in a large bowl.
- In a small bowl, combine milk, butter, and eggs. Add to the dry ingredients.
- Spoon batter into greased mini muffin tins. Bake 14-16 minutes. Cool for 5 minutes. Remove from tins.
- Cut muffins in half. Place turkey and a dab of chutney on each muffin bottom. Replace tops of muffins. Serve while still warm or at room temperature.

Yield: 3½ dozen

Great to pass at a party!

Zesty Pork Pastries

¹/₄ cup minced onion
1 clove garlic, minced
¹/₄ cup peeled and chopped
tomato
1 tablespoon minced red bell
pepper
1 tablespoon vegetable oil
¹/₄ teaspoon chili powder
³/₄ teaspoon Worcestershire
sauce
¹/₄ cup beef broth
2 teaspoons chili sauce
¹/₄ pound lean ground pork
1¹/₂ teaspoons chopped green
olives
2 teaspoons chopped raisins
1 teaspoon pickle relish
1 teaspoon sugar
¹/₈ teaspoon cayenne pepper
1 egg, beaten
1 sheet of puff pastry

- Puree the onion, garlic, tomato, red bell pepper, vegetable oil, chili powder, Worcestershire sauce, beef broth, and chili sauce in a blender.
- Brown pork. Add blender mixture. Simmer 15-20 minutes, or until very thick. Stir in green olives, raisins, relish, sugar, and cayenne pepper. Cool completely.
- Preheat oven to 375°.
- Roll out puff pastry sheet to a 12-inch square and cut into sixteen 3-inch squares.
- Put a teaspoonful of meat mixture on each square and fold over pastry to form a triangle. Brush corners with egg and press sides together with a fork to seal.
- Brush tops with egg and bake for 10-12 minutes.

Yield: 16 pastries

These may be prepared ahead and frozen prior to baking. When ready to serve, remove from freezer and bake.

Brie with Sun-Dried Tomato Topping

2 pounds Brie

5 tablespoons minced parsley leaves

2 tablespoons grated Parmesan cheese

10 sun-dried tomatoes packed in oil, minced

2½ tablespoons oil from sun-dried tomatoes

6 cloves garlic, minced

2 tablespoons minced fresh basil

3 tablespoons coarsely chopped toasted pine nuts

- Chill Brie before handling. Remove rind from top and place cheese on serving platter.
- Combine parsley, Parmesan cheese, tomatoes, oil, garlic, basil, and pine nuts. Spread on top of Brie.
- Serve at once or refrigerate for later use. For optimum flavor, allow Brie to stand 30-60 minutes at room temperature when removed from refrigerator.
- Serve on crackers or baguette slices.

Yield: 16 servings

Cheese, Pesto, and Sun-Dried Tomato Mold

2 (8 ounce) packages cream cheese, room temperature

1 (8 ounce) container ricotta cheese

1 cup freshly grated Parmesan cheese

1 tablespoon Worcestershire sauce

Hot pepper sauce to taste

2 (8 ounce) containers pesto, well drained

16 ounces sun-dried tomatoes packed in oil, drained and diced

- Mix cheese, Worcestershire sauce, and hot sauce in food processor until smooth.
- Line a round cake pan or quiche dish with plastic wrap.
- Spread tomatoes on bottom of pan in a single layer. Spread cheese mixture over tomatoes. Spread pesto over cheese. Cover and chill several hours or overnight.
- Invert on platter and serve with Bremner wafers or Stoned Wheat Thins.

Yield: 20-25 appetizer servings.

Can be easily halved.

Very colorful, festive presentation!

Brie with Brown Sugar

1 small round of Brie
3 tablespoons butter
3 tablespoons brown sugar
3 tablespoons chopped nuts
  (pecans or walnuts)
1 tablespoon honey

- Microwave Brie on high for 15 seconds. Place on serving dish.
- Combine butter, brown sugar, nuts, and honey in a small microwave container. Microwave on high for 15 seconds. Spread on top of Brie.
- Serve with sliced apples and plain crackers.

Yield: 8 servings

Very attractive.

Melted Brie Loaf

1 pound round of French
  bread
1/3 cup melted butter
2 cloves garlic, minced
1 1/2 pounds Brie
Grapes and apple slices for
  garnish

- Preheat oven to 350°.
- Cut a 5-inch diameter opening into the top of the loaf. Cut bread to leave a shell about ½" thick on sides without cutting into bottom. Pull bread out to leave a hollow shell and set aside. Make cuts approximately 1½ inches deep and 1½ inches apart around the top of hollow shell.
- Mix butter and garlic. Slice bread that was set aside. Brush garlic and butter on inside of shell and on top of bread slices. Cut Brie into chunks and place in hollowed bread shell.
- Place Brie loaf and bread slices on rectangular cookie sheet. Bake for 10 minutes. Remove bread slices and return Brie loaf to bake for another 10 minutes.
- Place Brie loaf and bread slices on serving platter. Garnish with grapes and apple slices.

Yield: 16 servings

Soft breads cut more easily with a slightly heated bread knife.

Sun-Dried Tomato Pâté

4 ounces sun-dried tomatoes packed in oil, drained (reserving oil), and finely chopped
2 (8 ounce) packages cream cheese, softened
¼ cup grated Romano cheese
1 tablespoon reserved tomato oil
¼ cup chopped fresh basil

- Mix all ingredients. Cover and chill.
- Serve with crackers, water crackers, or pita chips.

Yield: 8-10 servings

Can be made in food processor. Chop tomatoes first, then grate cheese and add cream cheese and other ingredients. Very quick and easy.

Marinated Goat Cheese with Cognac and Red Onion

½ pound soft goat cheese (Bucheron)
1 small red onion, thinly sliced
1 bay leaf, split in two for enhanced flavor
1 teaspoon thyme
1 teaspoon rosemary
⅛ teaspoon freshly ground black pepper
2 cloves garlic, minced
½ cup cognac or brandy
1 cup dry white wine
1 cup extra virgin olive oil
Sprig of rosemary

- Slice cheese into 16 rounds. Fill two 1-cup jars with cheese and onions.
- Combine bay leaf, thyme, rosemary, pepper, garlic, cognac, and wine in a medium saucepan. Boil until reduced to a syrup. Add olive oil and swirl to mix. Cool to room temperature.
- Pour marinade over cheese and onions. Cover tightly. Chill for a minimum of 2 days or up to 4 weeks. Flavor increases over extended time.
- Before serving, drain some of the marinade from the cheese mixture. Serve at room temperature as a spread for mild crackers or thin slices of French bread. Garnish with a sprig of rosemary.

Yield: 2 cups

Toasted Almond Party Spread

*1 (8 ounce) package cream
  cheese, softened*
6 ounces grated Swiss cheese
*1/4 cup mayonnaise-type salad
  dressing*
*2 tablespoons chopped green
  onion*
1/8 teaspoon ground nutmeg
1/8 teaspoon pepper
1/3 cup toasted sliced almonds
*Extra toasted almonds for
  garnish*

- Preheat oven to 350°.
- Combine all ingredients and mix well.
  Spread into 9-inch pie plate.
- Bake for 15 minutes, stirring after 8
  minutes.
- Garnish with additional toasted
  almonds. Serve with assorted
  crackers or toasted bread cut-outs.

Yield: 2 cups

Cheddar Cheese Spread

*1 pound sharp Cheddar
  cheese, grated*
*1 (3 ounce) package cream
  cheese, softened*
1 cup mayonnaise
1 small onion, grated
1 teaspoon minced garlic
*2 teaspoons Worcestershire
  sauce*
1/2 cup chopped pecans
*1/8 teaspoon hot pepper sauce
  or to taste*
*1/8 teaspoon cayenne pepper or
  to taste*
*1/8 teaspoon Cavenders All-
  Purpose Greek Seasoning or
  to taste*

- Combine all ingredients; mix well.
- Refrigerate overnight.
- Serve with crackers.

Yield: 8 servings

*For added color, sprinkle with
paprika before serving. Makes a
great spread for sandwiches.*

Mexican Cheesecake

1½ cups finely crushed tortilla chips
¼ cup butter, melted
2 (8 ounce) packages cream cheese, softened
2 cups grated Monterey Jack cheese
1 (8 ounce) carton sour cream
3 eggs
1 (8 ounce) jar mild salsa
1 (4 ounce) can chopped green chilies
1 (8 ounce) carton sour cream
1 (6 ounce) container frozen avocado dip, thawed
1 (8 ounce) jar mild salsa, drained
Tortilla chips or large corn chips

- Preheat oven to 350°.
- Combine tortilla chips and butter. Press into bottom of a lightly greased 9-inch springform pan. Bake for 10 minutes.
- Combine cream cheese and Monterey Jack cheese in a large bowl. Beat with an electric mixer until light and fluffy. Beat in one carton sour cream.
- Add eggs all at once; beat at low speed only until ingredients are combined.
- Stir in salsa and green chilies.
- Pour mixture on top of tortilla crust in springform pan. Place on baking sheet and bake for 40-45 minutes or until the center is almost set.
- Spread remaining sour cream immediately over top of the hot cheesecake.
- Cool on a wire rack.
- Cover pan and refrigerate for 3 to 24 hours.
- To serve, remove sides of pan. Dollop avocado dip and drained salsa alternately around edge of cheesecake. Serve with tortilla chips or corn chips.

Yield: 20 servings

After adding the eggs, beat the mixture just until combined; the cheesecake is less likely to crack after baking and cooling.

Red Bell Pepper Cheese Spread

2 teaspoons olive oil
½ small onion, quartered
3 large garlic cloves, chopped
2 large red bell peppers
1½ cups grated sharp
  Cheddar cheese, firmly
  packed
½ teaspoon salt
¼ teaspoon cayenne pepper
2 tablespoons chopped fresh
  chives
Salt and pepper to taste

- Heat olive oil in a small skillet. Sauté onion and garlic for 10 minutes. Cool.
- Char peppers over gas flame or under broiler until blackened on all sides. Wrap peppers in plastic wrap. Cool for 10 minutes. Peel and seed peppers; pat dry.
- Place all ingredients (except chives, salt, and pepper) in food processor. Puree until almost smooth. Transfer to bowl.
- Stir in chives. Season with salt and pepper. Cover and refrigerate for at least 2 hours.
- Serve with crackers, crusty country bread, or as a dip for fresh vegetables.

Yield: 1½ cups

Can be prepared one day ahead.

Champagne Punch

2 *(12 ounce) cans frozen*
   lemonade concentrate,
   thawed
2 *(12 ounce) cans frozen*
   pineapple juice concentrate,
   thawed
6 *cups water*
2 *liters chilled ginger ale*
1 *liter chilled tonic water*
1 *(.75 ml.) bottle chilled*
   Champagne

- Combine first three ingredients. Mix well and pour over ice (or an ice ring) in a large punch bowl.
- Gently pour in ginger ale, tonic water, and Champagne.
- Add orange or lemon slices for garnish. Serve.

Yield: 20 servings

When making an ice ring, use boiled water for clearer ice.

New Year's Punch

1 *fifth Jack Daniels*
1 *fifth water*
1 *cup sugar*
12 *lemons*

- Pour Jack Daniels, water, and sugar into a large container.
- Cut the lemons in half. Squeeze all of the juice from the lemons into the container. Drop the lemon halves into the container. Leave the lemon halves in the container for 24 hours.
- Refrigerate overnight.
- Before serving, squeeze the lemon halves again, then discard.
- Pour into a pitcher, and serve.

Yield: 8-10 servings

Also great for football Saturdays! Rumor has it that the lemons in this recipe prevent a hangover!

Festive Eggnog

10 eggs, separated
1½ cups sugar, divided
1 cup good whiskey
1 cup milk
1 cup heavy cream
Nutmeg

- Beat egg whites until stiff. Add ¾ cup of sugar gradually to egg whites and beat well.
- In another bowl, beat egg yolks until creamy yellow. Add ¾ cup of sugar gradually to yolks and beat a long time or until fluffy and pale yellow.
- Add whiskey to yolks mixture. Combine whites mixture with yolks and whiskey mixture. Stir in milk.
- Whip cream; gently fold into egg mixture until well blended. Chill for 2 to 3 days.
- Before serving, mix with a spoon and sprinkle with nutmeg.

Yield: 12 punch-cup servings

Raw eggs are easily separated while still cold. Allow whites to reach room temperature before beating to achieve maximum volume.

Strawberry Punch

1 bottle Boone's Strawberry
  Hill wine
1 liter 7-Up
1 package frozen sliced
  strawberries

- Combine wine and 7-Up in punch bowl.
- Float block of frozen strawberries on top.

Yield: 8 servings

Your guests will never guess the secret ingredient!

Magnolia Blossoms

1 (6 ounce) can frozen orange
  juice concentrate
3 cups Chablis
1½ cups water
½ cup Triple Sec

- Mix ingredients well and serve over ice.
- Garnish with orange slices, if desired.

Yield: 6 cups

A delicious breakfast or brunch beverage!

Famous Mint Iced Tea

4½ cups water, divided
6 sprigs of fresh mint
3 individual tea bags
¾ cup sugar
Juice of 3 lemons
2 cups cold water

- Make two separate pots of boiling water, each containing 2¼ cups of water.
- Put mint and tea bags in first pot. Cover and steep for 15 minutes.
- In the second pot, add sugar and lemon juice.
- Pour contents of the first pot through a strainer into the second pot.
- Add 2 cups of cold water. Refrigerate.
- Serve over ice, garnish with lemon slices or mint sprigs.

Yield: 6 servings

If tea clouds, add some boiling water.

Holiday Tea

1½ cups boiling water
6 tea bags
10 whole cloves
2 cinnamon sticks
2 cups cranberry juice cocktail
1½ cups unsweetened grape juice
¼ cup light brown sugar
2 oranges, sliced and studded with whole cloves for garnish

- Place tea bags, whole cloves, and cinnamon sticks in boiled water; brew for 5 minutes. Remove tea bags.
- Stir in cranberry juice and grape juice. Heat thoroughly.
- Remove spices.
- Garnish with clove-studded orange slices.
- Serve in a punch bowl.

Yield: 8 servings

Soups, Salads & Breads

The Great Southwest

Southern cooking is rooted in hard times. No times were harder and no cooking better than in Southwest Virginia's mountains.

Joe Smiddy, former chancellor of Clinch Valley College in Wise, let his mind run to those times with home fries, potatoes cut in disks and fried on both sides in the skillet; soup beans (pintos and brown beans), and cornbread.

"You'd bridle a mule, fill a tow sack with shelled corn, and go to the grist mill," Smiddy said. "The miller ground the corn and took out a bucket of it as his toll. You'd sling the sack of meal over the mule's back, which, after you hurried home, was wet with perspiration. Nobody minded. It dried and contributed to the flavor. The meal, ground coarse, had bits of husks, but that was good for you. People are back to fiber today, and that coarse-ground meal had plenty of it."

Joe's wife, Reba, uses buttermilk in cornbread. Just before she pours the batter into a hot iron skillet greased with corn oil, she sprinkles corn meal atop the oil; so when the cornbread is done, the bottom is crusty.

Kathleen Sturgill, 85, explained how cooks preserved "leather britches" or dried string beans. You removed the strings, and put the whole beans, one by one, on threads and hung them to dry by a fireplace or in the attic or sun porch, or in the back window of a car. Her mother hung them around a porch that embraced the house. What a glorious scene that tasseled fringe must have been.

In cooking leather britches, she lets them soak overnight and boils them with a piece of meat or seasoning. "Lots of people love them," she said.

Lore informs her talk. In making biscuits, scoop a hole in the flour in which to pour the other ingredients for mixing. In making gravy, as she did every morning for her four sons, "sometimes the sausage sticks a little and when the bits are stirred up, that makes the gravy better." In cutting biscuits out of the dough, don't twist the cutter in your hand. "My mother taught me that. I don't really know the reason. It works." When her son in Charlottesville is coming to visit, he calls ahead to make sure she'll have chicken and dumplings on the table.

Neighbors watch her every step of the way preparing a dish, yet they can't replicate her results. Well, no wonder. She doesn't cook by recipes, she cooks by feel and intuition. She has a knowing hand. You might as well expect someone, having watched Picasso paint, to be able to produce a masterpiece on canvas. Cooking, too, is an art inspired by the cook's love of those she has in mind.

Gateway to the Great Southwest is Roanoke. A river runs through the city; a mountain, shaped like a slumbering elephant, crouches in its midst. Residents and tourists throng the downtown Center in the Square which offers a museum, concerts, and drama. Roanoke had the good sense to retain its historic market that farmers fill with a cornucopia of fresh vegetables and fruit.

Southwest Virginians walk with a trace of a lope that eats up the miles. They speak straight-forward and love the land.

A Southwest Virginian went to a big city to work in an icebox factory and quit the next week to go back home to the mountains. "Why?" the foreman asked. "The pay is better here, but the day is better there," the Southwest Virginian said.

The natives, by the way, pronounce it "Ro-noke."

-Guy Friddell

Cold Cucumber and Dill Soup

*4 cups pureed cucumbers,
  peeled and seeded*
1 quart heavy cream
3 cups sour cream
2 teaspoons minced garlic
2 teaspoons salt
½ teaspoon white pepper
*2 teaspoons Worcestershire
  sauce*
4 cups chicken stock
⅓ cup cider vinegar
½ cup chopped fresh dill
Hot pepper sauce to taste
*Thin cucumber slices for
  garnish*

- Puree cucumbers in food processor until smooth.
- Whip cream in a large bowl until thickened. Add sour cream; mix.
- Add remaining ingredients except dill. Season with hot pepper sauce and additional salt, pepper, or Worcestershire sauce if desired.
- Add dill. Chill several hours. Flavor intensifies as it chills.
- Serve in chilled cups. Garnish with thin cucumber slices.

Yield: 4 quarts

Make a delicious cucumber and watercress soup by substituting ½ cup chopped fresh watercress for the dill in the recipe.

White Gazpacho

3 cucumbers
3 cups chicken broth
3 cups sour cream
3 teaspoons white vinegar
2 teaspoons salt
1 clove garlic, minced
2 tomatoes, chopped
½ cup chopped green onions
¾ cup toasted almonds
½ cup chopped fresh parsley

- Puree cucumbers and chicken broth in food processor.
- Add sour cream, vinegar, salt, and garlic. Mix until completely blended.
- Pour into individual bowls. Sprinkle with tomatoes, onions, almonds, and parsley.

Yield: 6 servings

This summer soup is easy and delicious! Impress your friends by serving it at an outdoor buffet.

To substitute dried herbs for fresh, use 1 teaspoon dried herbs for 1 tablespoon fresh.

Chilled Strawberry Soup with Cinnamon Croutons

Croutons

2 slices whole wheat bread, cubed in ½-inch squares
1 tablespoon ground cinnamon
2 tablespoons granulated sugar
3 tablespoons melted butter

Soup

1 pint fresh strawberries, stemmed and washed
1 pint heavy cream
1½ cups powdered sugar
1 teaspoon vanilla extract
3 fresh medium-sized strawberries, cut in half
Mint sprigs, optional

- Preheat oven to 350°.
- Place wheat bread cubes in a small bowl. Add cinnamon, granulated sugar, and melted butter. Mix until bread is saturated.
- Place cubes on a cookie sheet. Bake until croutons are crunchy.
- Remove from oven; set aside.

- Place pint of strawberries into a food processor or blender. Use pulse button only to chop strawberries into ¼-inch sized pieces.
- Pour strawberries and any liquid into a cooled mixing bowl. Add cream, powdered sugar, and vanilla. Mix with mixer on medium speed until mixture is only halfway whipped with no peaks.
- Immediately pour into individual serving bowls. Garnish with 5 or 6 cinnamon croutons, half of a fresh strawberry, and fresh mint sprigs.

Yield: 6 cups

A specialty of Hermitage Country Club. Beautiful and delicious for a summer luncheon.

When purchasing fresh strawberries, choose those that are fully ripened with a deep red color and fresh looking caps. Unlike many fruits, strawberries do not continue ripening after being picked.

Chilled Peach Orchard Soup

10 peaches; peeled, pitted, and
  sliced (about 5 cups),
  reserving 8-10 slices for
  garnish
2 cups fresh orange juice,
  divided
3/4 cup unsweetened pineapple
  chunks, drained, reserving
  1/2 cup juice
1 teaspoon ground ginger
1 cup sour cream
Confectioners' sugar to taste
Fresh mint sprigs for garnish

- Puree the peaches and 1/2 cup of the orange juice. Transfer to a large bowl. Add the remaining orange juice.
- Puree the pineapple with 1/4 cup of the reserved juice. Add the pineapple puree to the peach puree.
- Whisk in the ginger, sour cream, and remaining pineapple juice.
- Stir in confectioners' sugar, to taste.
- Chill, covered, until thoroughly cold.
- Serve in chilled bowls, garnished with peach slices and mint sprigs.

Yield: 6-8 servings

A flavorful, chilled summer soup!

Black Bean Soup

6 slices bacon, chopped
4 cloves garlic, minced
1 large onion, chopped
2 (16 ounce) cans black beans
6 cups beef bouillon
1 (16 ounce) can Italian
  stewed tomatoes
1-2 tablespoons chopped sun-
  dried tomatoes
1/2 teaspoon celery seed
1/2 teaspoon seasoning salt
1/2 pound smoked sausage,
  chopped
1/2 pound cooked turkey,
  chopped
1/2 cup long-grain white rice,
  uncooked
1/2 teaspoon ground oregano
1 tablespoon sugar
4-6 dashes hot pepper sauce
Salt and pepper to taste

- Cook bacon in Dutch oven or large soup pot: remove bacon pieces.
- Sauté garlic and onion in bacon grease. Drain grease and add remaining ingredients. Cook 2 hours over low heat.

Yield: 4 servings

This soup is even better the second day!

Cream of Carrot Soup

5 cups peeled, sliced carrots
1 cup peeled, chopped potato
¾ cup chopped onion
¼ cup butter
4 cups chicken broth
Salt and white pepper to taste
1 bay leaf
1 cup milk
Whipped cream and parsley
  for garnish

- Melt butter in a large skillet. Sauté carrots, potato, and onion for 10 minutes.
- Butter a piece of wax paper, place over skillet with buttered side down, then place lid on top of paper. Continue cooking vegetable mixture on low heat for 10 minutes. Transfer to a large pot.
- Add chicken broth, salt, pepper, and bay leaf. Simmer, covered, for 45 minutes.
- Remove bay leaf. Puree mixture in blender or food processor. Return mixture to pot and stir in milk over low heat. Heat thoroughly.
- Garnish with whipped cream and parsley.

Yield: 4-6 servings

Carrots with the darkest orange color have the highest Vitamin A content.

Lean's Corn Chowder

½ onion, chopped
3-4 slices bacon, cut into
  1-inch pieces
2 (16 ounce) cans corn
2 cans condensed cream of
  chicken soup
½ cup light cream

- In a medium skillet, brown onion and bacon. Do not drain.
- In a separate pot, bring undiluted chicken soup and corn to a boil. Add undrained bacon and onion to pot; cook 2 minutes.
- Stir in cream and heat to boiling.

Yield: 6 servings

Great while watching football on a lazy Sunday afternoon.

To lower the fat content in recipes using bacon, substitute lean Canadian bacon or baked ham.

White Onion Soup

4 large white onions
3 tablespoons butter
3 tablespoons all-purpose flour
2 cups milk
¾ teaspoon salt
¼ teaspoon white pepper
1½ cups chicken broth
2 tablespoons grated
  Parmesan cheese

- Steam onions until tender. Cool onions, then chop coarsely. Set aside.
- Melt butter in a small saucepan. Stir in flour with wooden spoon until smooth. Add milk gradually, stirring constantly. Cook until sauce thickens. Stir in salt and pepper. If white sauce contains lumps, strain through a fine sieve.
- Add onions. Stir in chicken broth. Heat thoroughly.
- Stir in Parmesan cheese with a wooden spoon until smooth.
- Serve hot.

Yield: 6 servings

Never cover the pot! Great as small first-course soup. Very tasty!

Chunky Potato Soup

1 stick margarine
1 cup finely chopped onion
4 large potatoes; peeled,
  boiled, and diced
1 tablespoon garlic salt
½ tablespoon white pepper
6 cups hot water
3 chicken bouillon cubes
1½ cups milk
1 cup half and half
1 cup cold water
½ cup all-purpose flour
¼ cup sherry, optional
⅛ cup parsley flakes

- Melt margarine and sauté onions until soft. Add diced potatoes, garlic salt, and pepper.
- Dissolve chicken bouillon cubes in hot water, then add to potato mixture along with milk and half and half. Stir well and bring to a boil.
- Whisk flour into cold water, then stir into potato mixture. Stir constantly until soup is thick.
- If desired, add sherry and stir well. Add parsley flakes just before serving.

Yield: 8 servings

A great cold weather soup!

Lemaire's Peanut Soup

48 ounces peanuts, divided
½ cup clarified butter, divided
½ cup finely diced onion
¼ cup finely diced celery
¼ cup finely diced carrots
4 cups chicken stock
¼ cup all-purpose flour
Salt and pepper to taste
Smooth peanut butter,
  optional
Cream, optional

- Chop 12 ounces of the peanuts. Set aside.
- Heat a large stock pot. Add ¼ cup clarified butter, onions, celery, carrots, and 12 ounces chopped peanuts. Sauté, but do not brown.
- Add chicken stock. Heat well.
- In a food processor, puree remaining peanuts into a paste and reserve.
- Over moderate heat, combine remaining butter and flour to make a roux. Add to chicken stock to thicken. Bring to a boil.
- Add pureed peanuts. Reduce heat and simmer for 1 hour.
- Strain and season with salt and pepper. Add peanut butter and a little cream to smooth your mixture out a little, if desired.

Yield: 6 servings

This recipe from Mark Langenfeld, chef at Lemaire restaurant, is superb! Lemaire, a four-star restaurant located in the historic Jefferson Hotel in Richmond, is widely credited for introducing to America the fine art of cooking with wines.

• • •

Peanuts grow in the south-central section of Virginia and are among the state's most important products. Pigs raised in the town of Smithfield are fed peanuts which provide a distinctive flavor to the hams that are known worldwide as Smithfield hams.

Spinach, Leek, and Red Potato Soup

*2 tablespoons butter or
   margarine*
4 slices Canadian bacon, diced
2 cups finely diced leeks
*1½ cups finely diced white
   onion*
1½ cups finely diced celery
1 tablespoon dried tarragon
1 tablespoon thyme
Salt and pepper to taste
5 cups chicken broth
*2½ cups thinly sliced red
   potatoes*
*1 pound fresh spinach, rinsed,
   stemmed, and divided*
*½ cup heavy cream, half and
   half, or milk*

- Melt butter in a large pot. Cook the Canadian bacon in the butter for 3 minutes over low heat. Add the leeks, onions, and celery. Cook over low heat for 15 minutes.
- Add tarragon, thyme, salt, and pepper.
- Stir in the chicken stock and potatoes. Simmer, covered, until potatoes are tender but not mushy, 10-20 minutes.
- Add half of the spinach. Simmer one minute. Remove soup from heat.
- Puree half of soup mixture in a blender or food processor. Return to pot.
- Add remaining spinach and cream. Heat thoroughly over low heat. Do not boil.
- Season with additional salt and pepper, if desired.

Yield: 6 servings

**Unlike many soups, this one does
not require hours of simmering. It
should be served immediately.**

Cheesy Vegetable Chowder

½ cup chopped onion
1 clove garlic, minced
1 cup sliced celery
¾ cup sliced carrots
1 cup cubed potatoes
3½ cups chicken broth
1 (17 ounce) can whole kernel
   corn, drained
¼ cup butter or margarine
2 cups milk
¼ cup all-purpose flour
1 tablespoon prepared
   mustard
¼ teaspoon white pepper
⅛ teaspoon paprika
2 tablespoons diced pimientos
2 cups (8 ounces) grated
   Cheddar cheese

- Combine onion, garlic, celery, carrots, potatoes, and chicken broth in a large pot; bring to a boil. Cover, reduce heat, and simmer 15-20 minutes or until potatoes are tender.
- Stir in corn. Remove from heat.
- Melt butter in a heavy saucepan over low heat. Add flour, stirring constantly. Stir in milk gradually. Cook until thick and bubbly.
- Stir in remaining ingredients. Cook just until cheese is melted.
- Gradually stir cheese mixture into vegetable mixture. Cook over medium heat, stirring constantly, until thoroughly heated.

Yield: 4 servings

Do not overcook the vegetables in this superb chowder.

Vegetable Soup

1 pound ground beef
1 onion, chopped
1 (16 ounce) package frozen
   mixed vegetables
1 (16 ounce) can whole
   tomatoes
2 cans condensed tomato soup
1½ cups water
½ teaspoon pepper
½ teaspoon chili powder
¼ teaspoon garlic salt
¼ teaspoon oregano

- Brown the ground beef. Mix with all other ingredients, and bring to a boil.
- Reduce heat and simmer 1½ to 2 hours uncovered, or all day in a crock pot.

Yield: 8 servings

This quick homemade soup is even better the second day, if there are leftovers!

New England Clam Chowder

5 cans condensed cream of
   potato soup
3 cups half and half
3 cups milk
2 (10 ounce) cans whole baby
   clams, with liquid
1 tablespoon dried minced
   onions
1 tablespoon parsley flakes
1/2 teaspoon garlic powder
1/2 teaspoon seasoned salt
Hot pepper sauce to taste
Salt and pepper to taste
1/4 cup butter, melted

- Heat soup, half and half, and milk in a heavy saucepan over medium heat.
- Add clams, onions, parsley flakes, garlic powder, seasoned salt, hot pepper sauce, salt, and pepper.
- Reduce heat to low. Simmer gently until thickened, stirring frequently, about 15 minutes.
- Drizzle butter on top, stir and serve.

Yield: 10-12 servings

Tastes like you labored over it for hours!

May be easily halved or doubled.

Crab Bisque

6 tablespoons butter
3 tablespoons grated onions
6 tablespoons all-purpose flour
1/2 teaspoon dry mustard
4 cups half and half, warmed
2 cups whole milk, warmed
2 tablespoons ketchup
1 1/2 teaspoons tomato paste
2 teaspoons chopped fresh
   parsley
1 pound crabmeat
2 tablespoons dry sherry
2 teaspoons Worcestershire
   sauce
1/4 teaspoon hot pepper sauce
1 teaspoon salt
1 teaspoon pepper

- Melt butter in a large saucepan; add onions and sauté 5 minutes.
- Add flour and cook 2 minutes.
- Stir in mustard.
- Lower temperature and whisk in half and half, milk, and ketchup.
- Pour one-fourth of mixture into a small bowl. Add tomato paste to small bowl and blend well. Pour mixture back into large saucepan.
- Add remaining ingredients.
- Serve hot or cold.

Yield: 6-8 servings

Wonderfully rich! Serve with a salad and French bread for an easy, elegant dinner.

She-Crab Soup

2 cans condensed cream of
   celery soup
2 cups milk
1 cup half and half
1/2 cup butter
1/2 teaspoon Old Bay seasoning
1/2 teaspoon Worcestershire
   sauce
1/4 teaspoon garlic salt
1/4 teaspoon white pepper
1 cup crabmeat, drained and
   flaked
1/4 cup dry sherry
Marigold or parsley leaves for
   garnish

- Combine soup, milk, half and half, butter, Old Bay, Worcestershire sauce, garlic salt, and pepper in a large Dutch oven. Bring to a boil.
- Add crabmeat. Cook over medium heat, stirring occasionally, until heated thoroughly.
- Stir in sherry.
- Ladle into individual bowls. Sprinkle each serving with marigold or parsley leaves.

Yield: 2 quarts

For a slightly different taste and texture, add 2 finely chopped hard-boiled eggs to the soup or use as additional garnish.

Oyster Stew

3 tablespoons butter
1 (8 ounce) can oysters
1 teaspoon salt
1/8 teaspoon pepper
2 cups milk
1 cup heavy cream
Chopped fresh parsley or
   paprika for garnish

- Melt butter over low heat. Add oysters, bring to a boil, and cook 3 minutes.
- Add salt, pepper, milk, and cream. Bring to boiling point, but do not allow stew to boil.
- Garnish with fresh parsley or paprika.

Yield: 4 servings

Great with hearty bread and robust wine!

Frozen Cranberry Salad

6 ounces cream cheese,
  softened
2 tablespoons mayonnaise
2 tablespoons sugar
1 (20 ounce) can crushed
  pineapple, drained
1 pound whole cranberry
  sauce
½ cup chopped nuts
8 ounces frozen whipped
  topping
Lettuce leaves

- Combine cream cheese, mayonnaise, and sugar. Add pineapple, cranberry sauce, nuts, and whipped topping. Mix well.
- Pour into an 8½"x4½" loaf pan.
- Freeze for 6 hours or overnight.
- Let stand at room temperature for 15 minutes before removing from pan.
- Slice and serve on lettuce leaves.

Yield: 8-10 servings

Delicious and refreshing! Perfect for a summer luncheon served with chicken salad and fruit wedges.

Strawberry Banana Gelatin Salad

1 (6 ounce) package
  strawberry gelatin
1 cup boiling water
2 (10 ounce) packages frozen
  strawberries, thawed and
  drained
1 (20 ounce) can crushed
  pineapple, drained
3 ripe bananas, mashed
1 cup chopped pecans

- In a large bowl, dissolve gelatin in 1 cup boiling water. Place bowl in the refrigerator and allow gelatin to partially gel.
- Add remaining ingredients; blend well.
- Pour mixture into a large ring mold or rectangular dish. Refrigerate until firm.

Yield: 8-10 servings

For an elegant presentation, place molded gelatin ring on a bed of lettuce.

Curried Chicken Salad

1 cup mayonnaise
3 tablespoons honey
Juice of 1 lemon
1½ teaspoons curry powder
¼ teaspoon ground ginger
4 chicken breast halves,
   cooked and cubed
2 stalks celery, chopped
1 green apple, peeled and
   diced
3 slices bacon, cooked crisp
   and crumbled
¼ cup almond slices

- In a small bowl, combine mayonnaise, honey, lemon juice, curry powder, and ground ginger. Blend well.
- In a large mixing bowl, combine chicken, celery, apple, bacon, and almonds.
- Add dressing mixture to chicken mixture. Blend well.

Yield: 4 servings

Excellent chicken salad!

Grilled Chicken and Fusilli

4 boneless, skinless chicken
   breast halves
2 tablespoons fresh lemon
   juice
1 pound fusilli (or twists)
2 large red bell peppers, cut
   into strips
2½ cups thinly sliced celery
1 red onion, chopped
1¼ cups black olives, pitted
   and thinly sliced
¼ cup minced fresh dill
3 tablespoons white wine
   vinegar
2 tablespoons mayonnaise
2 tablespoons Dijon mustard
½ cup olive oil
Salt and pepper to taste

- Grill chicken breasts 5-6 minutes on each side. Transfer to a dish and sprinkle with lemon juice. Allow to cool, then cut into thin slices, reserving the juices.
- Cook pasta in boiling salted water until tender. Immediately rinse under cold water.
- In a large bowl, toss together the pasta, bell peppers, celery, onion, olives, and dill.
- Add thinly sliced chicken.
- To juices, add the vinegar, mayonnaise, mustard, and olive oil. Salt and pepper to taste. Mix well.
- Add the dressing to the pasta salad.

Yield: 8-10 servings

A delightful change from the usual summer picnic fare.

Stir-Fried Turkey Salad

4 slices bacon, cut into slivers
1 pound turkey, cut into thin
  strips
2-3 heads butter lettuce,
  rinsed and torn into bite-
  size pieces
1 large tomato, diced
1 avocado, peeled and sliced
¼ cup chopped green onion
¼ cup grated Parmesan cheese

- In a 12-inch skillet, fry bacon until crisp. Remove bacon with a slotted spoon and drain on paper towel. Set aside. Discard all but 1 tablespoon grease.
- Turn heat to high, add turkey and stir-fry until lightly browned, 3-4 minutes. Remove from heat; set aside.
- Arrange lettuce on individual servings plates. Top with tomato, avocado, and onion.
- Arrange turkey over greens. Spoon juices over turkey. Top with bacon and cheese.
- Serve dressing on the side.

Yield: 2-3 servings

Dressing
¼ cup olive oil
3 tablespoons mayonnaise
3 tablespoons wine vinegar
1 tablespoon Dijon mustard
1 teaspoon thyme

- Blend all ingredients. Chill.

Yield: 1 cup
A delicious light entree salad.

Garlic Chicken Pasta Salad with Artichokes and Hearts of Palm

2 cups mayonnaise
3 cloves garlic, minced
2 (6 ounce) jars marinated
artichoke hearts, drained
(reserving oil) and sliced
1 pound bow tie pasta
1 (7 ounce) can hearts of
palm, drained and sliced
4 chicken breast halves,
cooked and cubed
2 heads Bibb lettuce
1 pint cherry tomatoes

- Combine mayonnaise with garlic and oil drained from marinated artichokes; chill.
- Cook pasta in 4 quarts boiling water until al dente. Drain and rinse well with cold water, then drain again.
- Place pasta in a large bowl and cool to room temperature, stirring occasionally to keep pasta from sticking.
- With hands, blend one-third of the garlic-flavored mayonnaise gently with the pasta. In a separate bowl, combine artichoke hearts, hearts of palm, chicken, and remaining garlic-flavored mayonnaise. Chill both combinations several hours or overnight. Remove from refrigerator 30 minutes before serving.
- Combine artichoke hearts mixture with pasta.
- Serve over Bibb lettuce. Garnish with cherry tomatoes.

Yield: 4-6 servings

The elegant appearance of this dish makes it as appealing for a formal dinner party as a summertime picnic.

Salad spinners are excellent for all types of lettuce except the delicate Bibb lettuce which bruises easily. Soak and rinse well to clean, wrap in paper towels, and store in a sealed plastic bag until ready to use. Bibb lettuce leaves should be used whole, not torn.

Tomato and Feta Pasta Salad

*12 ounces penne or
   mostaccioli*
*¹/₂ pound crumbled Feta cheese
   (Corsican or the least salty
   Feta is best)*
2 large ripe tomatoes, chopped
¹/₄ cup extra virgin olive oil
*2 tablespoons red wine
   vinegar*
1 clove garlic, minced
2 tablespoons fresh basil
2 tablespoons fresh oregano
Fresh ground pepper to taste

- In a large pot, cook pasta in boiling water. Rinse with cold water; drain.
- In a large bowl, toss pasta with Feta and tomatoes. Set aside.
- To make dressing, combine remaining ingredients in a separate bowl; mix well.
- Add dressing to pasta; toss.
- Refrigerate salad until ready to serve.

Yield: 6-8 servings

Add fresh chopped parsley for more color. Add cherry tomatoes and black olives if serving as a light entree.

A wonderful accompaniment to a grilled entree, or as a luncheon or tailgate dish.

Stunning Pasta Salad

*1 pound trio corkscrew pasta,
   cooked and drained*
*¹/₂ jar McCormick's Salad
   Supreme seasoning*
*1 (8 ounce) bottle Kraft Zesty
   Italian salad dressing*
1 cucumber, diced
1 Bermuda onion, diced
1 red bell pepper, chopped
1 green bell pepper, chopped
1¹/₂ cups sliced baby carrots
1 pint cherry tomatoes, halved

- Mix all ingredients and toss well.
- Refrigerate at least 1 hour before serving.

Yield: 6-8 servings

This pasta salad tastes as wonderful as it looks! Great for parties or just to have in the refrigerator.

Pasta may be cooked and mixed with seasoning and ¹/₂ bottle salad dressing the day before a party, adding the remaining salad dressing and vegetables prior to serving.

Spinach and Strawberry Crunch Salad

1 pound fresh spinach, rinsed
and stemmed
1 pint fresh strawberries,
sliced

- Tear spinach into bite-size pieces.
- In a large bowl, combine spinach, strawberry slices, and dressing. Toss well. Serve immediately.

Yield: 6 servings

Dressing

¼ cup sugar
1 tablespoon sesame seeds
½ tablespoon poppy seeds
¼ teaspoon paprika
½ cup vegetable oil
¼ cup red wine vinegar
¼ teaspoon Worcestershire
sauce
½ teaspoon minced onion

- Combine all ingredients; mix well.
- Use immediately or chill.

Yield: 1 cup

A special treat any time, but especially attractive during the holidays with the deep green of the spinach and the bright red of the strawberries.

Gruyère and Walnut Salad

1 head Boston lettuce
½ pound watercress, trimmed
½ cup chopped walnuts
4 ounces Gruyère cheese, cut
into matchstick-size pieces

- Tear lettuce into bite-size pieces.
- Add watercress, walnuts, and cheese.
- Prepare vinaigrette dressing.
- Add vinaigrette to greens; toss well.

Yield: 4 servings

Vinaigrette Dressing

¼ cup olive oil
1 tablespoon red wine
1 tablespoon red wine vinegar
1 tablespoon Dijon mustard
½ teaspoon pepper

- Combine all ingredients; blend well.

Yield: ½ cup

Very simple, but distinctive! The watercress makes this salad special.

Gruyère cheese has a nutty aroma and flavor. It is often used in cooking because of its excellent melting qualities.

Spinach and Bacon Salad

1½ *pounds spinach, rinsed*
and trimmed
4 *ounces arugula, rinsed and*
trimmed
2 *small red onions, thinly*
sliced
1 (3½ *ounce) package enoki*
mushrooms
4 *ounces fresh white*
mushrooms, thinly sliced
1½ *cups Warm Champagne*
Vinegar Dressing
8 *ounces bacon, cooked crisp*
and crumbled
2 *hard-boiled eggs, finely*
chopped
½ *cup toasted sesame seeds*

- Tear the spinach and arugula leaves into bite-size pieces and place in a large salad bowl.
- Add the onions and mushrooms; toss well.
- Prepare dressing. Pour 1½ cups of the dressing over the salad and toss to coat.
- Sprinkle with bacon, eggs, and sesame seeds.

Yield: 6 entree servings or 10
side-dish servings

Present this on individual salad
plates. Arrange spinach mixture
on plates, drizzle each serving with
dressing, and top with bacon, eggs,
and sesame seeds. Garnish with
cherry tomatoes.

Warm Champagne Vinegar Dressing

1 *cup Champagne vinegar*
2 *tablespoons sugar*
1½ *tablespoons all-purpose*
flour
2 *teaspoons dry vermouth*
1 *teaspoon Dijon mustard*
(2 teaspoons for a zestier
dressing)
1 *egg, beaten*
3 *tablespoons heavy cream*
2 *cups olive oil*
Salt and freshly ground
pepper to taste

- Combine vinegar, sugar, flour, vermouth, and mustard in a small saucepan. Heat to simmering over medium heat.
- Reduce heat to low, and gradually whisk in the egg and the cream.
- Whisk in the oil in a thin, steady stream.
- Season with salt and pepper to taste.
- Remove from heat.
- Serve immediately over salad.

Yield: 3 cups

The dressing recipe makes twice
what is needed for the spinach
salad. The remaining dressing can
be reheated for later use.

The dressing is the highlight of
this salad. Truly outstanding!

Boston Lettuce with Avocado, Hazelnuts, and Raspberry Vinaigrette

2 heads Boston lettuce
2 ounces hazelnuts
2 ripe avocados

- Rinse lettuce and tear into bite-size pieces. Chill.
- Preheat oven to 350°. Place hazelnuts on a cookie sheet. Bake for 15 minutes. Wrap nuts in a tea towel and let cool. Rub the nuts in the towel to remove the skins. Chop nuts coarsely in a food processor.
- Peel and slice the avocados.
- Combine the lettuce, avocado slices, and hazelnuts in a salad bowl. Toss with Raspberry Vinaigrette.

Creamy Raspberry
Vinaigrette
4 tablespoons raspberry
  vinegar
1 tablespoon Dijon mustard
Salt and pepper to taste
1 cup avocado or peanut oil
1 tablespoon heavy cream

- Combine the vinegar, mustard, salt, and pepper in a blender or food processor. Slowly add the oil and cream, blend for 30 seconds or until smooth.

Yield: 1½ cups

Cutting salad greens with a knife will cause discoloration and bruising of the leaves. Tear the leaves for better results.

Feta and Vegetable Salad

7 ounces Feta cheese,
  crumbled
1 cucumber, peeled and
  chopped
½ large red onion, chopped
3 tablespoons olive oil
2 tablespoons fresh lemon
  juice
Pepper to taste
Chopped fresh parsley for
  garnish

- In a large bowl, combine Feta cheese, cucumber, onion, oil, and lemon juice. Season with pepper. Toss well.
- Garnish with parsley. Serve chilled.

Yield: 4 servings
Very refreshing on a hot day!

Endive Salad with Toasted Walnuts

⅓ cup walnuts
1 head Belgian endive

- Preheat oven to 375°. Toast walnuts for 5-7 minutes. Remove and let cool.
- Arrange endive on plate, sprinkle walnuts on top, and drizzle with dressing.

Yield: 4 servings

Dressing
4 tablespoons walnut oil
1 tablespoon Champagne vinegar
2 tablespoons orange marmalade
2 green onions (white part only), minced
Salt and freshly ground black pepper

- Combine all dressing ingredients in a small bowl; whisk until well mixed. Refrigerate for at least 4 hours.
- Add another tablespoon of orange marmalade if a sweeter dressing is desired.

Yield: 1 cup

This salad is wonderful with fish!

Red Onion and Blue Cheese Salad

½ head red leaf lettuce
½ head romaine lettuce
1 head Belgian endive
5 tablespoons olive oil
1 tablespoon red wine vinegar
1 teaspoon Dijon mustard
1 teaspoon sugar
Salt and pepper to taste
½ red onion, thinly sliced
⅓ cup crumbled blue cheese

- Rinse salad greens. Slice red leaf and romaine horizontally into ¼-inch strips. Slice endive vertically into ¼-inch strips.
- Combine olive oil, vinegar, mustard, sugar, salt, and pepper in bottom of salad bowl.
- Place greens on top of dressing, followed by onions and blue cheese.
- Toss just before serving.

Yield: 4-6 servings

Add more cheese for real blue cheese lovers!

Green Bean and Tomato Salad with Bacon and Pine Nut Dressing

¼ cup pine nuts
1¼ pounds green beans
2 medium tomatoes, cut into wedges
6 ounces smoked bacon, cooked crisp and crumbled
2 tablespoons bacon grease
3 tablespoons extra virgin olive oil
3 tablespoons red wine vinegar
½ teaspoon sugar
½ teaspoon salt
¼ teaspoon freshly ground pepper

- Preheat oven to 375°.
- Spread pine nuts on a baking sheet, toast in oven until golden brown, about 10 minutes. Set aside.
- In a large saucepan of boiling water, cook beans, stirring once, about 5 minutes. Drain immediately and rinse beans under cold water. Drain again thoroughly and arrange on platter.
- Place tomato wedges around beans.
- In a small skillet, heat bacon grease and olive oil. Stir in remaining ingredients. Bring to a boil and simmer 1 minute, stirring until sugar dissolves. Add pine nuts. Pour over beans.

Yield: 4 servings

Broccoli Bacon Salad

2 large heads broccoli, chopped
½ cup raisins
¼ cup chopped red onion
1 cup mayonnaise
¼ cup sugar
2 tablespoons cider vinegar
12 slices bacon, cooked crisp and crumbled

- In a large bowl, combine mayonnaise, sugar, and vinegar; mix well.
- Add broccoli, raisins, and onion to bowl. Toss with mayonnaise mixture.
- Cover and chill several hours or overnight.
- Top with bacon before serving.

Yield: 8-10 servings

For a different flavor, substitute 1½ cups grated Cheddar cheese for raisins.

For a slightly softer texture, blanch the broccoli for 1 minute, then plunge into ice water before adding to other ingredients.

Zucchini Salad

3 medium-sized zucchini,
  thinly sliced
½ cup shredded green pepper
½ cup shredded celery
½ cup shredded yellow onion
⅔ cup cider vinegar
⅓ cup oil
¼ cup Burgundy wine
2 tablespoons red wine
  vinegar
½ cup sugar
1 teaspoon salt
½ teaspoon freshly ground
  pepper

- Combine vegetables in a large bowl.
- Combine remaining ingredients in a separate bowl; mix well. Add to vegetables; mix thoroughly.
- Cover and refrigerate at least 6 hours before serving.

Yield: 6 servings

Very easy! Vegetables can be chopped instead of shredded, if desired.

Gazpacho Salad

4 large tomatoes, unpeeled,
  seeded and diced
1 green bell pepper, diced
1 red bell pepper, diced
1 medium-sized onion, diced
1 medium-sized cucumber,
  seeded and diced

Dressing
¼ cup red wine vinegar
2 teaspoons minced garlic
½ teaspoon sugar
½ teaspoon salt
¼ cup extra virgin olive oil

- Place all ingredients in a glass bowl.
- Pour dressing over salad.
- Cover and chill.

Yield: 4-6 servings

- Combine vinegar, garlic, sugar, and salt. Whip in olive oil.

Yield: ½ cup

Serve salad on lettuce leaves and top with lots of croutons!

24 Hour Slaw

1 *large head of red or green*
  cabbage, shredded
1 *large sweet onion, chopped*
1 *large green bell pepper,*
  chopped
1 *cup sugar*
1 *cup vinegar*
1 *teaspoon dry mustard*
1 *teaspoon celery seed*
1 *teaspoon salt*
1 *cup vegetable oil*

- Place cabbage, onion, and bell pepper in a large bowl.
- In a medium saucepan, combine sugar, vinegar, mustard, celery seed, and salt. Bring to a boil and cook until sugar is dissolved. Remove from heat, add oil, and pour over vegetables. Do not toss.
- Cover and chill for 24 hours before tossing and serving.

Yield: 10-15 servings

This is a fantastic picnic or vacation dish. It will keep for almost a week in the refrigerator!

Black Bean and Corn Vinaigrette Salad

1 *(15 ounce) can black beans*
1 *(11 ounce) can white shoe*
  peg corn
1 *(10 ounce) can diced*
  tomatoes and green chilies
1 *bunch green onions, chopped*
½ *cup chopped fresh cilantro*
½ *cup finely chopped fresh*
  parsley

- Drain and rinse black beans and corn.
- Combine all ingredients in a large bowl. Pour vinaigrette dressing over salad and toss.
- Serve at room temperature or prepare ahead of time and refrigerate.

Yield: 4-6 servings

In the summer, replace the can of tomatoes and chilies and the canned corn with diced fresh tomatoes and 3 ears of cooked fresh corn.

Vinaigrette Dressing
⅓ *cup olive oil*
Juice from 2 lemons
Sea salt to taste

- Mix all ingredients.

Yield: ⅔ cup

This quick, easy salad has great flavor and color!

Fiesta Bean Salad

1 pound fresh green beans
1 (10 ounce) package frozen
  lima beans
1 small onion, minced
$^1/_4$ cup olive oil
1 tablespoon chili powder
$^1/_3$ cup white vinegar
$1^1/_2$ teaspoons sugar
$1^1/_2$ teaspoons salt
1 (16 ounce) can corn,
  drained
1 (16 ounce) can red kidney
  beans, drained
1 (16 ounce) can white kidney
  beans, drained
1 (16 ounce) can black beans,
  drained
2 tablespoons chopped fresh
  cilantro or parsley

- Parboil green beans until crisp, 5-10 minutes.
- Prepare lima beans as directed, do not overcook.
- In a medium saucepan, heat olive oil. Sauté onion until tender but not brown. Stir in chili powder; cook for 1 minute. Remove pan from heat.
- Stir in vinegar, sugar, and salt.
- Place corn, red kidney beans, white kidney beans, black beans, green beans, lima beans, and cilantro or parsley in a large bowl. Toss with dressing.
- Chill for at least 1 hour before serving.

Yield: 6-8 servings

A deluxe bean salad! Always a hit!

Black-Eyed Pea Salad

4 (15 ounce) cans black-eyed
  peas, drained
1 red bell pepper, chopped
1 green bell pepper, chopped
1 yellow bell pepper, chopped
3 stalks celery, chopped
1 bunch green onions, chopped
1 bunch fresh parsley or
  cilantro, chopped

Dressing
$^1/_3$ cup olive oil
$^1/_3$ cup red wine vinegar
$^1/_4$ cup sugar
2 cloves garlic, minced

- Combine all ingredients. Toss with dressing.

Yield: 8-10 servings

- Combine oil, vinegar, sugar, and garlic. Mix well.

Yield: $^3/_4$ cup

Spice this up with salsa or jalapeño peppers. Keeps for weeks!

Melanie's Salad

1 (16 ounce) can cut green beans, drained
1 (16 ounce) can tiny green lima beans
1 (16 ounce) can tiny green peas
1 (2 ounce) jar sliced pimientos
1 bunch celery, chopped
1 green pepper, chopped
2 medium onions, chopped
Salt, pepper, and garlic salt to taste
1 cup sugar
1 cup vinegar
1 cup vegetable oil

- Mix vegetables; place one-fourth of mixture in the bottom of a salad bowl. Sprinkle with salt, pepper, and garlic salt. Repeat layers until all is used. Set aside.
- Combine sugar, vinegar, and oil; mix well. Pour over vegetables.
- Marinate overnight. Drain well before serving.

Yield: 10 servings

Will keep indefinitely!

Seasons Cafe Red Potato Salad

5 pounds small red potatoes, each cut into 6 wedges
1/2 pound red onions, thinly sliced
1 (16 ounce) can French-style green beans, drained
4 ounces bacon, cooked crisp and crumbled
2 tablespoons chopped fresh parsley
1 cup mayonnaise
4 teaspoons salt
1/2 cup vegetable oil
1/2 cup red wine vinegar

- Cook potatoes until tender. Drain and cool.
- In a large mixing bowl, combine potatoes, onions, green beans, bacon, and parsley; set aside.
- In a small bowl, mix mayonnaise, salt, oil, and vinegar.
- Pour dressing over potato mixture. Blend with a rubber spatula.

Yield: 20 servings

Excellent potato salad from Seasons Cafe in historic Williamsburg, Virginia.

Celery Seed Dressing

½ cup sugar
1 teaspoon dry mustard
1 teaspoon salt
½ onion, grated
⅓ cup vinegar
1 cup oil
1 tablespoon celery seed

- Combine sugar, mustard, and salt in a small bowl.
- Add onion and a small amount of the vinegar. Mix well.
- Add remaining vinegar. Mix well.
- Add oil slowly while continuing to blend.
- Add celery seeds.

Yield: 1½ cups

Spectacular on fruit or green salad.

Parmesan Pepper Dressing

1½ cups oil
½ cup white wine vinegar
Juice of 1½ lemons
½ teaspoon Worcestershire sauce
3 tablespoons chili sauce
1 teaspoon prepared mustard
¼ cup grated Parmesan cheese
Salt and pepper to taste

- Combine all ingredients in a blender or food processor; blend well.
- Cover and chill for at least 1 hour.
- Serve with fresh green salad.

Yield: 2 cups

Outstanding flavor...you'll never buy a bottled version again!

Cranberry Chutney

½ *cup white or cider vinegar*
4 *cups cranberries*
2½ *cups sugar*
1 *cup water*
10 *whole cloves*
½ *teaspoon salt*
2 *tart apples, cut into* ¼-*inch*
  pieces
2 *ripe pears, cut into* ¼-*inch*
  pieces
1 *small onion, cut into* ¼-*inch*
  pieces
½ *cup raisins*
1 *(2-inch) piece of ginger root,*
  peeled and grated
Grated peel of 1 orange

- Combine vinegar, cranberries, sugar, water, cloves, and salt in a medium saucepan. Bring to a boil over medium heat.
- Add apple, pear, and onion pieces along with raisins to cranberry mixture; mix well.
- Stir in grated ginger root and orange peel. Cook over low heat until chutney thickens, approximately 30 minutes. Cook and transfer to a storage container.
- Cover and refrigerate.

Yield: 5 cups

Delightful on ham biscuits, turkey sandwiches, pork or lamb chops, or with cream cheese and crackers.

Rosy Relish

2¼ *cups sugar*
1 *cup chopped green pepper*
4 1-*inch cinnamon sticks,*
  broken
2 *tablespoons mustard seed*
10 *cloves*
1 *tablespoon salt*
1½ *cups dark vinegar*
4 *cups peeled, chopped green*
  cooking apples
1 *cup chopped celery*
2 *tablespoons chopped red bell*
  pepper

- Combine all ingredients. Bring to a boil in an uncovered pot. Simmer until thick, about 4½ hours. Stir every 15 minutes. Be careful not to burn the relish in the last hour of cooking.
- Cool and store in jars in refrigerator.

Yield: 2 pints

An excellent relish for hamburgers and hot dogs. Also good as an hors d'oeuvre served on cream cheese with crackers. This is an old Virginia recipe and a favorite from **Virginia Seasons.**

Sweet Potato Biscuits

1½ cups all-purpose flour
2½ teaspoons baking powder
½ teaspoon cinnamon
½ teaspoon salt
¼ teaspoon allspice
¼ teaspoon nutmeg
⅓ cup brown sugar
½ teaspoon lemon peel
1 stick butter, room
*   temperature*
¾ cup pureed baked sweet
*   potato*
2 tablespoons heavy cream

- Preheat oven to 350°.
- In a large bowl, sift together flour, baking powder, cinnamon, salt, allspice, and nutmeg.
- Stir in brown sugar and lemon peel.
- Cut in butter until mixture becomes a coarse meal.
- Add sweet potato and cream. Mix until evenly moist.
- Turn out and knead 12 times. Add more flour to mixture to knead, if necessary. Knead by pushing center of dough and folding outside dough inward. Roll dough with rolling pin on lightly floured surface.
- Cut dough with biscuit cutter and place on an ungreased baking sheet.
- Bake 25 minutes or until brown.

Yield: 1 to 2 dozen, depending on biscuit size

Good sliced with turkey or ham.

Marian's Sour Cream Biscuits

1 cup biscuit baking mix
½ stick butter, softened but
*   not melted*
4 ounces sour cream

- Preheat oven to 400°.
- Mix all ingredients.
- Spray miniature muffin tins with non-stick vegetable spray. Fill tins half full with batter.
- Bake for 9-11 minutes. Do not overcook...they will get too dry.

Yield: 24 muffins

Perfect for luncheons. A quick and easy way to dress up any meal.

The Roanoker Buttermilk Biscuit Mix

1 pound Big Spring Mill
  self-rising flour
1¹/₂ teaspoons sugar
1¹/₂ teaspoons baking powder
4¹/₂ ounces vegetable
  shortening
³/₄ cup cold buttermilk
All-purpose flour

- Preheat oven to 400°.
- Combine self-rising flour, sugar, and baking powder in a large bowl.
- Cut in shortening with pastry blender or 2 knives until mixture resembles coarse meal.
- Use immediately or store in an airtight container in a cool place.
- To prepare biscuits, combine the biscuit mix and ¾ cup cold buttermilk. Work the mixture until the dough is slightly sticky.
- Spread a light layer of all-purpose flour on a flat work surface.
- Form dough into a ball and place in the middle of the floured work surface.
- Knead the dough with the flour, bringing the outside into the center and pressing downward. Repeat 10 times.
- Roll dough until ½" to ¾" thick.
- Cut with a 3-inch biscuit cutter. Place biscuits on an ungreased baking sheet.
- Bake 12-14 minutes or until browned on top and bottom.
- Serve hot with butter, jelly, or The Roanoker Red Eye Gravy, page 175.

Yield: 6-8 biscuits

From the "Home of Good Food", The Roanoker Restaurant in Roanoke, Virginia.

Fairlea Farm's "Upside-Down" French Toast

Syrup

1 cup dark brown sugar
½ cup butter
2 tablespoons light corn syrup

- Combine ingredients in medium saucepan. Simmer until thickened and syrupy.
- Spread mixture over bottom of a 9"x13" baking pan.

Toast

1 loaf French or Italian bread
1½ cups milk
5 eggs
1 teaspoon vanilla
¼ teaspoon salt

- Slice bread into eight ½-inch thick slices. Place over syrup in baking pan.
- Beat milk, eggs, vanilla, and salt. Pour mixture over bread.
- Cover and refrigerate overnight.
- Preheat oven to 350°.
- Bake, uncovered, for 45 minutes.
- Cut and serve with bacon, sautéed apples, or sliced fresh fruit.

Yield: 6 servings

Use day-old bread. It will keep its form better.

A delicious "do-ahead" breakfast or brunch favorite from Fairlea Farm Bed and Breakfast in Washington, Virginia.

Rugelah

1 (8 ounce) package cream
   cheese, softened
2 sticks sweet butter, softened
2 cups all-purpose flour
1/2 cup sugar, divided
2-3 tablespoons cinnamon
1/2 cup raisins
1/2 cup walnuts

- In a large mixing bowl, combine cream cheese, butter, flour, and 2 tablespoons sugar.
- Remove dough from bowl; knead well into a ball.
- Wrap ball in wax paper. Refrigerate overnight.
- Bring dough to room temperature and divide into four equal parts.
- Preheat oven to 350°.
- In a small mixing bowl, combine remaining sugar, cinnamon, raisins, and nuts.
- Roll out each of the portions of dough and cut into triangles or strips. Fill centers of triangles or strips with cinnamon mixture (1-2 teaspoons each). Roll up triangles or strips and place on a large ungreased cookie sheet.
- Bake for 20-25 minutes.

Yield: 24-30 servings

Your family will rave! Delicious when heated in the microwave for breakfast and spread with butter.

Sour Cream Muffins

1 stick margarine
1 1/2 cups sugar
1/2 teaspoon salt
4 eggs, beaten
1 1/2 cups sour cream
2 3/4 cups all-purpose flour
1/3 cup nutmeg
1 teaspoon baking soda

- Preheat oven to 450°.
- Combine margarine, sugar, and salt.
- Combine eggs and sour cream.
- Combine flour, nutmeg, and baking soda.
- Mix all ingredients. Line muffin tins with paper baking cups. Fill each baking cup 3/4 full with batter.
- Bake for 15 minutes.

Yield: 2 dozen

Brown Sugar Oatmeal Pancakes

1 egg, beaten
2 tablespoons vegetable oil
1 cup buttermilk (may
substitute powdered form)
½ cup whole wheat flour
½ cup all-purpose flour
½ teaspoon baking soda
½ teaspoon salt
⅓ cup brown sugar, firmly
packed
½ cup plus 2 tablespoons
quick-cooking oats

• In a large mixing bowl, combine egg, vegetable oil, and buttermilk.
• In another bowl, combine the flours, baking soda, salt, and brown sugar; mix well. Add to liquid mixture.
• Stir in oats.
• Pour onto a hot griddle; turn pancakes when bubbles form on top.

Yield: 10 pancakes

The dry ingredients may be mixed the night before. Add egg, oil, and buttermilk in the morning for a quick, nutritious breakfast.

Chunky Apple Muffins

4 cups unpeeled, diced sweet
red and green apples (not
tart)
1 cup sugar
2 large eggs, lightly beaten
½ cup corn oil
2 teaspoons vanilla
2 cups all-purpose flour
2 teaspoons baking soda
2 teaspoons cinnamon
1 teaspoon salt
1 cup raisins
1 cup walnut pieces

• Preheat oven to 325°.
• In a large mixing bowl, combine apples and sugar. Set aside.
• In another bowl, stir eggs, oil, and vanilla until well blended.
• In a third bowl, combine flour, baking soda, cinnamon, and salt; stir with a fork until blended.
• Stir the egg mixture into the apples; mix well. Sprinkle the flour mixture over the apple mixture; mix well, using your hands if necessary.
• Sprinkle raisins and walnuts over the batter and mix until they are evenly distributed.
• Spoon batter into greased muffin tins almost to the top. Bake 25 minutes.
• Serve warm.

Yield: 1½ dozen

Particularly nice as a gift or with Sunday brunch.

71

Poppy Seed Muffins

½ cup all-purpose flour
1 package vanilla / white cake mix
3 tablespoons butter or margarine, softened
⅔ cup water
⅓ cup vegetable oil
2 eggs
1 tablespoon poppy seeds
1 tablespoon almond extract

- Preheat oven to 375°.
- Mix all ingredients in order listed. Pour batter into muffin tins.
- Bake for 25-30 minutes.

Yield: 18 muffins

These muffins are wonderfully light and flavorful!

Blueberry Muffins

1 cup fresh blueberries
1 tablespoon sugar (for topping)
1 teaspoon grated lemon peel
2 cups sifted all-purpose flour
⅓ cup sugar (for batter)
1 tablespoon baking powder
1 teaspoon salt
1 egg, well beaten
1 cup milk
¼ cup (½ stick) butter or margarine, melted

- Preheat oven to 425°.
- Wash berries and drain on paper towels. Set aside.
- Combine 1 tablespoon sugar and lemon peel; set aside.
- Sift flour, ⅓ cup sugar, baking powder, and salt into a bowl.
- Combine egg, milk, and melted butter in a small bowl; add immediately to dry ingredients. Stir quickly and lightly until liquid is absorbed (batter will be lumpy).
- Fold in berries.
- Spoon batter into a greased muffin tin, filling each cup ⅔ full. Sprinkle reserved lemon-sugar over all.
- Bake 20 minutes or until golden brown. Remove from pan at once.
- Serve hot.

Yield: 12 muffins

Incredible Edibles' Sour Cream Coffee Cake

½ cup sugar
1 tablespoon cinnamon
1 cup chopped pecans
1 cup semi-sweet chocolate
  chips
Extra chocolate chips for
  topping
2 cups all-purpose flour
2 cups sugar
1 tablespoon baking powder
¼ teaspoon salt
1 cup butter, softened
2 cups sour cream
2 eggs
2 teaspoons vanilla extract

- Preheat oven to 375°.
- To prepare topping, combine ½ cup sugar, cinnamon, pecans, and 1 cup of chocolate chips; set aside.
- Sift together flour, 2 cups sugar, baking powder, and salt in a large bowl. Add butter, sour cream, eggs, and vanilla; beat for 2 minutes.
- Spoon half the batter into a greased 10-inch tube pan. Sprinkle half of the topping over the batter. Add extra chocolate chips if desired. Spoon remaining batter on top of the chocolate chip mixture. Sprinkle with remaining topping and chocolate chips.
- Bake 60 minutes or until a toothpick inserted in the center comes out clean.

Yield: 12-18 servings

This delectable coffee cake is a specialty of Incredible Edibles in the Carytown section of Richmond, Virginia.

73

Tropical Coffee Cake

½ cup chopped pecans
½ cup flaked coconut
¼ cup sugar
2 teaspoons grated orange peel
1 teaspoon ground cinnamon
½ cup butter or margarine
1 cup sugar
2 eggs
8 ounces sour cream
1 teaspoon vanilla extract
2 cups all-purpose flour
1 teaspoon baking soda
1 teaspoon baking powder
Dash of salt

- Preheat oven to 350°.
- Combine pecans, coconut, sugar, orange peel, and cinnamon in a small bowl; set aside.
- Cream butter and sugar using an electric mixer at medium speed. Add eggs one at a time, beating after each addition. Add sour cream and vanilla; blend well. Set aside.
- In a separate bowl, combine flour, baking soda, baking powder, and salt. Add to creamed mixture, beating well.
- Spoon half of batter into a well-greased 9-inch cake pan. Sprinkle with half of the pecan mixture. Repeat with remaining batter and pecan mixture. Gently swirl with a knife to create a marbled effect.
- Bake 35 minutes or until a wooden toothpick inserted in the center comes out clean.

Yield: 8-12 servings

Very pretty cake. This is a wonderful cake to welcome new neighbors, take to a church supper, or give as a gift.

Cranberry Orange Bread

2½ cups sifted all-purpose flour
1 cup sugar
2 teaspoons baking powder
½ teaspoon baking soda
¼ teaspoon salt
½ cup chopped pecans
2 teaspoons grated orange peel
2 eggs
¾ cup orange juice
½ cup mayonnaise
1½ cups chopped fresh cranberries
2 tablespoons sugar, for topping
½ teaspoon grated orange peel, for topping

- Preheat oven to 350°.
- In a large mixing bowl, combine flour, sugar, baking powder, baking soda, and salt.
- Stir in pecans and 2 teaspoons orange peel; set aside.
- Combine the eggs, orange juice, and mayonnaise; mix well. Stir into flour mixture, mixing until just moistened. Fold in cranberries.
- Spoon into a greased and floured 9"x5" loaf pan.
- Combine 2 tablespoons sugar and ½ teaspoon orange peel; sprinkle on top of loaf.
- Bake 55 minutes. Cover with foil and continue baking 10 more minutes. Cool on wire rack.

Yield: 1 loaf

When baking loaves of bread, let the batter sit in the pan for 20 minutes before baking to lessen the size of the crack in the top of the loaf.

Pumpkin Bread

1¾ *cups all-purpose flour*
1½ *cups sugar*
1 *teaspoon baking soda*
½ *teaspoon baking powder*
1 *teaspoon cinnamon*
¾ *teaspoon salt*
½ *teaspoon ground cloves*
½ *teaspoon nutmeg*
½ *teaspoon allspice*
1½ *cups canned pumpkin*
½ *cup vegetable oil*
½ *cup water*
2 *eggs*

- Preheat oven to 350°.
- Grease 2 small loaf pans and line with wax paper.
- Sift dry ingredients into a large mixing bowl. Add the pumpkin, oil, water, and eggs to the dry ingredients; beat until well blended.
- Pour into loaf pans. Bake approximately 1 hour or until a knife inserted in loaf comes out clean. Do not overcook.

Yield: 2 loaves

Delicious spread with cream cheese for breakfast or with a midmorning cup of coffee.

Carrot Bread

3 *cups all-purpose flour*
2 *cups sugar*
2 *cups shredded carrots*
1½ *cups vegetable oil*
1 *(8 ounce) can crushed pineapple*
3 *eggs*
3 *tablespoons cinnamon*
1 *teaspoon baking soda*
1 *teaspoon salt*

- Preheat oven to 325°.
- Grease and flour 2 loaf pans or 6 mini loaf pans.
- Combine all ingredients in a large mixing bowl. Pour batter into loaf pans.
- Bake 45-60 minutes, until toothpick inserted in center comes out clean.

Yield: 2 loaves or 6 mini loaves

These rich, moist loaves freeze beautifully.

Sally Lunn Bread

1 stick butter or margarine
1 cup milk
⅓ cup sugar
1 (¼ ounce) package active
dry yeast
3 eggs, room temperature
4 cups sifted all-purpose flour
1 teaspoon salt

- Melt butter in a small saucepan. Add milk and sugar, stirring to dissolve sugar. When mixture is lukewarm, pour into mixer bowl and add yeast.
- Beat on low speed 3 minutes.
- Beat in eggs. Add flour and salt, continue beating on medium speed for 10 minutes.
- Cover mixer bowl with damp tea towel and set in a warm place to rise until dough is doubled in bulk and very spongy.
- Beat another 10 minutes on medium speed, then turn into a well-buttered 10-inch tube or Bundt pan. Set in warm place to rise.
- When Sally Lunn is doubled, place very gently in oven and bake 40-50 minutes, or until toothpick inserted in center comes out clean and bread is richly browned on top. Remove from oven; cool in pan 5 minutes. Turn onto rack to finish cooling, or turn onto serving platter, cut into wedges and serve immediately.

Yield: 12 servings

Sally Lunn may be frozen and reheated from frozen state, tightly wrapped in heavy-duty aluminum foil, in a preheated 350° oven for 15-20 minutes, or until piping hot throughout. Slice and serve hot.

A Virginia favorite perfected by food editor Frances Price.

Easy French Bread

2 (¼ ounce) packages active
  dry yeast
½ cup warm water
½ teaspoon sugar
2 tablespoons sugar
2 tablespoons shortening,
  butter, or margarine
2 teaspoons salt
2 cups boiling water
6-7 cups bread flour
1 egg
2 tablespoons milk
Poppy seeds or sesame seeds

- Dissolve yeast in ½ cup warm water with ½ teaspoon of sugar. Set aside.
- Combine 2 tablespoons sugar, shortening, salt, and boiling water. Cool to lukewarm. Add yeast mixture. Yeast mixture should be foamy before adding.
- Stir in bread flour. Knead for 10 minutes or until smooth and elastic. Place in a greased bowl, turning once. Cover with a dishtowel and let rise until doubled in a warm place (80-85 degrees) for an hour to an hour and a half.
- Punch down dough and let rest 15 minutes.
- Divide dough in half. On a floured surface, roll each half into 12"x15" rectangle. Roll up starting at the 15-inch edge. Place the loaves on a greased cookie sheet.
- Make 4 or 5 diagonal slashes with a knife across the tops of both loaves. Let rise until doubled, 45-60 minutes.
- Preheat oven to 400°.
- Beat egg with milk. Brush egg mixture on top of both loaves.
- Sprinkle with poppy seeds or sesame seeds.
- Bake for 20 minutes.
- Remove loaves to a cooling rack. Slice with a bread knife (serrated-edged knife).

Yield: 2 loaves

Thalhimers' Richmond Room Popovers

8 tablespoons vegetable oil,
  divided
2 cups all-purpose flour
6 eggs
3 cups whole milk, divided
½ teaspoon sugar
2 tablespoons baking powder
  (Rumford brand is
  recommended)

- Preheat oven to 400°.
- Pour 1 teaspoon vegetable oil into each of 24 (2½-inch) muffin cups. Place cups in oven and heat until hot.
- In bowl of electric mixer at medium speed, beat flour, eggs, 1½ cups milk, sugar, and baking powder for 15 minutes. Add remaining milk and beat 5 minutes longer.
- Pour batter into sizzling hot oil in muffin cups, filling each cup half-full.
- Bake until golden brown and popped, about 20 minutes.

Yield: 24 popovers

The secret is lots of eggs and lots of beating!

This recipe is also found in Virginia Seasons.

Thalhimers' Richmond Room Spoonbread

¼ cup margarine, melted
¾ cup white cornmeal
1½ cups boiling water
½ cup all-purpose flour
1½ cups whole milk
4 eggs
½ teaspoon sugar
1½ teaspoons baking powder
  (Rumford brand is
  recommended)
Pinch of salt

- Preheat oven to 350°.
- Melt margarine and pour into an 8-inch square baking pan.
- Place cornmeal in a mixing bowl. Pour boiling water over cornmeal; mix well. Stir in flour, milk, eggs, sugar, baking powder, and salt. Beat with a wire whisk until smooth.
- Pour into prepared pan. Bake until firm and golden brown, 30-35 minutes.

Yield: 9 servings

A fondly remembered bit of Richmond's history...the Richmond Room at Thalhimers' department store.

Mexican Cornbread

1 cup cream-style corn
⅓ cup vegetable oil
½ medium-sized banana
  pepper, chopped
1 cup grated sharp Cheddar
  cheese
½ cup milk
2 eggs, beaten
1 cup self-rising corn meal
1 cup chopped onion
Extra sharp Cheddar cheese,
  optional

- Preheat oven to 425°.
- Combine all ingredients in a large mixing bowl.
- Bake in a lightly greased jelly roll pan for 25 minutes. Additional cheese may be shredded on top of cornbread just before baking is complete, if desired.

Yield: 20 pieces

Lacy Cornbread Wafers

1 cup cornmeal
1¾ cups water
½ tablespoon salt
Dash of pepper
1 small onion, finely chopped
Vegetable oil for frying

- Mix all ingredients except vegetable oil to form a thin batter.
- Heat ½" vegetable oil in a skillet over medium-high heat.
- Drop batter by the tablespoonful into the hot oil. Fry until golden brown, turning once. Drain on paper towels.
- Serve immediately.

Yield: 6 servings

These unusual wafers taste just like hush puppies.

Traditional Southern cooking at its best!

Eggs, Cheese, Rice & Pasta

Southside Hospitality

Is any food more American than peanut butter? The young, eager to be on the move, eat it with jelly in sandwiches slapped together. Their mothers, feeding them and eating the smidgen of leftover peanut butter in the jar, form a hankering for it. The impatient elderly rely on it for quick and easy nourishment between soda crackers. Eight Virginia counties raise peanuts and in most seasons Southampton County produces more than any other county in the United States, save, now and then, one in Georgia. "In hard times," a Southampton farmer told me, "we live on peanuts and past recollections."

Explorers took the peanut from South America to Spain. It spread to Africa as goobers (ground nuts) or pindas and came to Virginia in ships as food for slaves in the holds.

In 1844, Dr. Matthew Harris harvested in Sussex County the first commercial crop. During the Civil War, goober peas whetted appetites of soldiers on both sides, which created a postwar demand for them nationwide. Circus wagons carried them coast to coast and missionaries took them to Asia. They have accompanied a spacecraft beyond the moon.

Suffolk became the peanut capital of the world with the arrival of Amedeo Obici, who had been roasting and bagging peanuts in Pennsylvania. To learn more about them, he visited Suffolk - and stayed. In 1913 he borrowed $ 25,000 to buy a brick factory. Pondering what to name his firm, he mused: "Planters raise peanuts. Why not call it Planters Peanuts?" A school boy won $ 5 with a sketch of a peanut in human guise. An artist added a cane, spats, top hat, and monocle and, presto, there was Mr. Peanut, a deliciously scary apparition to children.

A stocky figure, 5 feet tall, with an imposing air, voluble talk, and a large nose, Obici had an even larger heart and funded many charities for his adopted city. He and his tall, stately wife, Louise, enjoyed entertaining. One evening, noticing that guests hesitated to open small bottles of wine for fear of spilling liquid on the linen, expansive Amedeo arose and, holding his thumb loosely over the mouth of the bottle, shook drops over the tablecloth.

His beloved wife dreamed of a hospital for Suffolk. After her death in 1936, he provided funds for building the Louise Obici Memorial Hospital and a nursing school and a $ 20 million endowment to run the hospital. Later, his foundation provided $ 32 million to expand it.

Festivals are rampant through rural Southside. Each October Suffolk hosts a week-long Peanut Fest. Wakefield has a shad planking in April when the shad and the politicians run and the shad bush comes into bloom. In July, Halifax celebrates the super sweet gourmet cantaloupes raised in Turbeville, the copyrighted name that the delicacy bears. Smithfield has a gourmet festival of ham products. Lawrenceville holds the Virginia Beef and Dairy Products festival in late April. Surry offers a Pork, Pine, and Peanut Festival in July.

Sometimes you feel that what Virginians do most is eat. From spring to fall, Ruritan Clubs, churches, and other civic groups hold weekly barbecues and suppers dedicated to turnips or pancakes or chicken and dumplings or blue crabs so that one could live by sitting down each day to a feast in another town. Many a congregation has built its sanctuary on a foundation of sweet potato pies. Fabled Virginia hospitality traces to colonial times when visitors, after traveling long distances, stayed and stayed and ate and ate.

Sometimes they stayed so long they became members of the family.

-Guy Friddell

Cheesy Eggs

4 eggs, beaten
¼ cup grated Cheddar cheese
¼ cup chopped tomatoes
3 ounces cream cheese
4 drops hot pepper sauce
4 tablespoons butter, optional

- In a medium skillet, scramble eggs slowly over low heat until almost all moisture has evaporated. Remove eggs from heat.
- Stir in Cheddar cheese, tomatoes, cream cheese, and hot pepper sauce. Cover until cheeses are melted. Stir again.
- Dot with butter, if desired. Cover until melted.

Yield: 2 servings

Add your favorite ingredients...diced ham, green pepper, onions, chives, jalapeños! Use your imagination!

Very tasty served over a toasted English muffin. A nice alternative to scrambled eggs or an omelette.

Governor's Egg Casserole

½ cup chopped onion
2 tablespoons butter
2 tablespoons all-purpose flour
1¼ cups milk
1 cup grated sharp Cheddar cheese
6 hard-boiled eggs, sliced
1½ cups crushed potato chips
10-12 slices bacon, cooked crisp and crumbled

- Preheat oven to 350°.
- Sauté onion in butter until tender, not brown.
- Stir in flour. Add milk. Cook, stirring constantly, until thickened.
- Add cheese; stir until melted.
- Layer half of eggs, cheese sauce, potato chips, and bacon in a 10"x6"x2" casserole dish. Repeat layers.
- Bake for 30 minutes.

Yield: 6 servings

May be refrigerated overnight and baked the following day.

When hard-boiling eggs, add one teaspoon salt to water to prevent whites from draining through cracks in the shells.

Healthy Brunch Casserole

*4 slices low-fat whole wheat
  bread*
1 medium onion, chopped
*2 tablespoons low-fat,
  cholesterol-free cooking oil*
1 cup sliced fresh mushrooms
*1 cup low-fat ham slices, cut
  into small pieces*
*1 cup (4 ounces) grated low-
  fat Cheddar cheese*
*1 cup (4 ounces) grated low-
  fat Swiss cheese*
1 tablespoon all-purpose flour
1¼ cups skim milk
*Eggbeaters, amount
  equivalent to 4 eggs*
*1 tablespoon prepared
  mustard or 1 teaspoon dry
  mustard*
½ teaspoon garlic salt
*Parsley sprigs or fresh fruit
  slices for garnish*

- Place bread slices in bottom of a lightly greased (or sprayed with non-stick vegetable spray) 8-inch square baking dish. Set aside.
- Sauté onions and mushrooms in oil until tender; spoon evenly over bread. Top with ham.
- Combine cheese and flour; sprinkle over ham.
- Combine milk, Eggbeaters, mustard, and garlic salt. Pour over cheese.
- Cover and chill for 8 hours. Remove from refrigerator and let stand at room temperature for 30 minutes.
- Preheat oven to 375°.
- Bake for 35 minutes or until light golden brown, being careful not to overbake.
- Let stand for 10 minutes before serving. Garnish and serve.

Yield: 4-6 servings

Sausage and Green Chili Quiche

1 9-inch pie shell, unbaked
½ pound cooked sausage
*2 ounces canned chopped
  green chilies*
¾ cup grated Swiss cheese
¼ cup Parmesan cheese
1¼ cups evaporated milk
2 eggs

- Preheat oven to 450°.
- Line bottom of pie shell with cooked sausage. Top with green chilies.
- Combine the cheeses; sprinkle on top of chilies.
- Beat the evaporated milk and eggs together; pour over top of cheese.
- Bake for 15 minutes at 450°. Lower heat to 350° for an additional 10 minutes of baking.

Yield: 6 servings

For easy cleanup, brush your grater with vegetable oil before grating cheese.

Brookside Breakfast Pie

1 9-inch pie shell, unbaked
2 (21 ounce) cans apple pie
  filling
1 (8 ounce) package link
  sausage, cooked
1 cup grated Cheddar cheese
½ cup all-purpose flour
¼ cup sugar
1 teaspoon cinnamon
3 tablespoons margarine
Cinnamon and nutmeg to
  taste

- Preheat oven to 350°.
- Fill pie shell with apple pie filling.
- Place cooked link sausages in a pinwheel formation on top of pie filling. Sprinkle with Cheddar cheese.
- Prepare a streusel topping by combining flour, sugar, and cinnamon in a small bowl. Add margarine and mix together with a fork until pea-sized crumbs are formed. Cover top of pie with streusel. Sprinkle with cinnamon and nutmeg to taste.
- Bake for 35 minutes or until golden brown.

Yield: 6 servings

This recipe is a favorite at Brookside Bed and Breakfast. Built in 1780, the Brookside is near the northern end of the beautiful Shenandoah Valley, a few miles from the Appalachian Trail.

Smithfield Ham Quiche

1 cup grated Swiss cheese
1 cup chopped Smithfield ham
½ cup chopped onion
1 9-inch pie shell, unbaked
1 (12 ounce) can evaporated
  milk
3 eggs
1 cup hot cooked quick grits
1 tablespoon chopped parsley
½ teaspoon salt
¼ teaspoon dry mustard
⅛ teaspoon cayenne pepper

- Preheat oven to 375°.
- Sprinkle cheese, ham, and onion over bottom of pie shell.
- Beat remaining ingredients together and pour into pie shell.
- Bake for 45-50 minutes, or until knife inserted into center comes out clean.
- Cool 10 minutes before serving.

Yield: 6 servings

A new twist on basic quiche. Great served with fresh fruit for weekend guests!

Spanish Omelette

1 tablespoon olive oil
½ cup minced onion
1 large clove garlic, minced
¼ teaspoon salt
½ teaspoon basil
½ teaspoon oregano
Black pepper and cayenne
   pepper, to taste
½ small green bell pepper, cut
   into very thin strips
½ small red bell pepper, cut
   into very thin strips
1 medium-sized ripe tomato,
   chopped
4-6 green olives, minced
2 tablespoons tomato paste
4 eggs, brought to room
   temperature, then beaten
2 tablespoons butter
⅓ cup grated Cheddar cheese

- Heat olive oil in a medium skillet. Sauté onion and garlic with salt, herbs, black pepper, and cayenne pepper until the onion is soft, about 5 minutes.
- Add bell peppers, tomato, olives, and tomato paste; mix well and cover. Cook over low heat 8-10 minutes.
- Heat a heavy omelette pan gradually until it is very hot. Melt butter. It will make a sizzling noise when it is finished melting. As soon as the sizzling stops, add the beaten eggs.
- Keep the heat constant as you cook. Working quickly, lift the omelette sides and tilt the pan to let the uncooked egg flow into contact with the hot skillet.
- As soon as all the egg is set, place the vegetable filling on one side of the eggs, fold the other side over the top, and slip or flip the omelette onto a plate. Top with grated cheese.

Yield: 2 servings

The filling may be made ahead of time and stored in the refrigerator for several days.

When preparing multiple omelettes, you can make one large omelette and split it, have two frying pans going at once, or work quickly and keep the prepared omelettes warm in a low oven until all omelettes are ready.

To bring eggs to room temperature, place them in a bowl of hot tap water. They will be ready to use in 5 minutes.

Crab, Cream Cheese, and Avocado Omelette

4 eggs, room temperature
¼ cup milk
Salt to taste
Dash white pepper
⅛ teaspoon paprika
1½ tablespoons butter
2 ounces cream cheese,
  softened
½ avocado, sliced
½ cup crabmeat
2 teaspoons lemon juice
Chopped chives

- In a large bowl, beat eggs, milk, salt, pepper, and paprika.
- Melt butter in a large skillet over medium heat. Tilt pan to coat all sides evenly.
- Pour egg mixture into pan; tilt to permit uncooked egg to run to sides and bottom. Pierce egg with a fork to let heat through.
- Lower heat and cook 2-3 minutes or until egg is slightly firm.
- Spoon or drop cream cheese across the center of eggs. Top with avocado slices and crabmeat, drizzle with lemon juice. Roll the edges of egg over filling.
- Remove from heat and cover 2-3 minutes until cheese is melted.
- Sprinkle with chopped chives.
- Serve hot.

Yield: 2 servings

A rich brunch omelette, Virginia style!

Spinach Frittata

*2 (10 ounce) packages frozen
chopped spinach*
3 cups cottage cheese
*1 cup plain bread crumbs,
divided*
*½ cup grated Monterey Jack
cheese (any other type may
be substituted except
Mozzarella)*
5 eggs
¼ teaspoon paprika
Salt and pepper to taste

- Preheat oven to 350°.
- Cook and drain spinach thoroughly. Blend with cottage cheese, ¾ cup bread crumbs, and Monterey Jack cheese. Beat three eggs in a separate bowl, then add to the spinach mixture.
- Lightly oil the bottom of an 8-inch square baking dish; sprinkle it with the remaining ¼ cup bread crumbs. Place pan in oven until bread crumbs are golden brown, 3-5 minutes.
- Spread spinach mixture evenly in baking dish.
- Beat remaining eggs and pour evenly over spinach. Sprinkle with paprika, salt, and pepper.
- Bake 45 minutes. Cool 10 minutes before serving.

Yield: 8 servings

This is tasty right out of the oven or may be cut into wedges and served cold as a summer appetizer.

Pepper Jack Cheese and Herb Presnik

1 pound pepper jack cheese,
  cut into cubes
3 ounces cream cheese, cut
  into cubes
2 tablespoons butter, cut into
  very small pieces
1 cup cottage cheese
8 eggs, lightly beaten
Salt and pepper to taste
Herbs to taste (suggest sage,
  dill, cilantro, thyme,
  rosemary, or parsley in any
  combination)
1 cup milk
½ cup flour
1 tablespoon baking powder

- Preheat oven to 350°.
- Combine pepper jack cheese, cream cheese, butter, and cottage cheese. Place in a buttered 9"x13" non-stick baking dish (or in individual buttered ramekins, cutting down recipe as appropriate).
- In a large bowl, combine eggs, salt, pepper, selected herbs, milk, flour, and baking powder; mix well. Mixture will be a bit lumpy.
- Pour egg mixture over cheese mixture in the baking dish. Mix all together being sure to break up clumps of flour.
- Can be refrigerated at this point for later use, or baked for 40-45 minutes, until the presnik is puffy and golden.

Yield: 8 servings

Can be reheated the next day for approximately 2 minutes on high in the microwave.

Superb with salsa on top!

Chili Relleno Casserole

4 (4 ounce) cans whole green chilies

1 pound Monterey Jack cheese, grated

1 pound Cheddar cheese, grated

4 eggs

2 tablespoons flour

2 (13 ounce) cans evaporated milk

2 (8 ounce) cans tomato sauce

- Preheat oven to 400°.
- Grease a 9"x13" baking dish.
- Split chilies and remove seeds.
- Combine grated cheeses.
- Layer chilies and cheese beginning with half of the chilies in the bottom of the baking dish, top with ⅓ of the mixed cheese, top with remaining half of the chilies, finish layers with ⅓ of the cheese. Set aside remaining ⅓ of the cheese.
- In blender, mix eggs, flour, and milk. Pour over the top of chili/cheese layers.
- Bake 30 minutes. Remove from oven. Pour on tomato sauce and top with remaining cheese. Bake 15 minutes longer.

Yield: 10 servings

Great as a side dish with steaks, grilled fish, or hamburgers in lieu of a potato or vegetable.

Huevos Rancheros

6 8-inch soft corn tortillas
2 tablespoons vegetable oil
1/2 cup chopped onion
1 clove garlic, minced
3 large tomatoes, peeled and chopped (fresh or canned)
1 (4 ounce) can chopped green chilies
1/4 teaspoon salt
6 eggs
1/2 cup grated Cheddar or Monterey Jack cheese

- Preheat oven to 350°.
- In a large skillet, fry tortillas one at a time in hot oil for 5 seconds on each side, or until softened. Drain tortillas on paper towels.
- Lightly grease a 12"x8"x2" baking dish. Line baking dish with tortillas, letting tortillas extend ½ inch up sides of dish. Set aside.
- Sauté onion and garlic in skillet used for frying tortillas until slightly softened. Add tomatoes, chilies, and salt. Simmer uncovered for 10 minutes, stirring occasionally, or until most of liquid is reduced.
- Pour mixture over tortillas in baking dish. Make 6 indentations in tomato mixture and break an egg into each. Cover and bake for 25 minutes.
- Sprinkle with cheese. Return to the oven and bake an additional 2 minutes. Serve immediately.

Yield: 6 servings
Very colorful!

Breakfast Strata

1 cup milk
½ cup dry white wine
1 day-old loaf French bread,
  cut into ½-inch slices
8 ounces Smithfield ham,
  thinly sliced
1 pound basil torta cheese,
  thinly sliced
3 ripe tomatoes, sliced
½ cup basil pesto
4 eggs, beaten
Salt and freshly ground black
  pepper to taste
½ cup heavy cream

- One day before serving, mix the milk and wine in a shallow bowl. Dip 1 or 2 slices of bread in the milk mixture. Place bread slices between paper towels, gently press to squeeze as much liquid as possible from the bread. Be careful not to tear bread when handling it.
- Place the bread in a 12-inch round or oval au gratin dish. Cover with a slice of ham, some slices of basil torta, and a few tomato slices. Drizzle lightly with pesto. Repeat the layering overlapping the bread slices slightly until the dish is filled, ending with a bread layer on top.
- Beat the eggs with salt and pepper to taste. Pour over bread in the baking dish. Cover and refrigerate overnight.
- The following day, remove from the refrigerator and bring to room temperature.
- Preheat oven to 350°.
- Drizzle the cream on top. Bake until puffy and lightly browned, 45 minutes to 1 hour. Serve immediately.

Yield: 6 servings

Leek, Herb, and Gouda Cheese Tart

1 prepared refrigerated pie crust, unbaked
2 tablespoons olive oil
4 large leeks (white and pale green part), thinly sliced and separated into rings
2 large garlic cloves, minced
1½ (7 ounce) wheels Gouda cheese, grated
1 tablespoon chopped fresh rosemary
1 tablespoon chopped fresh oregano
1 tablespoon chopped fresh sage

- Preheat oven to 450°.
- Bring the pie crust to room temperature. Roll out on a lightly floured surface to a 13-inch round. Place in a 9-inch tart pan with removable bottom. Trim edges. Pierce dough all over with fork. Set aside.
- Heat oil in a large skillet over medium-low heat. Sauté leeks and garlic in oil until tender and golden. If this becomes too dry, add one or two tablespoons water. Set aside to cool. Stir cheese and herbs into cooled leek mixture.
- Bake crust until golden, piercing with fork if bubbles form, about 15 minutes. Spoon filling into crust. Bake until cheese melts and filling is heated, 15-20 minutes. Remove pan sides. Cut into wedges.

Yield: 8 servings

Very rich! A delicious accompaniment to any simple beef or chicken dish.

Noodle Casserole Florentine

*1 (8 ounce) package medium
wide egg noodles*
*4 tablespoons margarine or
butter, divided*
½ cup chopped onion
1 small clove garlic, minced
*1 (10 ounce) package frozen
chopped spinach, slightly
defrosted*
¾ teaspoon salt
¼ teaspoon black pepper
*¼ teaspoon crumbled
tarragon*
⅛ teaspoon ground nutmeg
*1 (16 ounce) carton creamed
cottage cheese*
½ cup nonfat sour cream
*4 tablespoons packaged bread
crumbs*
*2 tablespoons grated
Parmesan cheese*

- Preheat oven to 375°.
- Cook noodles in a large kettle following package directions. Drain and return to kettle. Toss noodles with 1 tablespoon margarine.
- Sauté onion and garlic in 2 table-spoons margarine in a large skillet until golden and soft. Add spinach and seasonings. Cover and cook over moderate heat for 5 minutes.
- Uncover skillet and continue cooking for 1 minute longer to evaporate the liquid. Add spinach mixture to noodles. Stir in cottage cheese and sour cream. Blend thoroughly.
- Turn mixture into a greased 2-quart casserole dish.
- Melt remaining 1 tablespoon marga-rine in a small skillet, add bread crumbs and Parmesan cheese. Blend with a fork until thoroughly mixed. Sprinkle over top of casse-role.
- Bake for 30 minutes or until bubbly and lightly browned.

Yield: 4 servings

Walnut Brown Rice with Mushrooms

5-6 servings brown rice (do not use quick-cooking variety)
2 tablespoons butter
2 shallots, chopped
8 ounces fresh mushrooms, chopped
2 tablespoons soy sauce
1 tablespoon white wine vinegar
1 cup coarsely chopped walnuts

- Prepare rice according to package directions.
- Fifteen minutes before the rice is finished cooking, sauté shallots in butter until tender. Add mushrooms and cook until tender.
- When rice is finished, add shallots and mushrooms to rice. Add vinegar and soy sauce, stirring well. Add walnuts just before serving.

Yield: 5-6 servings

Superb with grilled Cornish game hens.

Carrot Risotto

5 tablespoons butter or margarine
1 onion, chopped
1 clove garlic, pressed
½ teaspoon rosemary
2½ cups brown rice, uncooked
3 cups "chicken" style broth
1 cup non-alcoholic or regular beer
1½ cups finely grated carrots
1 cup grated Parmesan cheese
Pinch of nutmeg
Salt and pepper to taste

- Preheat oven to 350°.
- Melt butter or margarine in a large saucepan and sauté onion until clear. Add garlic and sauté until both onion and garlic are light brown.
- Stir in rosemary and brown rice. Add broth and beer to the mixture.
- Add carrots, Parmesan cheese, nutmeg, salt, and pepper to the rice mixture. Stir well.
- Pour into a greased 3-quart casserole dish. Bake 50-60 minutes or until the liquid is absorbed. Stir once during baking.

Yield: 8-10 servings

Not only a great side dish, but perfect as a vegetarian entree.

Browned Rice with Artichokes

*1½ cups long-grain white
  rice, uncooked
1 stick margarine
2 small onions, cut into rings
2 cans condensed beef
  consommé
1 can water
2 (4 ounce) cans sliced
  mushrooms, drained
1 (14 ounce) can artichokes,
  drained*

- Preheat oven to 300°.
- Mix all ingredients in a 2-quart casserole dish.
- Bake uncovered for 1 hour.

Yield: 6 servings

Watch this carefully; do not let it get dry while baking!

Carolyn's Rice Pecan Pilaf

*8 tablespoons butter or
  margarine, divided
1 cup chopped pecans
½ cup chopped onion
2 cups long-grain white rice,
  uncooked
4 cups chicken broth
1 teaspoon salt
¼ teaspoon thyme
⅛ teaspoon pepper
2 tablespoons chopped fresh
  parsley*

- In a large pot, melt 3 tablespoons butter. Add pecans; sauté for 10 minutes. Remove pecans, cover, and set aside.
- Melt remaining butter in same pot. Add onions; sauté until tender.
- Add rice. Stir to coat grains thoroughly. Add broth, salt, thyme, and pepper. Cover and simmer 18 minutes or until rice is tender and all liquid is absorbed. Remove from heat.
- Stir in nuts and parsley.

Yield: 8 servings

To prepare ahead, cover and refrigerate up to 24 hours before adding nuts and parsley. To heat, add ¾ cup of water to cooked rice. Cover and heat 5-8 minutes until hot. Stir in nuts and parsley just before serving.

Lemon Rice

1 cup long-grain white rice,
  uncooked
1 teaspoon grated lemon peel
1 tablespoon lemon juice
1 tablespoon butter, melted
2 tablespoons minced fresh
  parsley

- Prepare rice according to package directions.
- Add remaining ingredients. Blend well.

Yield: 3-4 servings

Garnish with lemon twists or parsley sprigs. A light, fresh taste. A nice change of pace from plain rice or potatoes.

Paella Rice

¼ cup vegetable oil
1 medium-sized onion,
  chopped
1 clove garlic, minced
1 cup long-grain white rice,
  uncooked
1 cup chicken broth
1 (16 ounce) can tomatoes, cut
  up, reserving liquid
½ teaspoon salt
⅛ teaspoon crushed red pepper
¼ teaspoon dried oregano
⅛ teaspoon ground cumin
1 cup frozen green peas,
  rinsed
1 (10 ounce) can chickpeas,
  drained
⅓ cup pitted black olives

- Heat oil in deep, heavy skillet. Add onion and garlic. Cook over medium-high heat until onion is softened, about 3 minutes.
- Add rice and cook 5 minutes or until rice starts to brown. Add broth and liquid from tomatoes.
- In a bowl, gently mix tomatoes, salt, red pepper, oregano, and cumin. Add to rice mixture. Cover skillet and bring mixture to a boil. Reduce heat to low and cook 15 minutes.
- Sprinkle green peas, chickpeas, and olives over rice; pressing down slightly. Cover and cook 5 minutes longer or until liquid is absorbed and rice is tender.
- Let stand covered for 5 minutes before serving.

Yield: 8 servings

Store red-colored spices in the refrigerator to maintain flavor and color.

Chinese Chicken Fried Rice

¾ cup long-grain white rice, uncooked
7 tablespoons peanut oil
2 eggs, lightly beaten
1 (6 ounce) chicken breast, cut into ½-inch cubes
1 clove garlic, minced
4 ounces mushrooms, sliced
1½ teaspoons ginger root, chopped
1½ tablespoons soy sauce
1½ teaspoons bead molasses (thick soy molasses)
½ cup bean sprouts, rinsed and dried
2 green onions (including green tops), chopped

- Bring 3 quarts water to a rolling boil in a stock pot.
- Wash rice well under cold water and sprinkle into the boiling water. Boil rice for 10 minutes. Pour cooked rice into a metal colander, saving the hot water from the pot.
- Return 1 quart of hot water to the pot. Place colander with rice into the pot, cover, and steam rice for 8 minutes. Remove colander from pot. Refrigerate rice until very cold.
- Heat 2 tablespoons peanut oil in a hot wok; swirl. Add eggs and scramble until just done. Remove eggs and set aside.
- Pour 2 more tablespoons peanut oil into wok and swirl. Add chicken and garlic. Stir-fry until chicken changes color all over; add mushrooms and ginger root and continue to stir-fry until mushrooms are light brown and chicken is just done. Remove and set aside.
- Add 3 remaining tablespoons peanut oil to wok; swirl. Add rice, stir-fry 1 minute then add soy sauce and bead molasses. Combine well until rice is evenly colored.
- Add reserved eggs and chicken/mushroom mixture; combine well. Add bean sprouts; combine well. Remove from heat.
- Garnish with chopped green onions. Serve.

Yield: 8 servings

After rice is added to the recipe, stir constantly while cooking over medium or medium-low heat to avoid burning and sticking of rice.

Lentils and Rice

1 cup lentils
Water
3 cloves
1 onion, whole
1 clove garlic, whole
½ large bay leaf
Juice of 1 lemon
2 green onions with tops,
   finely chopped
½ teaspoon olive oil
2 cups cooked rice
1 tablespoon chicken bouillon
   powder
Salt and pepper to taste

- Place lentils in a saucepan; add water to cover to a depth of ½ to 1 inch.
- Stick cloves in onion; add onion, garlic, and bay leaf to lentils. Simmer until lentils are tender but not mushy, about 30 minutes. Do not overcook; add more water if necessary.
- Discard onion, garlic, and bay leaf.
- Drain lentils. Add lemon juice, green onions, olive oil, and rice.
- Sprinkle with bouillon powder, salt, and pepper. Mix gently.

Yield: 4-6 servings

Raisin Rice Pudding

2 cups milk
½ cup sugar
¼ teaspoon salt
2 eggs
2 cups cooked rice
¾ cup raisins
Nutmeg or cinnamon,
   optional

- Preheat oven to 350°.
- Combine milk, sugar, salt, and eggs in a large bowl. Mix well.
- Stir in rice and raisins.
- Pour mixture into a 1-quart baking dish.
- Set baking dish in a large pan with an inch of water in it.
- Sprinkle with nutmeg or cinnamon, if desired.
- Bake for 1 hour and 15 minutes.
- Serve warm or cold.

Yield: 6 servings

When reheating, add a little milk to the pudding.

Very simple and delicious!

Shrimp and Pasta with Cilantro

6 plum tomatoes
¼ cup olive oil
20 large fresh shrimp, peeled
and deveined
1 large shallot, chopped
1 tablespoon minced garlic (or
more to taste)
⅓ cup dry white wine
⅓ cup chopped fresh cilantro
2 tablespoons fresh lemon
juice
½ cup heavy cream
6 tablespoons butter, cut into
pieces
Salt and pepper to taste
12 ounces fresh fettuccine,
linguine, or angel hair
pasta

- Drop tomatoes in a saucepan of boiling water for 10 seconds. Transfer to a bowl of cold water. Remove skins, seed, and chop tomatoes.
- Heat oil in a medium skillet over medium-high heat. Add shrimp and cook until pink, no more than 2 minutes. Transfer to a platter and tent with foil to keep warm.
- Add shallot and garlic to skillet; sauté 1 minute. Add tomatoes, wine, cilantro, and lemon juice. Cook until reduced by half.
- Add cream. Boil until mixture is reduced by half, stirring frequently. Remove from heat.
- Add butter one piece at a time, whisking until melted.
- Season with salt and pepper.
- Cook pasta according to package directions. Drain.
- Mound pasta on individual dinner plates. Top with shrimp. Spoon sauce over the top.

Yield: 4 servings

• • •

Norfolk, Virginia is the site of the world's largest naval base and NATO's Atlantic headquarters.

Herbed Shrimp and Pasta

1 pound medium-sized fresh
*   shrimp, unpeeled*
4 ounces angel hair pasta
½ cup butter
2 cloves garlic, minced
1 cup half and half
¼ cup chopped fresh parsley
1 teaspoon fresh dill weed
¼ teaspoon salt
⅛ teaspoon pepper
1 yellow or red bell pepper, cut
*   into strips then steamed or*
*   sautéed*

- Peel and devein shrimp. Set aside.
- Cook pasta according to package directions. Drain and set aside, keeping warm.
- Melt butter in a heavy skillet over medium-high heat. Add shrimp and garlic. Cook 3-5 minutes, stirring constantly. Remove shrimp and set aside, reserving garlic and butter in skillet.
- Add half and half to skillet, bring to a boil, stirring constantly. Reduce heat to low and simmer for about 15 minutes or until thickened, stirring occasionally.
- Add shrimp, parsley, and seasonings. Stir until blended.
- Serve over angel hair pasta with pepper strips.

Yield: 3 servings

Top each serving with freshly grated Parmesan cheese.

Four stars! This colorful recipe is easily doubled. Perfect for a small dinner party.

Shrimp Vermicelli with Sun-Dried Tomatoes

9 ounces vermicelli
1/4 cup olive oil
3 cloves garlic, chopped
1/2 yellow bell pepper, seeded
    and sliced
1/3 cup chopped sun-dried
    tomatoes
1 cup broccoli florets
6 ounces fresh shrimp, peeled
    and deveined
1/2 cup white wine
2 tablespoons lemon juice
5 fresh basil leaves, chopped
    (or 1/2 teaspoon dry basil)
Salt and pepper to taste

- Cook pasta according to package directions. Drain and set aside.
- Heat olive oil in a sauté pan. Sauté garlic, peppers, sun-dried tomatoes, and broccoli florets for approximately 3 minutes.
- Add shrimp. Continue to sauté 2-3 minutes, stirring frequently.
- Add wine, lemon juice, and basil. Continue cooking until shrimp is no longer transparent and fully cooked. Add pasta and mix well.
- Season with salt and pepper.

Yield: 2 servings

Serve with Caesar salad and French bread.

Quick Shellfish Pasta Paella

2 cups chicken broth
3/4 cup dry white wine
1/2 teaspoon crumbled saffron
3 tablespoons olive oil
6 ounces thin spaghetti,
    broken into 2-inch lengths
6 large fresh shrimp, peeled
6 large fresh sea scallops
6 fresh clams in shell,
    scrubbed
4 1/2 ounces frozen artichoke
    hearts, thawed
1 tablespoon minced fresh
    chives

- Preheat oven to 400°.
- In a medium saucepan, bring broth and wine to a boil. Stir in saffron. Reduce heat to simmer.
- In a heavy 8-inch ovenproof skillet, heat oil over medium-high heat until hot but not smoking. Sauté uncooked pasta, stirring until golden, about 2 minutes.
- Pour simmering broth mixture over pasta and continue to simmer 5 minutes.
- Nestle shellfish and artichoke hearts into pasta and bake, uncovered, in middle of oven until liquid is reduced to a syrupy glaze, about 20 minutes.
- Sprinkle with chives before serving.

Yield: 2 servings

Light and Delicious Seafood Fettuccine

6 tablespoons corn oil margarine

3 cloves garlic, minced

1 pound sliced fresh asparagus

½ cup fresh or frozen peas

½ cup sliced green onion

½ pound fresh shrimp, peeled and deveined

½ pound fresh scallops

2 tablespoons parsley

1 tablespoon basil

4 tablespoons chicken broth

1 tablespoon wine vinegar

½ teaspoon salt

⅛ teaspoon freshly ground black pepper

1 pound fettuccine, cooked and drained

⅓ cup freshly grated Parmesan cheese

- Melt margarine in a large skillet; sauté garlic.
- Add asparagus, peas, and green onions; stir-fry until vegetables are crisp-tender, about 5 minutes.
- Stir in shrimp, scallops, parsley, basil, broth, and vinegar. Cook on high 2-4 minutes, stirring constantly until seafood is thoroughly cooked. Do not overcook.
- Season with salt and pepper.
- Serve over pasta. Sprinkle with Parmesan cheese.

Yield: 4 servings

Fabulous! A healthy favorite for family or guests.

• • •

Virginia's Eastern Shore is a 70-mile peninsula and string of barrier islands that remains a haven for herds of wild ponies. This beautiful area of small fishing villages and unspoiled beaches is known for its fresh oysters, fried eel, steamed clams, and chowder. The Wild Pony Roundup, held every summer in Chincoteague and Assateague, features great local food, carnival festivities, and other entertainment.

Linguine with Shellfish

2 shallots, chopped

2-3 tablespoons extra virgin olive oil

2 cloves garlic, chopped

2 fresh basil leaves, finely chopped

1 (16 ounce) can tomatoes, drained and diced

2-3 ounces heavy cream

4-6 ounces cooked whole shrimp (lobster or crabmeat may be used)

Dash of sea salt, optional

1/8 teaspoon cayenne pepper (or a dash of hot pepper sauce)

1/2 pound linguine, cooked and drained

3-4 fresh basil leaves, julienned

- Sauté shallots in olive oil 2-3 minutes over medium heat. Add garlic and continue to sauté 1-2 minutes. Do not burn!
- Add chopped basil and tomatoes. Reduce heat and simmer for 4 minutes.
- Add cream and bring to a boil for 2 minutes.
- Reduce heat; add shrimp and cayenne pepper. Cook only until shrimp is heated.
- Toss mixture with pasta and julienned basil. Serve immediately.

Yield: 2 servings

Very easy, very tasty!

Seashell Pasta with Salmon and Dill

1 (8 ounce) salmon fillet,
  ³/₄-inch thick
Olive oil
Salt and pepper to taste
4 ounces small pasta shells
¹/₂ cup chopped red onion
¹/₂ cup chopped celery
¹/₂ cup mayonnaise
3 tablespoons chopped fresh
  dill
1 tablespoon country-style
  Dijon mustard

- Preheat broiler.
- Brush both sides of salmon with olive oil. Season with salt and pepper. Broil until just cooked through, about 3 minutes on each side. Cool slightly.
- Meanwhile, cook pasta according to package directions. Drain, rinse with cold water, and drain again. Transfer to a large bowl.
- Add onion and celery to pasta.
- Skin salmon and break into pieces. Add to pasta.
- Whisk mayonnaise, dill, and mustard in a small bowl. Add to pasta; toss. Cover and chill.

Yield: 2 servings

Canned salmon may be substituted.

Grill the salmon for optimum flavor. For a special luncheon entree, line individual plates with lettuce leaves, top with salmon pasta salad. Attractive presentation!

Blushing Clam Sauce with Linguine

½ *cup extra virgin olive oil*
5-6 cloves garlic, minced
½ *cup minced onion*
4 tomatoes, peeled and minced
1 teaspoon dried oregano
1 cup dry white wine
2 (10½ ounce) cans minced
  clams, juice reserved
Salt and pepper to taste
½ *cup minced fresh parsley*
1½ pounds linguine, cooked
  and tossed with 2 teaspoon
  olive oil
Grated Parmesan cheese

- Heat olive oil in a large skillet; sauté garlic and onion in oil for 5 minutes.
- Add tomatoes, oregano, white wine, clam juice, salt, and black pepper. Bring to a gentle boil. Stir, reduce heat, and simmer uncovered 35-40 minutes. Remove from heat.
- Stir in clams and fresh parsley. Toss with hot, oiled linguine.
- Top with a generous sprinkling of freshly grated Parmesan cheese.

Yield: 6-8 servings

Spectacular with fresh clams! Prepare fresh clam sauce as follows: substitute 18-24 whole chowder clams (enough to make 2 cups shucked) for the canned clams. Scrub the clams and place in cold salted water to which ¼ cup cornmeal has been added. Soak for several hours. Steam clams until shells open. Remove meat and mince. Use 2 cups bottled clam juice in place of the reserved canned clam juice.

Excellent and very easy.

Fettuccine with Bacon, Peas, and Red Peppers

4 slices bacon
1 tablespoon olive oil
1 small red onion, sliced
3 cloves garlic, minced
1 (7 ounce) jar roasted red bell peppers, drained and sliced
1 cup frozen peas, thawed
¼ cup chicken broth
1 pound fettuccine, cooked and drained
Salt and pepper to taste
Freshly grated Parmesan cheese

- Cook bacon in a large skillet over medium-high heat. Remove bacon slices, reserving grease. Drain and crumble bacon. Set aside.
- Add olive oil to bacon grease. Sauté onion and garlic, stirring occasionally, until onion is tender. Remove from heat; add bacon.
- Stir in peppers, peas, and broth. Simmer 1 minute.
- Transfer mixture to a large bowl. Add pasta and toss well.
- Season with salt and pepper.
- Serve immediately, passing grated Parmesan cheese separately.

Yield: 4 servings

Beautiful and delicious!

Governor Allen's Lasagne

Sauce

1 tablespoon olive oil
1 large onion, finely chopped
1 large garlic clove, minced
2 (28 ounce) cans tomatoes,
   coarsely chopped
1 (12 ounce) can tomato paste
1 (12 ounce) can water
1 tablespoon oregano
1½ tablespoons basil
1 bay leaf
1 teaspoon garlic powder
2 teaspoons sugar
1½ teaspoons salt
Black pepper to taste

- Sauté onions and garlic until transparent in olive oil.
- Combine remaining ingredients. Simmer several hours until smooth and thick.

Lasagne

1 (16 ounce) box lasagne,
   parboiled and drained
Olive oil
1 large onion, chopped
1 clove garlic, minced
1½ pounds ground beef
1½ pounds Italian sausage
1 pound mushrooms, sliced
½ pound Mozzarella cheese,
   grated
½ cup grated Parmesan cheese
½ cup grated Romano cheese
2 eggs, beaten
Salt and pepper to taste

- Sauté onions in a small amount of olive oil. Add garlic.
- Brown ground beef, sausage, and mushrooms. Cool mixture.
- Mix the 2 beaten eggs into the mixture. Add salt and pepper.
- Toss cheeses together. Set aside.
- Preheat oven to 350°.
- Spread small amount of sauce in the bottom of a 9"x13" pan. Line it with lasagne. Layer half the meat mixture, ⅓ the sauce, and ⅓ the combination of cheeses. Repeat layering with lasagne, meat, sauce, and cheese. Place remaining lasagne on top. Spread with remaining sauce, top with the rest of the cheese.
- Bake for 1 hour.

Yield: 6-8 servings

A favorite recipe from the kitchen of Governor and Mrs. George Allen. Virginia's Governor Allen was inaugurated in January of 1994.

Twist and Shout Italian Pasta

1 pound extra lean ground beef
1/3 pound pork sausage
1/4 cup water
1 (6 ounce) can tomato paste
1 (27 ounce) jar spaghetti sauce
3/4 cup diced cooked pepperoni
2 cups grated Mozzarella cheese
3/4 cup grated Parmesan cheese
1/2 cup grated sharp Cheddar cheese
1/3 cup red wine
1 1/2 teaspoons Worcestershire sauce
1 teaspoon garlic salt
1 teaspoon oregano
1 teaspoon lemon pepper
2 teaspoons Italian seasoning
12 ounces twist trio pasta (semolina, spinach, and tomato twists)

- Sauté ground beef and pork sausage in a large skillet over medium-high heat until lightly browned, about 10 minutes. Drain.
- In a large saucepan, combine water, tomato paste, and spaghetti sauce. Cook over medium heat.
- Add beef and sausage mixture, pepperoni, and all three cheeses. Stir well.
- Add wine, Worcestershire sauce, garlic salt, oregano, lemon pepper, and Italian seasoning. Bring to a boil. Reduce heat to low; cover and simmer 10-15 minutes, stirring occasionally.
- Cook pasta according to package directions. Drain.
- Pour sauce over pasta and serve hot.

Yield: 6 servings

Very spicy and flavorful! Excellent for freezing in loaf containers. Makes a nice gift.

Dried pasta may be stored for up to one year in a cool, dry place.

Robbin Thompson's Rock 'n Roll Spaghetti Sauce

1 pound extra lean ground beef, browned
½ pound Italian sausage, chopped and browned
1 (15 ounce) can stewed tomatoes
1 (15 ounce) can tomato sauce
1 (6 ounce) can tomato paste
1-2 cups red wine
1 green bell pepper, chopped
1 large onion, chopped
1-2 cups sliced fresh mushrooms
1 cup chopped celery
1-2 tablespoons fresh garlic
2 bay leaves
2 tablespoons Italian seasoning
1 tablespoon olive oil

• Combine all ingredients in a large pot. Let simmer for at least 2 hours.

Yield: 6 servings

Robbin Thompson is a well-known recording artist and actor. He also writes and produces music for radio and television commercials. When not touring, Mr. Thompson is at home in Richmond, Virginia.

Mr. Thompson likes to make his Rock 'n Roll Spaghetti Sauce at halftime of the first Sunday afternoon football game and then serve it after the second game. He prefers to use a good red Virginia wine with this sauce.

Country Dijon Chicken and Pasta

2 tablespoons flour
1/4 teaspoon cracked pepper
1 pound boneless, skinless
  chicken breasts, cut into
  1-inch pieces
3 tablespoons butter, divided
1 medium onion, chopped
1 clove garlic, minced
1 1/4 cups heavy cream
1/3 cup country Dijon mustard
1/4 cup grated Parmesan cheese
8 ounces fettuccine, cooked
  and drained
3 tablespoons chopped fresh
  parsley, divided

- Combine flour, pepper, and chicken in a plastic bag. Shake to coat chicken.
- Brown chicken in 2 tablespoons butter in a large skillet. Remove chicken to heated platter and keep warm.
- Add remaining 1 tablespoon butter to skillet. Sauté onion and garlic until soft. Stir in cream, mustard, and cheese. Add chicken. Keep warm.
- Toss hot pasta with 2 tablespoons parsley. Place on a serving platter and top with chicken mixture. Sprinkle remaining parsley over chicken.

Yield: 4 servings

Mexican Chicken Manicotti

8 ounces chicken, cooked and
  chopped
2 cups low-fat ricotta cheese
1/3 cup thinly sliced green
  onions
2 teaspoons dried cilantro
1 teaspoon garlic salt
1 (16 ounce) jar picante sauce
  (mild or hot)
8 manicotti shells, cooked and
  drained
1/2 cup grated Cheddar cheese

- Preheat oven to 350°.
- Mix chicken, ricotta cheese, onions, cilantro, and garlic salt.
- Pour a little picante sauce in an ungreased 9"x13" baking dish.
- Fill manicotti shells with chicken mixture.
- Arrange stuffed shells in baking dish. Pour remaining picante sauce over shells. Sprinkle with Cheddar cheese.
- Cover and bake 35-40 minutes or until hot in the center.

Yield: 4 servings

Ziti with Chicken and Peppers

1 pound ziti or macaroni
2 tablespoons virgin olive oil
4 boneless, skinless chicken
*   breast halves, cubed*
1 small red bell pepper, seeded
*   and sliced*
1 small yellow bell pepper,
*   seeded and sliced*
1-2 cloves garlic, chopped
2 green onions, sliced
1 (12 ounce) can tomato paste
1 tablespoon chopped black
*   Kalamata olives*
½ cup chicken broth
½ tablespoon chopped fresh
*   basil*
½ tablespoon chopped fresh
*   thyme*
½ tablespoon chopped fresh
*   rosemary*
Salt and pepper to taste
Chopped fresh parsley for
*   garnish*

- Cook pasta according to package directions until al dente. Drain and set aside.
- Heat olive oil in a large sauté pan. Add cubed chicken, bell peppers, garlic, and onion. Sauté until tender, about 4 minutes.
- Add pasta, tomato paste, olives, chicken broth, basil, thyme, and rosemary. Heat 2-3 minutes. Season with salt and pepper.
- Serve garnished with chopped parsley.

Yield: 4 servings

• • •

The College of William and Mary was founded in 1693. It is the second oldest college in America and is known for having initiated the honor system. The Phi Beta Kappa Society was founded at William and Mary in 1776.

Chicken and Swiss Spinach Fettuccine

1 cup chopped onion
4 tablespoons olive oil
4 tablespoons butter
8 chicken breast halves, cubed
¼ teaspoon garlic powder
½ cup cubed zucchini
2 teaspoons salt
Pepper to taste
1 teaspoon dried basil flakes
1 teaspoon oregano
1 pound spinach fettuccine
4 cups cherry tomatoes
2 cups grated Swiss cheese

- Sauté onion until tender in olive oil and butter.
- Add chicken pieces and garlic powder. Cook until chicken is just white on all sides.
- Add zucchini and seasonings. Continue cooking on low heat.
- Cook fettuccine according to package directions. Drain.
- Add tomatoes to chicken mixture.
- Toss chicken mixture with fettuccine and Swiss cheese.

Yield: 8 servings

Substitute red bell pepper slices for tomatoes.

Delicious chilled the next day!

Fresh and Light Tomato Pasta

1 pound angel hair pasta
2-3 cloves garlic, minced
1 onion, chopped
2 tablespoons olive oil
6-8 large ripe tomatoes,
  peeled, seeded and chopped
½ cup slivered fresh basil
1 teaspoon salt
Grated Parmesan cheese
Freshly ground black pepper

- Cook pasta according to package directions. Drain and set aside.
- Sauté garlic and onion in olive oil over medium-low heat until soft. Do not brown.
- Add tomatoes and their juices, basil, and salt. Simmer gently for 1 hour.
- Serve over pasta. Top with Parmesan cheese and fresh pepper.

Yield: 4 servings

Not a heavy casserole-type sauce. This light sauce glazes the pasta. Deliciously simple!

Avocado, Lemon, and Mushroom Pasta

½ cup vegetable oil
¼ cup fresh lemon juice
¼ cup minced fresh parsley
1 clove garlic, minced
1 teaspoon salt
½ teaspoon paprika
½ pound mushrooms, sliced
2 avocados, sliced
1 pound pasta

- Blend oil, lemon juice, parsley, garlic, salt, and paprika in a large bowl. Toss with mushrooms and avocado slices. Chill.
- Cook pasta according to package directions. Drain thoroughly.
- Toss pasta with avocado, lemon, and mushroom mixture. Serve.

Yield: 4 servings

Fusilli and Broccoli with Gorgonzola Cheese Sauce

1 pound fusilli (corkscrew pasta)
1 bunch broccoli, trimmed into small florets
1 cup heavy cream
1 stick unsalted butter, softened
½ pound Gorgonzola cheese, room temperature
¼ cup freshly grated Romano cheese
⅓ cup minced fresh parsley
1 (2 ounce) jar sliced pimientos, optional

- Cook fusilli in a large kettle of boiling salted water until al dente.
- Boil broccoli in a saucepan for 2 minutes while fusilli is cooking.
- Drain broccoli and refresh with cold water.
- Boil cream in a small saucepan for 5 minutes. Stir in Gorgonzola cheese and ½ stick of butter. Cook over low heat, stirring frequently, until mixture is smooth.
- Drain fusilli. Toss with broccoli and remaining ½ stick of butter in the large kettle.
- Add Romano cheese, parsley, and sliced pimientos; combine well. Stir in Gorgonzola cheese sauce; combine well.
- Serve immediately.

Yield: 6 servings

Very rich with a strong cheesy taste.

Roasted Red Pepper and Ricotta Puree with Linguine

1 pound linguine
1 pound ricotta cheese
1 (7 ounce) jar roasted red
* peppers*
½ cup grated Parmesan cheese
¼ cup chicken broth
1-2 tablespoons lemon juice
1 clove garlic, chopped
Salt and pepper to taste

- Cook linguine according to package directions until al dente. Drain, refresh with cold water, drain again. Set aside.
- Puree ricotta, roasted red peppers, Parmesan cheese, chicken broth, lemon juice, and garlic. Season with salt and pepper.
- Toss with pasta.
- Serve at room temperature.

Yield: 6 servings

Beautiful dish, especially when accented with fresh parsley.

Perfect Pesto

2 cups fresh basil
⅓ cup pine nuts
2 cloves garlic
¼ cup freshly grated
* Parmesan cheese*
¼ cup freshly grated Romano
* cheese*
½ cup extra virgin olive oil
1 pound linguine, cooked and
* drained*

- Mix all ingredients except linguine in food processor or blender.
- Serve over hot linguine.

Yield: 4 servings

Sesame Pasta

8 ounces angel hair pasta
2 tablespoons sesame oil
2 tablespoons rice vinegar
2 teaspoons hot oil
1½ tablespoons salt
1½ tablespoons pepper
1 tablespoon soy sauce
2 tablespoons sugar
4 tablespoons vegetable oil
4 tablespoons toasted sesame
  seeds
3-5 green onions, sliced

- Cook pasta according to package directions. Drain and set aside.
- Blend sesame oil, vinegar, hot oil, salt, pepper, soy sauce, and sugar. Stir until sugar is completely dissolved. Pour over pasta.
- Heat vegetable oil until smoking. Pour over pasta.
- Sprinkle with toasted sesame seeds and green onions. Toss well.

Yield: 6 servings

Toast sesame seeds by placing in a hot skillet and tossing until lightly toasted.

Barley Casserole

4-5 tablespoons butter or
  margarine
½ pound fresh mushrooms,
  sliced
1 large onion, finely chopped
1 cup quick-cooking barley
Salt and pepper to taste
2½ cups beef broth

- Melt butter in a large skillet. Sauté mushrooms and onions until tender.
- Mix in barley. Season with salt and pepper.
- Pour mixture into a 7"x11" baking dish.
- Pour beef broth over mushroom/barley mixture.
- Bake uncovered for 1 hour or until broth is absorbed.

Yield: 6-8 servings

Can be cooked in the microwave for 40 minutes on high power.

A refreshing and healthy alternative to rice. Good with all meats and poultry.

Garlic Cheese Grits

4½ cups water
1 teaspoon salt
1 cup quick grits
1 stick butter or margarine,
  divided
1 roll garlic cheese, sliced into
  chunks
2 eggs
1 scant cup milk
1 cup crushed corn flakes
½ cup grated Cheddar cheese

- Preheat oven to 350°.
- Bring water to a boil. Slowly stir in salt and grits. Reduce heat to medium-low and cover saucepan. Cook 5-7 minutes or until thickened, stirring occasionally.
- Add ¾ stick of butter and garlic cheese, heat until melted.
- Beat eggs in a measuring cup, adding milk to equal one cup, and beat again. Add to grits and stir well.
- Pour mixture into a buttered 2-quart casserole dish.
- Melt remaining ¼ stick of butter. Lightly sauté corn flakes in butter. Stir in Cheddar cheese.
- Cover grits evenly with corn flake/ Cheddar cheese mixture.
- Bake for 45 minutes.

Yield: 8-10 servings

May be prepared ahead of time and baked just before serving.

Spicy Vegetable Couscous

2 tablespoons olive oil
1 clove garlic, minced
1 medium-sized onion,
   coarsely chopped
½ medium-sized turnip, diced
   (about 2 cups)
2 carrots, sliced diagonally
1 (8 ounce) can tomatoes,
   drained
½ teaspoon salt
½ teaspoon ground cumin
¼ teaspoon crushed red pepper
   flakes
2½ cups chicken broth,
   divided
1 small zucchini, sliced
½ cup canned chickpeas
4 tablespoons butter or
   margarine
1 cup couscous
Fresh coriander or parsley
   sprigs for garnish
Sesame seeds for garnish

- Heat oil in a large skillet. Sauté garlic and onion until tender but not brown.
- Add turnip, carrots, tomatoes, salt, cumin, pepper flakes, and 1 cup chicken broth. Heat to boiling. Reduce heat to low, cover and simmer for 10 minutes or until vegetables are tender yet firm.
- Add zucchini and chickpeas. Cook until zucchini is just tender.
- Prepare couscous while vegetables are cooking. Heat remaining 1½ cups of chicken broth and butter in a large saucepan. Add couscous. Cover and remove from heat. Let stand 5 minutes.
- To serve, spoon some couscous onto a warm plate. Top with vegetables and some broth from the vegetables. Garnish with coriander or parsley and sesame seeds.

Yield: 4 servings

An outstanding vegetarian entree that is also delicious served with lamb.

Vegetables

Sisters by the Sea

In Hampton Roads, the seven sisters around the sea are about as different as sisters can be.

Clustering about the roadstead are Hampton with Langley Research Center, where the astronauts learned to walk on the moon; Newport News, where warships are built; Norfolk, where they are berthed; Portsmouth, which produces more celebrities per capita than any other city its size in the United States; Suffolk and Chesapeake sharing Dismal Swamp with 250 black bears; and Virginia Beach, a haven for tourists and, in 1607, the English Colonists who touched shore by its dunes.

One amenity all enjoy: dozens of produce farms that advertise in seasonal guides with their addresses and phone numbers and a listing of when they will be selling what. When stoop labor to pick the crops became scarce 40 years ago, enterprising farmers opened their fields to customers who pick their own and pay far less than retail prices. The practice spread throughout Virginia.

Virginia Beach has a regional year-round market and major farms have sizable sales facilities. Roadside stalls pop up along the margin of the fields. Good things to eat abound: May peas, a soft jade green, so delicate they may be eaten, uncooked, from the pod; sweet corn, fetched quickly from a boiling pot, their white kernels so tender they fall off the cob at a glance; fiery red tomatoes glowing in a bushel basket, miniature suns resplendent even in the deep shade of the old oak; musty, dusky okra with pearl-like seeds that pop in the mouth; early red-skinned bite-sized potatoes, simmered in butter and devoured whole, unpeeled; gold coins of squash.

Crisp cucumbers thinly sliced, iced in vinegar; spring onions competing for dominance with tongue-searing red radishes newly wrenched from the soil; fresh bell peppers to pep up bland dishes; butter beans scooped from amid juices of other viands. Nor eschew cabbages and cauliflowers.

Cherish as well a parade of fruits: peaches so juicy you'd best wear a bib while eating them; tart bronze scuppernongs and bitter sweet muscadines; cantaloupes whose aroma fills the room; figs that, with cream, make an epochal breakfast; watermelons great in girth and mirth, mayhap from Southampton County where Newsoms is the nation's watermelon capitol.

Did we overlook strawberries, so sweet and tart they make the jaws ache? Hampton Roads offers the greatest concentrations of strawberry fields in Virginia, dozens of them, each with an acre or more teeming with red berries peeping from amid green leaves. As your companions are driving along, car windows open, on a May day, or perhaps even the last week of April, a breeze wafts to you the sweet fragrance of strawberries perfuming fields yet a half mile away.

And what an exhilarating sight - people of all ages, brightly clad in a rainbow of colors, scattered across the green fields, absorbed in picking the berries, twinkling fiery as rubies. No one says much, except to yell: "Look at this berry! It's as big as a golf ball."

It is a stern puritan who can resist eating a strawberry on the spot now and then. And some gleaners eat one for every three they pick. When they finish, their containers are weighed for payment. Some of the customers ought to get on the scales, too, before and after picking.

In late May on Memorial Day, Virginia Beach hosts an annual strawberry festival at the hamlet of Pungo. There is unstinting consumption of strawberries as if people, like bears, are striving to stow away enough to last a year.

-Guy Friddell

Marinated Asparagus Medley

2 pounds fresh asparagus
1/3 cup chopped fresh parsley
1 (2 ounce) jar sliced
  pimientos, drained
2 tablespoons sliced green
  onion
1 1/2 cups vegetable oil
1/2 cup red wine vinegar
2 teaspoons lemon juice
1 teaspoon Worcestershire
  sauce
1 tablespoon dried basil
2 teaspoons ground pepper
1 teaspoon dried oregano
1/2 teaspoon garlic powder
1/2 teaspoon salt
1/4 teaspoon sugar
Bibb lettuce
12-16 large cherry tomatoes,
  sliced

- Snap off tough ends of asparagus. Remove scales with knife, if desired. Cook asparagus covered in boiling water 6-8 minutes or until crisp-tender. Drain.
- Place asparagus in a shallow lidded container. Sprinkle parsley, pimiento, and green onions over asparagus. Set aside.
- Combine vegetable oil with vinegar, lemon juice, Worcestershire sauce, basil, pepper, oregano, garlic powder, salt, and sugar in a large jar. Cover tightly and shake vigorously. Pour marinade over asparagus.
- Cover and chill for 8 hours.
- To serve, line individual plates with Bibb lettuce. Remove asparagus mixture from marinade and arrange on lettuce. Garnish with sliced tomatoes.

Yield: 8 servings

A colorful luncheon dish!

• • •

Virginia is the state of birth for eight United States Presidents: George Washington, first President, born February 22, 1732 in Westmoreland County; Thomas Jefferson, third President, born April 13, 1743 in Albemarle County; James Madison, fourth President, born March 16, 1751 in King George County; James Monroe, fifth President, born April 28, 1758 in Westmoreland County; William Henry Harrison, born February 9, 1773 in Charles City County; John Tyler, tenth President, born March 29, 1790 in Charles City County; Zachary Taylor, born November 24, 1784 in Orange County, and Thomas Woodrow Wilson, born December 28, 1856 in Staunton.

Savory Italian Asparagus

1 pound fresh asparagus
¼ cup water
1 medium-sized tomato,
  seeded and chopped
2 tablespoons chopped green
  onion
⅛ teaspoon dried oregano
⅛ teaspoon dried thyme
⅛ teaspoon pepper
2 teaspoons freshly grated
  Parmesan cheese

• Snap off tough ends of asparagus. Put asparagus into an 11"x7"x2" baking dish with stem ends toward outside of dish. Add water.
• Cover dish with heavy duty plastic wrap and vent. Microwave on high (100% power) for 6-7 minutes or until asparagus is tender. Let stand for 1 minute. Drain and set aside.
• Combine tomato, green onion, oregano, thyme, pepper, and Parmesan cheese. Stir well and mix with asparagus.

Yield: 4-6 servings

Slice asparagus into bite-size pieces before cooking, if desired.

Easy to prepare and low in calories.

Western Baked Beans

1 (31 ounce) can pork and
  beans, drained
2 tablespoons brown sugar
1 tablespoon sugar
4 tablespoons ketchup
1 tablespoon prepared
  mustard
1 cup chopped onion
½ cup chopped celery
¼ cup chopped green bell
  pepper
1 tablespoon chili powder
1 teaspoon hot pepper sauce
2 tablespoons Worcestershire
  sauce
3 slices bacon

• Preheat oven to 250°.
• Combine all ingredients except bacon. Pour into an 8-inch square baking dish.
• Place bacon slices on top of the bean mixture.
• Bake covered for 1 hour and 45 minutes. Uncover and continue baking for 15 minutes.

Yield: 6-8 servings

Spicy and delicious!

Pickled Snap Beans

2 (16 ounce) cans Blue Lake whole green beans
1 medium-sized onion, chopped
1 cup sugar
3/4 cup vinegar
1/4 cup water
4 tablespoons vegetable oil

- In a large bowl, combine beans and onion.
- Mix sugar, vinegar, water, and oil. Stir until sugar is completely dissolved. Pour over beans and onions.
- Cover and marinate 24 hours.
- Serve cold or at room temperature.

Yield: 6 servings

Lemon Basil Green Beans

1/4 cup chopped fresh basil
2 tablespoons lemon juice
1 tablespoon olive oil
1 clove garlic, cut into fourths
Salt and pepper to taste
1 pound green beans
Lemon wedges for garnish

- Combine basil, lemon juice, oil, garlic, salt, and pepper. Cover and let stand at room temperature for 2 hours.
- Cook beans, uncovered, in boiling salted water until crisp-tender.
- Pour marinade over beans. Cover and let stand at room temperature for 30-45 minutes. Serve at room temperature garnished with lemon wedges.

Yield: 6 servings

Green Beans with Herb Butter

1 pound fresh green beans
1/4 cup butter or margarine
3/4 cup finely chopped onion
1 clove garlic, minced
1/4 cup finely chopped celery
1/2 teaspoon parsley flakes
1/4 teaspoon dried rosemary
1/4 teaspoon dried basil
1/4 teaspoon dried thyme

- Cook beans, covered in water, for 15 minutes or until tender. Drain and set aside.
- Melt butter in a medium saucepan. Sauté onion, garlic, and celery for 5 minutes over medium heat.
- Add remaining ingredients and simmer 10 minutes.
- Toss well with beans.

Yield: 4 servings

Serve with fish or chicken.

Green Beans Viennese

1 (20 ounce) package frozen
  cut green beans
¼ cup chopped onion
1 tablespoon butter or
  margarine
1 tablespoon all-purpose flour
½ teaspoon salt
¼ teaspoon pepper
½ cup chicken broth
2 tablespoons snipped parsley
1 tablespoon vinegar
¼ teaspoon dried dill weed
½ cup sour cream

- Cook beans according to package directions. Drain and set aside.
- Sauté onion in butter until tender.
- Stir in flour, salt, and pepper.
- Add broth, parsley, vinegar, and dill weed. Cook, stirring frequently, until bubbly. Stir in sour cream.
- Add drained beans. Heat mixture through but do not boil.

Yield: 8 servings

Wonderful flavor for a family gathering or company dinner.

Italian Green Beans Sesame

2 (9 ounce) packages frozen
  Italian green beans
1 tablespoon toasted sesame
  seeds
1 tablespoon vegetable oil
1 tablespoon lemon juice
1 tablespoon soy sauce
4 teaspoons sugar

- Cook beans according to package directions. Drain and set aside.
- Toast sesame seeds in a preheated 350° oven for 15 minutes or until lightly brown. Do not overbake or the flavor is destroyed.
- Combine remaining ingredients in a small saucepan and bring to a boil. Stir in sesame seeds. Pour mixture over beans.

Yield: 5-6 servings

Bean Sprouts with Sesame

*1 pound bean sprouts, rinsed
  and drained*
2 green onions, thinly sliced
6 tablespoons soy sauce
1½ tablespoons vegetable oil
2 tablespoons sesame seeds
Salt and pepper to taste

- Bring a pot of salted water to a full boil. Drop in bean sprouts. Cook until water returns to a boil. Drain immediately.
- Add remaining ingredients. Mix well.

Yield: 6-8 servings

Serve with meat prepared with an Oriental-type marinade.

Green Bean and Red Pepper Bundles

*2 pounds whole green beans,
  trimmed*
*8 green onions including long
  stems*
*1 red bell pepper, cut into
  ¼-inch strips*
⅓ cup butter
1 clove garlic, minced
½ teaspoon crushed thyme
¼ teaspoon white pepper

- Preheat oven to 375°.
- Cook beans in boiling salted water for 3 minutes. Plunge into ice water. Drain and set aside.
- Blanch green onions 15 seconds. Remove and pat dry. Cut white part of onion off stem.
- Divide green beans into 8 serving-size bundles. Tie a green onion stem around each bundle of beans and tie a knot. Slip several pepper strips under each knot. Place bundles in a 9"x13" baking dish.
- Melt butter in a small saucepan. Sauté garlic for 3 minutes. Add thyme and pepper. Pour over beans.
- Bake for 7-10 minutes, or until heated through.

Yield: 8 servings

Elegantly simple.

Green beans no longer need stringing. For best results, trim the ends and cook whole in boiling salted water until crisp-tender.

Green Bean Bundles Wrapped in Bacon

2 pounds fresh green beans
6 slices bacon, cut in half
4 tablespoons butter, melted
3 tablespoons brown sugar
Garlic powder to taste
Salt and pepper to taste

- Preheat oven to 350°.
- Cook beans in boiling salted water for 3 minutes. Drain. Separate beans into 12 bundles.
- Wrap a piece of bacon around the middle of each bundle. Place bundles in the bottom of a buttered 9"x13" baking dish.
- Melt butter and brown sugar in a small saucepan. Drizzle over green bean bundles.
- Sprinkle with garlic powder, salt, and pepper.
- Bake for 20-30 minutes or until bacon is slightly crisp.

Yield: 6 servings

Western Style Black-Eyed Peas

½ pound bacon, cooked crisp
and crumbled
1½ quarts water
6 cups black-eyed peas, fresh
shelled or 3 (10 ounce)
packages frozen black-eyed
peas
2 ounces canned chopped
jalapeños
1 medium-sized yellow onion,
chopped
2 tablespoons sugar
1 teaspoon salt
½ teaspoon black pepper

- Combine all ingredients in a large saucepan. Bring to a boil over medium-high heat. Reduce heat to low, cover and simmer 2 to 2½ hours.

Yield: 6-8 servings

Excellent served with stewed tomatoes and rice.

Cheesy Broccoli

2 (10 ounce) packages frozen
  chopped broccoli
1 cup mayonnaise
1 cup grated sharp Cheddar
  cheese
1 can condensed cream of
  mushroom soup
2 tablespoons chopped onion
2 eggs, beaten
25 Ritz crackers, crushed

- Preheat oven to 350°.
- Cook broccoli according to package directions. Drain and set aside.
- Combine mayonnaise, cheese, soup, onions, and beaten eggs.
- Place broccoli in a buttered 1½-quart casserole dish. Pour cheese mixture over broccoli. Mix well. Cover with crushed crackers.
- Bake 45 minutes or until bubbly.

Yield: 6-8 servings

A very rich and delicious dish that can be "lightened" with low-fat mayonnaise, soups, and egg substitute.

Giselle's Marinated Broccoli

1 head fresh broccoli or 2 (10
  ounce) packages frozen
  broccoli spears, cooked and
  cooled in a colander
¾ cup sliced pitted black olives
1 (2 ounce) jar sliced
  pimientos, drained
2 teaspoons capers, drained
⅔ cup vegetable oil
¼ cup wine vinegar
1 tablespoon lemon juice
1 teaspoon salt
2 cloves garlic, minced
½ teaspoon pepper

- Layer cooked broccoli, olives, pimientos, and capers in a 9"x13" baking dish.
- Combine oil, vinegar, lemon juice, salt, garlic, and pepper. Pour marinade over broccoli.
- Chill for 1 hour or overnight. Serve cold or at room temperature.

Yield: 6 servings

Substitute canned roasted peppers for pimientos, if desired.

Unusual, and appealing!

Sautéed Brussels Sprouts with Garlic and Poppy Seeds

2 tablespoons olive oil
1 tablespoon minced fresh garlic
1 pound Brussels sprouts, thinly sliced
2 tablespoons poppy seeds
¼ cup lemon juice
⅛ teaspoon salt

- In a medium sauté pan, heat oil and sauté garlic. Cook over medium heat until tender.
- Add Brussels sprouts. Stir and cook until slightly crisp and cooked through, about 5 minutes.
- Stir in poppy seeds, lemon juice, and salt. Serve immediately.

Yield: 4 servings

For quick, easy preparation, slice Brussels sprouts in your food processor with a 2 mm. blade.

Beautiful presentation with a zingy, tart flavor!

Baked Carrots

3 cups carrots, sliced
¾ cup bread crumbs
2 teaspoons minced onion
2 tablespoons butter, melted
¼ teaspoon cracked pepper
½ cup reserved liquid from cooked carrots
4 tablespoons grated Parmesan cheese

- Preheat oven to 350°.
- Boil carrots in water until tender. Drain, reserving ½ cup liquid.
- Mash carrots and stir in bread crumbs, onions, butter, pepper, and reserved liquid.
- Spread into a greased 1-quart baking dish. Sprinkle with cheese.
- Bake 15 minutes.

Yield: 6 servings

Use Italian-style bread crumbs for a different flavor!

Excellent! An extraordinary side dish.

Company Carrots

2½ pounds carrots, peeled
½ cup reserved liquid from
  cooked carrots
½ cup mayonnaise
1 tablespoon chopped onion
1 tablespoon prepared
  horseradish
Salt and freshly ground black
  pepper
¼ cup crushed saltine crackers
2 tablespoons butter
Parsley
Paprika

- Preheat oven to 375°.
- Cook carrots in enough water to cover until crisp-tender, about 15 minutes. Do not overcook. Drain, reserving ½ cup liquid.
- Cut carrots into strips. Place in an ungreased 2-quart casserole dish.
- Combine reserved carrot liquid, mayonnaise, onion, horseradish, salt, and pepper. Pour over carrots.
- Sprinkle crackers on top. Dot with butter.
- Sprinkle with parsley and paprika.
- Bake 20 minutes.

Yield: 6-8 servings

Use baby carrots to make more elegant.

Very pretty!

Remove the tops from carrots before storing to prevent the carrots from becoming limp and dry. Small young carrots have the best flavor.

Tipsy Carrots

24 baby carrots
2 tablespoons orange-flavored
  liqueur (Triple Sec)
1/4 cup brandy
1/4 cup honey
Juice of 1 lemon
2 tablespoons chopped Italian
  parsley (flat-leaf parsley)

- Cook carrots until crisp-tender, about 10 minutes, in a small amount of water.
- Arrange carrots in a buttered 1-quart baking dish.
- Combine liqueur, brandy, honey, and lemon juice in a small saucepan. Bring to a boil. Boil slowly until mixture is reduced by half.
- Pour mixture over carrots and marinate overnight.
- Reheat in oven for 20 minutes at 350° or microwave until thoroughly heated. Sprinkle with parsley before serving.

Yield: 6-8 servings

Perfect for a dinner party...easy and delicious!

Corn Fritters

1 egg
1/4 scant cup milk
1 1/4 cups all-purpose flour
1 teaspoon baking powder
1/2 teaspoon salt
1 tablespoon butter, melted
1 cup cream-style corn
Vegetable oil for frying

- Combine egg, milk, flour, baking powder, salt, butter, and corn. Mix well.
- Heat 5-6 inches of oil in a large skillet. When the oil temperature reaches 375°, carefully drop batter from a tablespoon into the oil. Fry until golden brown.

Yield: 2 dozen small fritters

Serve with warm syrup and powdered sugar.

Green Chilies and Corn Casserole

2½ cups fresh corn kernels,
  divided
6 tablespoons butter, melted
2 eggs
1 cup low-fat sour cream
1 cup grated Monterey Jack
  cheese
½ cup yellow cornmeal
1 (4 ounce) can chopped green
  chilies
1½ teaspoons salt

- Preheat oven to 350°.
- Puree 1 cup of corn with butter and eggs in a food processor or blender.
- Combine remaining ingredients. Add to pureed mixture and stir until well blended.
- Pour into a 1-quart casserole dish sprayed with non-stick vegetable spray.
- Bake uncovered for 50-60 minutes.

Yield: 4 servings

Norie's Corn Pudding

2 cups corn, canned or fresh
4 eggs
4 cups milk
8 tablespoons all-purpose flour
1 teaspoon salt
3 tablespoons sugar
2 tablespoons butter

- Preheat oven to 325°.
- Combine corn, eggs, and milk.
- In a separate bowl, mix flour, salt, and sugar. Add to corn mixture.
- Pour into a 1-quart baking dish. Dot with butter.
- Bake for 1 hour, stirring 3 times during baking process.

Yield: 4 servings

This custard-like pudding is easy and delicious!

Southwest Lentil Burritos

1 cup lentils
2 cups water
1 (4 ounce) can chopped green chilies
1 packet chicken broth mix
2 tablespoons instant minced onion
1 teaspoon minced garlic
1 teaspoon ground cumin
½ teaspoon dried oregano leaves
4 large burrito tortillas, corn or flour
1 (4 ounce) can chopped green chilies or jalapeños
1 (10 ounce) can mild enchilada sauce
½ cup shredded Monterey Jack cheese
Shredded lettuce and chopped tomatoes for garnish

- Rinse lentils. In a large saucepan, combine lentils, water, 1 can green chilies, chicken broth mix, minced onion, garlic, cumin, and oregano leaves. Heat to boiling. Reduce heat, cover, and simmer 25-30 minutes until lentils are soft.
- Mash lentil mixture until almost smooth.
- Preheat oven to 350°.
- Spread lentils over burrito shells. Sprinkle with green chilies or jalapeños as desired. Fold ends inward and roll. Top with enchilada sauce and cheese.
- Bake for 15 minutes or until cheese is heated thoroughly.
- Serve topped with shredded lettuce and chopped tomatoes.

Yield: 4 servings

If desired, substitute 1 chicken bouillon cube or 1 teaspoon crystallized chicken bouillon for the chicken broth mix.

Mushroom Enchiladas

2 tablespoons olive oil
2 shallots, minced
1 pound fresh mushrooms,
thinly sliced
Dash thyme
¼ cup dry sherry
Salt and pepper to taste
1 cup strong vegetable broth
1 tablespoon cornstarch
1 tablespoon cold water
Juice of 1 lemon
Juice of 1 lime
1 cup sour cream
½ cup vegetable oil
8 corn tortillas
1½ cups grated Monterey
Jack cheese

- Heat olive oil in a large skillet over medium heat. Add shallots; sauté until soft.
- Add mushrooms, thyme, and sherry. Cook until mushrooms are tender, 8-10 minutes. Season with salt and pepper. Drain mushrooms; set aside.
- Heat vegetable broth in a medium saucepan over medium heat. In a small cup, mix cornstarch and water to make a smooth paste. Add cornstarch mixture to broth. Bring to a boil, stirring constantly.
- Remove broth mixture from heat. Stir in lemon and lime juices. Add sour cream. Blend well. Return to low heat and keep warm.
- Preheat oven to 400°.
- Heat vegetable oil in a skillet over medium heat. One at a time, add tortillas and fry gently to soften. Do not fry until crisp. Drain on paper towels to remove excess oil.
- Divide mushrooms and place on the centers of the tortillas. Roll each tortilla jelly-roll style. Arrange enchiladas seam sides down with sides touching in a shallow baking dish.
- Pour sour cream sauce over enchiladas. Sprinkle cheese on top.
- Bake until sauce is bubbly and cheese is melted and browned, about 10 minutes.

Yield: 4 servings

A substantial vegetarian entree.

Stewed Okra and Tomatoes

*2 slices bacon, cooked crisp
  and crumbled, reserving
  grease
1/2 medium-sized onion,
  chopped
3 cups chopped okra (fresh or
  frozen)
1 1/2 cups chopped tomatoes
2 cloves garlic, minced
Hot pepper sauce to taste
Salt and pepper to taste
1/3 cup water*

- Heat bacon grease in a large skillet. Sauté onion until clear. If bacon grease is insufficient, a little olive oil can be added.
- Add okra, tomatoes, garlic, hot pepper sauce, salt, pepper, and water. Stir gently. Let simmer 20-30 minutes until okra is tender.
- Sprinkle with crumbled bacon.

Yield: 6 servings

Delicious as a side dish served with marinated flank steak or as an entree served over rice.

Cheddar Onion Round

*1 1/2 cups crushed Ritz crackers
5 tablespoons butter, melted,
  divided
2 cups thinly sliced onions
2 eggs, lightly beaten
3/4 cup milk
1 teaspoon salt
Dash pepper
3/4 cup grated Cheddar cheese*

- Preheat oven to 350°.
- Mix cracker crumbs with 4 tablespoons butter. Press into an 8-inch pie plate. Cover and refrigerate until chilled.
- In a medium sauté pan, melt remaining 1 tablespoon butter. Sauté onions until soft. Spoon into crust.
- Combine eggs, milk, salt, and pepper. Pour over onions. Sprinkle with cheese.
- Bake uncovered for 30 minutes.

Yield: 6 servings

An excellent companion to steak or marinated chicken.

Vidalia Onion Casserole

1 stick butter
5 large Vidalia onions,
  coarsely chopped
¼ cup milk
24 Ritz crackers, crumbled
½ cup grated Parmesan
  cheese, divided

- Preheat oven to 325°.
- Heat butter in a large skillet. Sauté onions 15-20 minutes until clear. Stir in milk.
- Put half the onion mixture in the bottom of a 1-quart casserole dish. Spread half the crumbled crackers on top of the onions. Sprinkle with ¼ cup Parmesan cheese.
- Repeat layers, ending with cheese.
- Bake uncovered for 30 minutes

Yield: 8-10 servings.

Always a hit!

Italian Peppers and Onions

3 tablespoons olive oil
5 cloves garlic, chopped
1 tablespoon chopped fresh
  oregano
4 large red bell peppers,
  seeded and chopped
1 large yellow onion, sliced
Salt and pepper to taste

- Heat oil in a large pan. Add garlic and oregano. Sauté peppers for 10 minutes. Add onions and continue cooking 10 more minutes or until vegetables are tender.
- Season with salt and pepper.

Yield: 4 servings

Use green and yellow peppers with the red bell peppers for a beautifully colorful dish.

Serve as a side dish or as a topping for a hot submarine sandwich!

Baked Stuffed Potatoes

4 large baking potatoes
4 slices bacon, cooked crisp
*   and crumbled*
6 tablespoons sour cream
4 tablespoons butter
2 tablespoons finely cut chives
Pinch nutmeg
Salt
Freshly ground white pepper
2 teaspoons cracker meal
⅛ teaspoon paprika
1 teaspoon grated Parmesan
*   cheese*
1 tablespoon butter, melted

- Preheat oven to 350°.
- Bake potatoes for 45-50 minutes or until a fork poked into them meets no resistance.
- When the potatoes are done, remove them from the oven. Reduce heat to 325°. Let the potatoes cool until you can handle them. Using a paring knife, cut a slice about 1½ inches wide, and nearly as long as the potato, from the top.
- Scoop out the potato pulp with a soup spoon, being careful to leave the skin intact. Put the pulp into a mixing bowl.
- Add the bacon, sour cream, butter, chives, and nutmeg. Season carefully with salt and pepper. Blend well with a wooden spoon, breaking up the larger lumps. The potato mixture should be smooth and not too loose. If it seems too dry, add a little more butter and sour cream.
- Stuff the potato skins with the mixture and arrange them in a baking dish.
- Combine the cracker meal and paprika in a small bowl with the Parmesan cheese. Sprinkle this mixture over the potatoes. Drizzle the melted butter over the topping.
- Set the potatoes into the oven to bake for about 10 minutes or until very hot.
- Serve at once.

Yield: 4 servings

The potatoes may be stuffed hours before serving and kept covered and refrigerated until the final baking. In this case, allow 2-3 minutes more for them to get hot. One of our favorites from Albert Schnarwyler of The Homestead.

Potatoes for a Crowd

²/₃ cup olive oil
2 tablespoons lemon juice
2 tablespoons white wine
* vinegar*
1 clove garlic, minced
1 tablespoon finely chopped
* fresh tarragon*
1 teaspoon Dijon mustard
¹/₂ teaspoon salt
¹/₂ teaspoon pepper
1 cup grated Parmesan cheese,
* divided*
10 medium-sized red
* potatoes, unpeeled and cut*
* into quarters*

- Preheat oven to 350°.
- Combine oil, lemon juice, vinegar, garlic, tarragon, mustard, salt, and pepper in a large bowl. Toss with ²/₃ cup Parmesan cheese and the potato quarters.
- Spread potatoes in a shallow casserole dish. Sprinkle with remaining Parmesan cheese.
- Bake for 1 hour or until nicely brown on top.

Yield: 10-12 servings.

Roasted Potatoes with Orange Peel

4 teaspoons extra virgin olive
* oil*
2 teaspoons grated orange peel
1 teaspoon dried rubbed sage
¹/₂ teaspoon ground pepper
6 medium-sized red potatoes,
* each cut into 8 wedges*

- Preheat oven to 425°.
- Mix olive oil, orange peel, sage, and pepper in a medium bowl. Add potatoes. Toss well.
- Place potatoes on a baking sheet, spacing so they do not touch.
- Bake 40 minutes or until crisp and brown. Turn once during baking.

Yield: 4 servings

Serve with stuffed Cornish game hens.

For basic baked potatoes in a hurry, cut potatoes in half and place cut-side down on a greased baking sheet. Bake for 35 minutes at 425°.

Potato Gratin with Swiss and Cheddar Cheese

2 pounds baking potatoes,
peeled and thinly sliced
2 teaspoons minced garlic
1 teaspoon salt
½ teaspoon white pepper
1 cup heavy cream
½ cup grated Swiss cheese
½ cup grated Cheddar cheese

- Preheat oven to 375°.
- Place half of the potato slices in an ungreased 9"x9"x2" square baking dish. Sprinkle with half of seasonings (garlic, salt, and pepper).
- Cover with remaining potatoes. Sprinkle with remaining seasonings.
- Pour cream over potatoes.
- Cover tightly with foil and bake 1 hour or until potatoes are tender.
- Increase oven temperature to 450°.
- Uncover potatoes. Top with cheese.
- Bake uncovered until cheese melts, about 10 minutes.
- Cool slightly before serving.

Yield: 6 servings

Substitute evaporated skim milk for heavy cream to lighten this recipe.

Outstanding with beef or lamb.

Sweet Potato Balls

1 (17 ounce) can sweet
  potatoes
2 tablespoons butter or
  margarine, melted
1 teaspoon salt
Pinch nutmeg
Pinch cinnamon
3 tablespoons brown sugar,
  firmly packed
1½ tablespoons orange juice
¼ teaspoon grated orange peel
1½ cups crushed corn flakes
16 pineapple slices
4 large marshmallows, cut
  into quarters
8 maraschino cherries, cut in
  half
6 tablespoons butter, melted
  (for topping)

- Combine sweet potatoes, 2 table-spoons butter, salt, nutmeg, cinna-mon, brown sugar, orange juice, and orange peel. Roll mixture into balls slightly larger than golf balls.
- Roll sweet potato balls in crushed corn flakes until completely coated.
- Place pineapple slices on a greased baking sheet. Top each slice with a sweet potato ball.
- Make a thumbprint in the top of each ball and top with ¼ of a marshmallow and ½ of a maraschino cherry.
- Drizzle ½ teaspoon melted butter over each ball.
- Bake for 20 minutes.

Yield: 16 balls

Kids love these! Fun to make and fun to eat. A nice complement for poultry dishes.

• • •

St. John's Church, site of Patrick Henry's rousing "Give me liberty" speech is located in the Church Hill section of Richmond.

Melissa's Sweet Potato Fluff

4 cups cooked sweet potatoes,
  peeled and mashed
1/3 cup butter, melted
2 eggs, beaten
1/2 cup milk
1 teaspoon vanilla extract
1/2 cup sugar
1/2 cup chopped nuts
1/2 cup shredded coconut
3 tablespoons butter or
  margarine, melted (for
  topping)

- Preheat oven to 375°.
- In a large bowl, combine mashed sweet potatoes, 1/3 cup butter, eggs, milk, vanilla extract, and sugar.
- Spread into a greased 1½-quart casserole dish.
- Combine nuts, coconut, and 3 tablespoons butter. Sprinkle over sweet potato mixture.
- Bake for 25 minutes.

Yield: 8 servings

The recipe for Sweet Potato Fluff was submitted by national recording artist Bruce Hornsby. A leader in the popular music field, Mr. Hornsby is a native Virginian and lives in Williamsburg.

Artichokes Florentine

1 (10 ounce) package frozen
  chopped spinach
3 tablespoons butter
1/4 cup minced onion
1/4 cup sour cream
4 tablespoons grated
  Parmesan cheese
Salt and pepper to taste
2 (14 ounce) cans artichoke
  bottoms, drained
Grated Parmesan cheese

- Preheat oven to 350°.
- Cook spinach according to package directions. Drain well.
- Sauté onion in butter until tender.
- Combine spinach, onion, sour cream, Parmesan cheese, salt, and pepper. Stuff mixture into artichoke bottoms. Sprinkle with additional Parmesan cheese.
- Place in a shallow baking dish with a small amount of water in the bottom.
- Bake for 15-20 minutes. Serve hot.

Yield: 4-6 servings

Spinach on Tomato Rings

3 pounds fresh spinach or 2
   (10 ounce) packages frozen
   spinach.
3 tablespoons butter, melted
6 eggs, lightly beaten
1⅓ cups milk
2 medium-sized onions,
   minced
1 tablespoon white vinegar
1¼ teaspoons salt
¼ teaspoon pepper
¼ teaspoon savory
8 tomato slices, ¼-inch thick
   and slightly wider than
   custard cups
Salt and pepper to taste
Watercress for garnish

- Rinse and drain spinach. Cook spinach, covered, in just the water that clings to the leaves, 4-5 minutes. Squeeze all water from the spinach and finely chop. If using frozen spinach, thaw completely and drain, using the back of a spoon to press out all water. Do not cook it.
- Combine spinach, melted butter, eggs, milk, onions, vinegar, salt, pepper, and savory in a medium-sized bowl.
- Generously butter eight 5-ounce custard cups and fill with spinach mixture. Place the cups in a shallow roasting pan in 1 inch of hot water.
- Bake spinach custard 35-40 minutes or until custard is set. May be done ahead to this point. Reheat by covering with foil and setting in hot water in a 350° oven for 10 minutes.
- Cover roasting pan with foil. Set on back of stove to keep warm until serving.
- Sprinkle raw tomato slices with salt and pepper.
- Loosen the custard from the sides of each cup with a thin knife.
- Lay tomato slices over the tops of molds and invert onto a serving platter generously garnished with watercress.

Yield: 8 servings

A very colorful side dish. A unique way to prepare spinach!

Lynda J. Robb's Hot Spinach Casserole

2 (10 ounce) packages frozen
  chopped spinach
2-3 tablespoons chopped onion
4 tablespoons butter
2 tablespoons all-purpose flour
½ cup evaporated milk
Black pepper to taste
¾ teaspoon celery salt
¾ teaspoon crushed garlic
1 teaspoon Worcestershire
  sauce
Small dash cayenne pepper
1 (6 ounce) roll jalapeño
  cheese, cut into small pieces
Croutons

- Preheat oven to 350°.
- Cook spinach according to package directions. Drain well, reserving ½ cup cooking liquid.
- Sauté onion in butter. Add flour and mix well.
- Stir in the evaporated milk and the reserved spinach liquid.
- Season with pepper, celery salt, garlic, Worcestershire sauce, and cayenne pepper. Add jalapeño cheese. Stir until cheese is melted.
- Add cooked spinach. Blend well.
- Pour mixture into a 1½-quart casserole dish. Top with croutons.
- Bake for 30 minutes or until bubbly.

Yield: 6-8 servings

Excellent spicy dish! Very unusual!

Lynda Robb is the daughter of the late former President Lyndon Johnson and wife of Virginia's United States Senator Charles Robb.

Eggplant Tomato Casserole

1 large eggplant (about 1½
  pounds)
1½ teaspoons salt
2 eggs, beaten
2 tablespoons butter or
  margarine, melted
Dash pepper
3 tablespoons chopped onion
½ teaspoon oregano
½ cup dry bread crumbs (or
  wheat germ)
2 large tomatoes, thinly sliced
½ cup grated Cheddar cheese
¼ cup grated Parmesan cheese

- Peel eggplant and cut into thin slices. Place in about an inch of salted boiling water and cook covered until softened, about 10 minutes.
- Drain eggplant and mash thoroughly.
- Combine eggs, butter, pepper, onion, oregano, and bread crumbs. Add to mashed eggplant. May be prepared ahead of time to this point.
- Preheat oven to 375°.
- Grease a shallow 1½-quart baking dish. Cover the bottom with half the tomato slices followed by the egg-plant mixture. Top with remaining tomatoes.
- Combine the Cheddar and Parmesan cheeses. Sprinkle on top of the casserole.
- Bake for 45 minutes.

Yield: 4-6 servings

For a healthier version of this delicious casserole, use egg substitute in place of eggs.

Eggplants are available most of the year. For best results, purchase eggplants that are firm to the touch with smooth, unblemished skins.

Acorn Squash Baked with Honey

2 medium-sized acorn squash
4 teaspoons butter
4 teaspoons honey
4 pinches ground ginger
4 pinches ground cinnamon
Salt

- Preheat oven to 325°.
- Rinse the squash under cold running water, pat dry, and set on your work surface.
- Remove a ¼-inch thick slice from the blossom end of each squash to facilitate slicing them in half. Stand the squash on this level base and slice it evenly in half from the stem to the blossom end. Then cut a ⅛-inch thick slice from the bottom of each half so the squash will sit evenly in the baking pan (and on your plate).
- Scoop out the seeds and stringy insides with a teaspoon, set the squash halves into a baking pan, and put 1 teaspoon butter, 1 teaspoon honey, a pinch of ginger, a pinch of cinnamon, and a dash of salt into each cavity.
- Put the baking pan into the middle level of the oven and bake for 40-50 minutes or until the squash halves are soft and mushy and a knife point meets no resistance when thrust into the thickest part of the squash.
- Serve while very hot.

Yield: 4 servings

A simple and very tasty fall and winter vegetable recipe that has been handed down from generation to generation.

A specialty from Albert Schnarwyler, chef at The Homestead in Hot Springs, Virginia.

This recipe is reprinted from **Dining at the Homestead.**

Spaghetti Squash and Sun-Dried Tomatoes

1 spaghetti squash
1 (7 ounce) jar sun-dried
tomatoes packed in oil,
drained, reserving 1
tablespoon oil
1 tablespoon cider vinegar
¼ cup fresh orange juice
1 tablespoon olive oil
½ teaspoon cumin
½ teaspoon ground coriander
½ teaspoon crushed red pepper
flakes
Grated peel of 1 orange
2 cloves garlic, minced
2 green onions, finely sliced
12 basil leaves, shredded, for
garnish

- Preheat oven to 375°.
- Halve squash, discard seeds. Place halves, cut side down, in a large saucepan. Add 2 inches of water and bring to a boil. Cover saucepan, reduce heat to medium, and simmer squash for 20 minutes or until tender. Drain and let cool.
- Remove spaghetti-like fibers from squash with a fork. Set aside.
- Halve tomatoes and combine with spaghetti squash in a large bowl. Toss well.
- In a large jar, combine cider vinegar, orange juice, olive oil, sun-dried tomato oil, cumin, ground coriander, red pepper flakes, orange peel, garlic, and green onions. Cover jar and shake well. Add to squash mixture and toss.
- Bake in a large casserole dish for 30-45 minutes.
- To serve, mound squash and tomatoes onto individual plates and garnish with shredded basil.

Yield: 4 servings

The combination of the spaghetti squash, sun-dried tomatoes, and garlic produces a unique flavor.

Stuffed Squash

12 *small yellow squash*
2 *tablespoons finely chopped*
 onion
1 *teaspoon chopped fresh*
 parsley
2 *tablespoons butter*
2 *tablespoons bread crumbs*
1 *hard-boiled egg, finely*
 chopped
1 *teaspoon chopped pimiento*
Salt and pepper to taste
Buttered bread crumbs

- Cook squash in boiling salted water until tender. Drain and let cool. Cut an oval hole in the top of each squash. Spoon out the inside pulp and seeds, being careful not to break the squash. Finely chop the squash pulp and seeds. There should be 1 cup of pulp and seed. Set aside.
- Sauté onion and parsley in butter until onion is soft.
- Add squash pulp, 2 tablespoons bread crumbs, egg, and pimiento. Mix well. Season with salt and pepper.
- Fill the reserved squash cavities with squash filling. Sprinkle with buttered bread crumbs.
- Bake uncovered in a greased baking pan for 20 minutes or until bread crumbs are brown and sizzling.

Yield: 6 servings

To make buttered bread crumbs, melt butter and add bread crumbs. Cook until foamy.

Excellent dish! Very attractive for company!

• • •

Virginia has a prominent horse industry. Four Virginia-bred horses have won the Kentucky Derby...Reigh Count (1928), Secretariat (1973, also a Triple Crown winner), Pleasant Colony (1981), and Sea Hero (1993).

Summer Squash Casserole

2 pounds yellow summer
squash, sliced
1 medium onion, chopped
¾ cup mayonnaise
1 cup grated Cheddar cheese
1 egg, lightly beaten
Salt and pepper to taste
¾ cup herb-seasoned stuffing
mix
½ stick butter or margarine,
melted

- Preheat oven to 350°.
- Boil squash and onion in water for 10 minutes until tender.
- Drain squash and onions. Mix with mayonnaise, Cheddar cheese, egg, salt, and pepper.
- Place squash mixture in a buttered 1½-quart casserole.
- Mix melted butter with stuffing mix. Spread on top of squash.
- Bake uncovered for 30 minutes.

Yield: 6 servings

As a variation, top squash with crumbled cheese crackers and drizzle with 3 tablespoons melted butter instead of using the stuffing mix.

Surrey House Stewed Tomatoes

1 (28 ounce) can whole
tomatoes, undrained
4 tablespoons butter
1½ cups sugar, or to taste
1 teaspoon cinnamon
2 slices bread, torn into pieces

- Combine all ingredients and cook over low heat until thickened. If a thicker consistency is desired, add more bread.

Yield: 6 servings

The Surrey House, known for its true Southern cooking, has been serving travelers to the Southside of the James River in Surry, Virginia for 40 years.

Sautéed Zucchini and Tomatoes

*2 tablespoons olive oil or
butter*
1 clove garlic, minced
1 small onion, thinly sliced
*3 medium-sized zucchini,
thinly sliced*
*1 tomato, peeled, seeded, and
cut into small wedges*
Salt and pepper
½ cup grated Parmesan cheese

- Heat olive oil in a large skillet. Sauté garlic and onion until soft.
- Add zucchini; sauté until tender.
- Add tomatoes. Season with salt and pepper. Simmer for 5 minutes.
- Sprinkle with Parmesan cheese and serve.

Yield: 4-6 servings

A summer favorite!

Zucchini Custard

4 large zucchini, sliced
1 egg
½ cup sour cream
¾ teaspoon seasoned salt
¼ teaspoon pepper
*1 cup grated Parmesan cheese,
divided*
2 tablespoons butter

- Preheat oven to 400°.
- Cook zucchini in boiling salted water until tender. Drain.
- Place zucchini in a shallow baking dish.
- Combine egg, sour cream, seasoned salt, pepper, and ½ cup Parmesan cheese. Beat well. Pour mixture over zucchini.
- Dot with butter. Sprinkle with remaining ½ cup Parmesan cheese.
- Bake uncovered for 15 minutes or until set.

Yield: 4-6 servings

Poppy Seed Zucchini

1½ *pounds zucchini, sliced*
1 *onion, chopped*
1 *egg, lightly beaten*
1½ *tablespoons butter*
1 *teaspoon poppy seeds*
1 *clove garlic, minced*
Salt to taste
½ *teaspoon black pepper*
⅓ *cup grated Parmesan cheese*

- Preheat oven to 375°.
- Cook zucchini and onion in boiling salted water until tender. Drain.
- Add egg, butter, poppy seeds, garlic, salt, and pepper. Mix well and place in a 1-quart baking dish. Sprinkle with Parmesan cheese.
- Bake for 30 minutes.

Yield: 6 servings

Light Matchstick Zucchini

1½ *pounds zucchini*
1 *tablespoon olive oil*
2 *cloves garlic, minced*
Black pepper to taste
⅓ *cup grated Parmesan cheese*

- Cut zucchini lengthwise into thin slices. Cut slices into long matchstick pieces.
- Heat oil in a large non-stick frying pan over medium heat. Add zucchini and garlic. Cook, lifting and gently stirring, until zucchini is crisp-tender, 2-3 minutes.
- Season with pepper. Sprinkle with Parmesan cheese.
- Serve immediately.

Yield: 4 servings

Vegetarian Chili

1 tablespoon olive oil
1 onion, chopped
1 red bell pepper, chopped
1 green bell pepper, chopped
1 jalapeño pepper, seeded and
  chopped
2 garlic cloves, crushed
1 (16 ounce) can tomatoes
2 (15 ounce) cans red kidney
  beans
1 (15 ounce) can black beans
½ cup dried whole lentils
1 cup water
1 teaspoon paprika
2 teaspoons chili powder
½ teaspoon salt
1 teaspoon pepper
1 tablespoon sugar

- Heat oil in a large saucepan and sauté onion and peppers for 10 minutes.
- Add garlic; cook 1-2 minutes. Add tomatoes.
- Drain red kidney beans and black beans; reserve liquid.
- Simmer lentils in water for 40-45 minutes until tender. Drain lentils; reserve liquid.
- Add beans and lentils to tomato mixture. Season with paprika and chili powder. Simmer for 15 minutes.
- Add reserved bean and lentil liquid until chili is the desired consistency.
- Add salt, pepper, and sugar.

Yield: 6 servings

Delicious served over rice and topped with grated cheese, sour cream, and sliced jalapeños.

When selecting peppers, choose ones with smooth skins that have not shriveled.

Curried Baked Fruit

1 (16 ounce) can pear halves
1 (16 ounce) can cling peaches
1 (16 ounce) can pineapple
  chunks
1 (16 ounce) can apricot
  halves
13 maraschino cherries
⅔ cup blanched, slivered
  almonds
½ cup butter, melted
¾ cup light brown sugar
3 tablespoons curry powder

- Preheat oven to 325°.
- Drain all fruit.
- Arrange fruit and nuts in layers in a 1½-quart casserole dish.
- Melt butter in a saucepan; add sugar and curry powder. Blend well.
- Pour butter mixture over fruit and nuts.
- Bake for 1 hour.
- Refrigerate overnight. Reheat at 350° before serving.

Yield: 12 servings

A favorite from **Virginia Seasons!**

Bourbon Apples

1 can apple pie filling
⅓ cup bourbon
¼ cup brown sugar
2 tablespoons white sugar
Cinnamon and nutmeg to taste
2 tablespoons butter

- Mix all ingredients except butter. Let set in refrigerator 24 hours to mellow.
- Remove from refrigerator and dot with butter.
- Bake at 350° for 1½ hours. May need to put under broiler to crystallize top.

Yield: 6 servings

This dish is an excellent accompaniment for game and may also be used for brunch. Could also be a tasty dessert.

An easy treat from Virginia Seasons*!*

Apple Fritters

4 apples
1 cup prepared pancake mix
1 cup all-purpose flour
1⅓ cups water
Vegetable oil for deep frying
Confectioners' sugar

- Core the apples and cut into ⅜-inch slices.
- Combine pancake mix, flour, and enough water to make a thick batter to coat the apple slices.
- Heat vegetable oil in a large skillet for deep frying.
- Dip the apple slices in the batter. Deep fry until golden brown.
- Cool apples for a few minutes, then roll in confectioners' sugar.
- Delicious served hot or cold.

Yield: 6 servings

These batter-fried apples are a specialty of The Surrey House in Surry, Virginia, which is just a short ferry ride across the James River from Williamsburg and Jamestown.

Baked Curried Bananas

4 large firm bananas
¼ cup butter, melted
1 teaspoon curry powder
2 tablespoons light brown
*   sugar*

- Preheat oven to 350°.
- Cut bananas lengthwise and then in half.
- Combine butter and curry powder.
- Dip banana pieces in the curry sauce to coat. Sprinkle with sugar.
- Bake for 12-15 minutes.

Yield: 8 servings

Scalloped Pineapples

1 (20 ounce) can pineapple
*   chunks*
⅓ cup sugar
3 tablespoons all-purpose flour
1 cup grated Cheddar cheese
½ cup crumbled buttery
*   crackers*
¼ cup butter, melted

- Preheat oven to 350°.
- Drain pineapple, reserving 3 tablespoons of the juice.
- Combine pineapple juice with sugar and flour.
- Pour pineapple into a greased 1-quart casserole dish, and cover with the juice mix. Top with grated cheese.
- Combine cracker crumbs with the melted butter. Sprinkle on top of casserole.
- Bake for 20 minutes or until bubbly.

Yield: 4 servings

Serve with ham, chicken, or an Oriental meal!

Scenes of Virginia

Roanoke's Farmers Market

Fruits and vegetables fresh from the field are abundant at Roanoke's Farmers Market, one of the longest continually used farmers markets in the country. Known as the "Star City," Roanoke serves as the southern gateway to the Shenandoah Valley.

Governor's Palace

The Governor's Palace in Colonial Williamsburg offers tourists a taste of life in Virginia before the Revolutionary War. Along with Jamestown and Yorktown, Williamsburg marks the birthplace of America.

Azaleas In Bloom

Vibrant azaleas and delicate dogwood blossoms abound in Virginia during the spring. In keeping with their tradition as entertainers, Virginians proudly play host to one of the nation's oldest garden tour weeks.

Foxhunting

Cool autumn days laced with crisp, colorful leaves provide the perfect backdrop for the sporting life in Virginia's Hunt Country.

Schooner on Chesapeake Bay

The largest natural estuary in the United States, the Chesapeake Bay today yields a bounty of seafood, from oysters and crabs to fresh and saltwater fish.

Blue Ridge Mountains

Dominating the landscape with glorious peaks, spectacular fall foliage and painted skies, the Blue Ridge Mountains illustrate why Thomas Jefferson called Virginia "God's country."

Monument Avenue

Strolling down Richmond's Monument Avenue on a sunny afternoon, one can enjoy both the beauty and the heritage of Virginia's capital.

Virginia Fare

From a simple picnic to an elegant dinner, Virginians love to entertain. Fine Virginia wine, distinctive cuisine, and dramatically varied landscapes are just some of the ingredients that make Virginia unique.

Meat & Poultry

Where We Began

With the arrival of 100 or so English settlers in 1607, our nation was born at Jamestown on the Virginia Peninsula. The colonists began developing at Jamestown the process for curing country ham which later was refined across the James River at Smithfield. They had brought hogs from England and, seeing the Indians preserve venison by rubbing it with salt and smoking it, they tried it with pork and it worked.

The first marketer of Smithfield ham was Mallory Todd, born in Bermuda in 1749. A runaway, he became owner of ships trading with English colonies in America and by the time he was 25 was operating in Smithfield. He died in 1817 and his son, John R. Todd, continued the business in Smithfield. Heirs sold the business and after nearly a century the owners moved it to Richmond where it flourishes today as E.M. Todd. On the wall is an invoice dated April 10, 1779 for a shipment of several barrels of hams to St. Eustatius in the West Indies for which Todd received "various sundries, a two-pound cannon, and a hat." Today, when Virginia's governors go abroad on trade missions, they take along a Todd's to enhance state dinners.

Fame of the Smithfield ham spread. Queen Victoria was a regular customer. State officials took to carrying along a Smithfield when they attended a convention out of state. The room with the ham became the convention's informal headquarters. Fortunately, one ham can feed a multitude.

During curing anywhere from nine months to three years or more, the ham shrinks, concentrating its essence. A recent prize winner by A.D. Doggett of Smithfield shrank during a 14-month curing from 20 pounds to 14 pounds. A ham cured three months, a milder sort, is deemed a country ham. A ham cured within Smithfield's boundaries six months to nine months (most often, the latter time) is defined as a Smithfield. Those cured outside the city but over the same long period are called old Virginia hams. Any long-cure ham is so rich it must be carved, with a sharp knife, into well nigh veil-thin slices until, some purists say, a newspaper can be read through a slice of ham. Somebody in the family becomes, through innate talent and tenacious practice, a master carver who is excused from all other chores in preparing dinner.

Just before the meal, others watch in awe as he sharpens the knife and wields it slowly, surely, the pieces curling before the blade, falling into an exquisite pattern on the platter. The Smithfield or old Virginia ham, cured with loving care, is the Stradivarius of hams. The carver, bowing the thin knife, beginning at the shank end and working up into the ample cushion would, if he tucked it under his chin, appear to be Yehudi Menuhin playing the violin. Spectators break into applause after the virtuoso performance.

Thanks to two individuals, the colonists survived at Jamestown. Captain John Smith gave them discipline. The first American, he loved the land for itself, not out of just greed for gold. He explored its rivers and studied its Indians and wrote about it all in America's first masterpiece. Pocahontas, daughter of emperor Powhatan, gave them love, bringing the settlers food and warning them of impending attacks by her father's braves. "The mother of us all," poet Vachel Lindsay called her.

In Williamsburg was a galaxy of political genius unmatched by any other era of history. Other states boast of two or three of the nation's founders; Virginia contributed dozens to the American Revolution. At Yorktown, aided by Admiral DeGrasse's fleet that bottled up British General Cornwallis and by Rochambeau's siege guns, George Washington shaped a victory over the British. America came of age.

-Guy Friddell

Beef Medallions with Roquefort Sauce

8 (3 ounce) medallions of beef
  tenderloin
Salt and pepper to taste
2 tablespoons vegetable oil
1½ cups dry white wine
1 tablespoon Dijon mustard
4 ounces Roquefort cheese
1 cup heavy cream
Chopped parsley for garnish

- Lightly salt and pepper the beef.
- Heat oil in a large sauté pan. Place the medallions in the hot pan and sear them on both sides to the desired degree of doneness.
- Remove the beef from the sauté pan, place them on a serving platter and set aside.
- Add the white wine and mustard to the sauté pan. Gently rock it over medium heat to deglaze.
- Add the Roquefort and cream. Heat until sauce is reduced by half.
- Remove any meat juice from the platter. Spoon Roquefort sauce over the medallions. Garnish with parsley and serve.

Yield: 4 servings

Beautifully elegant dinner party fare!

Seafood Stuffed Beef Tenderloin

3-4 pounds beef tenderloin
8 ounces cooked lobster or
  crabmeat
1 tablespoon butter, melted
1½ teaspoons lemon juice
6 slices bacon, partially cooked
½ cup sliced green onions
½ cup butter
½ cup dry white wine
½ teaspoon garlic salt
Watercress for garnish
Fluted mushrooms for garnish

- Preheat oven to 425°.
- Cut tenderloin lengthwise to within ½ inch of bottom to "butterfly".
- Place lobster or crabmeat pieces end-to-end inside the tenderloin.
- Combine 1 tablespoon melted butter and lemon juice. Drizzle on seafood.
- Close meat around seafood and tie with string at 1-inch intervals.
- Place on rack and roast in a shallow roasting pan for 40-45 minutes.
- Lay bacon on top and roast for 5 more minutes.
- Meanwhile, sauté green onions in ½ cup butter over low heat until tender, stirring frequently.
- Add wine and garlic salt. Heat, stirring frequently.
- Spoon mixture over beef on serving platter.
- Garnish with watercress and fluted mushrooms.

Yield: 8 servings

Delightful and delicious!

Stuffed Flank Steak

4 tablespoons butter or
  margarine
1/2 cup chopped onion
3/4 cup chopped celery
1/2 cup chopped celery leaves
1 (4 ounce) can sliced
  mushrooms
1/2 teaspoon salt
Dash pepper
1/4 teaspoon thyme
1/4 cup chopped fresh parsley
2 cups (6 1/4 ounces) crumbled
  blue cheese crackers or 2
  cups crumbled saltine
  crackers mixed with 1 1/2
  tablespoons crumbled blue
  cheese
1/4 cup milk or water
1 (2 pound) flank steak,
  pounded to 1/4-inch thickness
  with one side scored
Vegetable oil
1 can condensed cream of
  mushroom soup
1/2 soup can water

- Melt butter in skillet; sauté onions and celery until tender but not browned.
- Add celery leaves, mushrooms, salt, pepper, thyme, parsley, crumbled crackers, and milk; toss well.
- Spread mixture on unscored side of flank steak. Roll the steak and fasten with toothpicks or tie with string.
- Brown the steak on all sides in vegetable oil in a large skillet or in a shallow baking dish in a hot oven (425°) for 30 minutes.
- Place meat on rack in a covered pan and roast at 350° for 1 1/2 to 2 hours, until tender.
- If gravy is desired, stir mushroom soup and water into roasting pan drippings about 15 minutes before removing steak from oven.
- Slice and serve.

Yield: 6-8 servings

Roasts, steaks, and chops will be more tender if they are brought to room temperature before cooking.

Blackened Prime Rib with Hot and Spicy Sauce

Creole Sauce

*1 (28 ounce) can whole
   tomatoes with juices*
1 tablespoon olive oil
½ cup sliced Bermuda onion
*½ cup green bell pepper, cut
   in strips*
½ cup celery, cut in strips
1 clove garlic, minced
½ teaspoon hot pepper sauce
⅛ teaspoon cayenne pepper
⅛ teaspoon black pepper
⅛ teaspoon white pepper
¼ teaspoon oregano
¼ teaspoon thyme
¼ teaspoon basil
1 small bay leaf

- Puree tomatoes with juices in a food processor; set aside.
- Heat oil in a heavy saucepan. Sauté onion, green pepper, celery, and garlic until softened, but not brown.
- Add tomato puree and spices. Simmer 45-60 minutes.

Seasoning Mix

4 tablespoons paprika
1 tablespoon oregano
1 tablespoon basil
1 tablespoon thyme
½ teaspoon cayenne pepper
½ teaspoon black pepper
½ teaspoon salt
1 tablespoon onion powder
1 tablespoon garlic powder

- Combine all ingredients; set aside.

Grilled Steak

*1 (16 ounce) ribeye steak, cut
   ¾"-1" thick*
Olive oil

- If meat is very lean, coat lightly with olive oil.
- Sprinkle meat lightly with seasonings.
- Heat an iron skillet over very high heat to an ashen gray. Cook meat on both sides to desired degree of doneness.

Continued on next page

Blackened Prime Rib with Hot and Spicy Sauce (continued)

- Serve by placing Creole sauce on individual warm plates and topping with cooked steak.

Yield: 2 servings

A tasty alternative to grilled steak. Use a heavy wok instead of the iron skillet, if desired, to reduce splattering.

If your dried herbs and spices are more than a year old, consider replacing them or using more than the recipe calls for to make up for their decreased pungency.

Beef Stroganoff

2-3 large onions, thinly sliced
4 tablespoons butter
3 tablespoons soy sauce
¾ cup ketchup
Generous dash nutmeg
1½ pounds beef tenderloin, cut into thin strips
2 cups sliced mushrooms
1 pint sour cream
Additional sour cream for garnish
1 (16 ounce) package egg noodles, cooked and drained

- Sauté the onions in butter.
- Add soy sauce, ketchup, and nutmeg to onions; blend well.
- Add tenderloin; cook on high heat 2-3 minutes.
- Add mushrooms and sour cream just before serving. Simmer over low heat 2-3 minutes.
- Serve over buttered egg noodles

Yield: 4-6 servings

From the home of J.E.B. Stuart IV, a direct descendant of Civil War cavalry leader, General J.E.B. Stuart. General Stuart's memorial equestrian statue graces Monument Avenue in Richmond.

Never allow sour cream to reach its boiling point or it will separate and curdle.

159

Beef Bourguignon for Twenty-Four

1½ cups all-purpose flour
4 teaspoons salt
1 teaspoon pepper
10 pounds beef chuck, cut in
1½-inch pieces
½ cup butter
½ cup olive oil
¾ cup cognac, warmed
1 pound bacon, diced
6 cloves garlic, mashed
8 carrots, coarsely chopped
4 leeks, coarsely chopped
4 large yellow onions, chopped
¼ cup chopped fresh parsley
3 bay leaves (or one per
casserole)
1½ teaspoons thyme
4 tablespoons tomato paste
7 cups Burgundy wine
6 cups beef broth
Salt and freshly ground
pepper
60 pearl onions, preferably no
larger than 1 inch in
diameter
½ cup butter
2 tablespoons sugar
3 pounds button mushrooms
½ cup butter
Juice of 1 lemon
Additional salt and freshly
ground pepper to taste
½ cup chopped fresh parsley

- Combine flour, salt, and pepper. Dredge meat in flour mixture.
- Brown meat on all sides in ½ cup butter and ½ cup oil using a heavy skillet over high heat. This must be done in several batches, adding butter and oil as needed.
- Place browned meat in two 5-quart casserole dishes or one large, deep roasting pan.
- Deglaze the skillet by pouring warmed cognac into it, lighting the cognac with a match, and stirring to loosen particles. It is best to add cognac in ¼-cup increments to avoid flames leaping too high! Pour this over meat.
- Add bacon, garlic, carrots, leeks, chopped yellow onion, and ¼ cup parsley to the same skillet. Cook, stirring, until bacon and vegetables are lightly browned.
- Add bay leaves, thyme, and tomato paste to skillet, stir well. Add to the beef mixture. Add wine and enough beef broth to barely cover the meat. Mix well. Season with salt and pepper.
- Cover casseroles and bake for 2 hours at 350°. Stir occasionally and add more beef broth if necessary. Cool, then freeze following this step, or freeze after entire dish is prepared.
- Peel the pearl onions by dropping them into boiling water for 1 minute. Cut off the ends and slip off the outer skin.
- Sauté the pearl onions in ½ cup

Continued on next page

Beef Bourguignon for Twenty-Four (continued)

butter with sugar, shaking the pan to caramelize the onions as evenly as possible.

- Pour a small amount of broth or water over pearl onions and simmer, covered, for 10-15 minutes or until they are barely tender. Set aside.
- Sauté the mushrooms in ½ cup butter until lightly browned. Sprinkle with lemon juice.
- Add mushrooms and pearl onions to beef. Cook 1 more hour or until beef is tender. Skim any fat from the casseroles and remove bay leaves.
- Season again with salt and pepper. Sprinkle with chopped parsley before serving.

Yield: 24 servings

This recipe can easily be reduced to serve 6.

This hearty dish freezes beautifully. Make it a few days ahead of time to allow flavors to fully develop.

To save time, have your butcher cut the beef into 1½-inch pieces.

Many fresh herbs can be frozen. Simply place 2-3 tablespoons of minced herbs in each compartment of an ice cube tray. Fill with water and freeze. When frozen solid, remove cubes from tray and store in a labeled sealable plastic bag or freezer container. When the herb is needed for a soup, stew, or cooked dish, simply drop in an herb cube!

"On The Go" Beef

3 tablespoons vegetable oil
1 (4½ pound) boneless beef
   chuck roast, cut into ¾-inch
   pieces
1 teaspoon salt
½ teaspoon pepper
4 cloves garlic, crushed
2 medium-sized onions,
   coarsely chopped
1½ cups water

- Heat oil in a Dutch oven over medium heat. Cook beef in batches until well browned. Season with salt and pepper; set aside.
- Sauté garlic and onion in same pan until onion is lightly browned. Pour off drippings.
- Return beef to pan. Add water. Bring to a boil, then reduce heat, cover tightly and simmer until meat is tender, 1½ to 2 hours. Let cool and skim off fat.
- Set out three 1-quart freezer containers. Put approximately 2 cups of beef mixture in each container. Cover tightly and freeze.
- Defrost and use beef mixture in "On The Go" Chili or "On The Go" Beef Stew.

Yield: 6-7 cups

Shoulder, arm, or blade pot roast may be substituted for beef chuck roast.

"On The Go" Beef Chili

2 cups "On The Go" Beef,
   thawed
1 (8 ounce) jar medium salsa
1 tablespoon chili powder
1 (15 ounce) can kidney
   beans, drained and rinsed
1 cup shredded Cheddar cheese
¼ cup sliced green onions

- Combine beef mixture, salsa, and chili powder in a medium saucepan. Bring to a boil. Reduce heat to low, cover tightly, and simmer 10 minutes.
- Add beans and heat through.
- Serve with Cheddar cheese and green onions.

Yield: 4 servings

"On The Go" Beef Stew

2 cups "On The Go" Beef,
  thawed
2 medium-sized red potatoes,
  cut into ¼-inch thick slices
1 cup sliced carrots
⅔ cup water
1 teaspoon dried oregano
  leaves
½ teaspoon salt
1 cup frozen peas, thawed
1 tablespoon lemon juice
2 teaspoons cornstarch

- Combine beef mixture, potatoes, carrots, water, oregano, and salt in a medium saucepan. Bring to a boil. Reduce heat to low, cover tightly, and simmer until potatoes are tender, 10-12 minutes. Add peas.
- Combine lemon juice and cornstarch in a small bowl. Stir into beef mixture. Bring to a boil; cook and stir 1 minute.

Yield: 4 servings

Broccoli Beef Stir-Fry

6 tablespoons peanut oil,
  divided
½ pound beef tenderloin,
  sliced and cut into bite-size
  pieces
4 teaspoons cornstarch,
  divided
1 teaspoon sugar
1½ pounds broccoli, sliced
1 (8 ounce) can sliced water
  chestnuts
½ cup beef stock
½ teaspoon salt
2 green onions, chopped

- Heat three tablespoons peanut oil in a wok until oil barely begins to smoke.
- Toss beef with 2 teaspoons cornstarch and sugar. Put in wok and stir-fry beef until just cooked. Remove from wok; set aside.
- Heat remaining oil, add broccoli and water chestnuts. Stir-fry until broccoli is crisp-tender, 3-4 minutes. Add beef stock and salt. Bring to a boil. Cover and steam 1 minute.
- Dissolve remaining cornstarch in 1 tablespoon water.
- Return beef to wok and mix with greens. Add cornstarch solution; toss to coat.
- Turn onto a warm serving platter, sprinkle with green onions, and serve immediately.

Yield: 2-3 servings

Equally delicious prepared with chicken instead of beef. Serve over steamed rice or with sesame noodles.

Beef Stir-Fry with Oyster Sauce

1 pound filet mignon, very
thinly sliced
2 tablespoons cornstarch,
divided
1 tablespoon soy sauce
1 teaspoon sugar
½ tablespoon peanut oil
4 tablespoons oyster sauce
½ cup water
3 cloves garlic, minced
1 tablespoon grated ginger
root
Peanut oil for frying
1½ pounds bok choy (Chinese
greens), sliced diagonally
4 ounces canned sliced bamboo
shoots
½ cup chicken stock
1 cup bean sprouts

- Combine beef, 1 tablespoon corn-starch, soy sauce, sugar, and ½ tablespoon peanut oil. Set aside.
- Combine oyster sauce, water, remaining 1 tablespoon cornstarch, garlic, and ginger root. Set aside.
- Heat 2 tablespoons peanut oil in a hot wok until oil barely begins to smoke. Add meat mixture and stir-fry briefly until meat changes color. Remove meat from wok; set aside.
- Heat an additional 2 tablespoons peanut oil in the same manner. Add bok choy and bamboo shoots, toss to coat with oil and add stock. Cover and simmer 1 minute.
- Return beef to wok and toss with vegetables. Add bean sprouts. Stir-fry for 30 seconds.
- Add oyster sauce mixture, toss to coat all pieces and allow sauce to thicken.
- Place on a warm serving platter. Serve immediately.

Yield: 4 servings

Easy Brisket Pot Roast

1 (8 ounce) jar chili sauce
1 (1 ounce) package dry onion
   soup mix
1 (12 ounce) can of beer
1 (2-3 pound) beef brisket
Sliced or quartered onions,
   carrots, and potatoes

- Preheat oven to 325°.
- Mix chili sauce, soup mix, and beer in a large roasting pan. Place brisket on top of the sauce mixture.
- Bake covered for 3 hours.
- Remove from roasting pan. Slice brisket on the diagonal; return slices to roasting pan. Add onions, carrots, and potatoes. Bake for an additional 1-2 hours.

Yield: 6 servings

To freeze, slice brisket and cool after the first 3 hours of roasting. Wrap tightly and freeze. When ready to use, thaw beef and sauce, add vegetables and bake for the extra hour or two. Adding the fresh vegetables when ready to continue the recipe assures a fresh taste.

Cabbage Goulash

1 pound bulk sausage
1 pound ground beef
1 clove garlic, finely minced
1 medium onion, cut in half
   and thinly sliced
2 tablespoons balsamic
   vinegar
1 (6 ounce) can tomato paste
1 (28 ounce) can tomatoes,
   drained and chopped
1 teaspoon red pepper flakes
1-2 teaspoons chili powder
1 medium head of cabbage,
   coarsely chopped to make
   8-9 cups

- Brown sausage, beef, garlic, and onion in a large skillet. Remove meat mixture and drain well.
- Return meat mixture to skillet. Add all other ingredients except cabbage. Heat thoroughly.
- Add cabbage and cook 15-20 minutes over medium heat.
- Serve hot or refrigerate overnight for even better taste. Reheat before serving later.

Yield: 8 servings

An excellent winter dish that freezes well.

Zesty Barbecued Meat Loaf

2 pounds ground beef
1½ cups bread crumbs
1 large onion, chopped
1 cup milk
¾ cup chopped green pepper
2 eggs
½ teaspoon salt
¼ teaspoon pepper
1 pound mushrooms, sliced

- Preheat oven to 350°.
- Combine the first eight meat loaf ingredients. Mix well.
- Shape into a loaf. Place in a baking dish larger than the loaf so the meat does not touch the sides of the pan.
- Place mushroom slices over meat loaf. Set aside.

Zesty Sauce

½ cup chopped onion
2 tablespoons butter
2 tablespoons sugar
½ tablespoon dry mustard
⅔ cup water
*1½ tablespoons
   Worcestershire sauce*
4 drops hot pepper sauce
½ teaspoon salt
¼ teaspoon pepper
1½ teaspoons paprika
¾ cup ketchup
1½ tablespoons vinegar

- To prepare the sauce, sauté onions in butter until translucent. Add remaining sauce ingredients. Cook 15 minutes over low heat.
- Pour sauce over meat loaf and mushrooms.
- Bake for at least 1 hour or until done.

Yield: 6-8 servings

Wonderful zippy taste!

Avoid excess handling when mixing and shaping ground meats or meat loaf mixtures to obtain a moister, lighter dish.

Meatloaf will slice easily if allowed to stand for 10 minutes after removing from the oven.

Herbal Leg of Lamb

½ cup Dijon mustard
2 tablespoons soy sauce
1 clove garlic, minced
1 teaspoon rosemary
¼ teaspoon ground ginger
2 tablespoons olive oil
1 (6 pound) leg of lamb
Watercress and mint leaves
*   for garnish*

- Blend mustard, soy sauce, garlic, rosemary, and ginger. Beat in olive oil by drops to make a creamy sauce.
- Dry lamb well with paper towels.
- Spread sauce over lamb using a pastry brush.
- Place lamb on a roasting rack and let rest several hours before roasting.
- Roast at 350° for 1¼ hours for medium doneness, or until a meat thermometer registers 170°. Do not overcook!
- Place lamb on a hot platter. Garnish with watercress and mint leaves.

Yield: 8 servings

Have lamb butterflied by butcher. Reduce roasting time since there will be no bone to absorb heat. This recipe also works well on the barbecue.

Marinate overnight or for up to 2 days in the refrigerator for extra flavor.

• • •

Alexandria, the heart of Northern Virginia, was settled in the 1740's by Scottish merchants whose clipper ships brought the tobacco trade to the shores of the Potomac River. Its rich heritage has been preserved through the restoration of 18th and 19th century buildings which now house numerous businesses, museums, homes, and shops. Nearby are Washington, D.C. and George Washington's Mount Vernon.

Veal Scallopini

Sauce

1 tablespoon chopped onion
1 tablespoon butter
1/4 cup chopped celery
1/4 cup chopped carrot
1 teaspoon chopped fresh
  parsley
1/2 teaspoon crushed bay leaf
1 tablespoon flour
1/2 cup beef stock
1 tablespoon tomato paste
1 teaspoon Worcestershire
  sauce
1 tablespoon dry red wine
Salt and freshly ground black
  pepper

- To prepare sauce, sauté onion in butter until soft. Add celery, carrot, parsley, and bay leaf.
- Stir in flour; cook for 2 minutes, browning slightly.
- Stir in stock; cook until smooth and thickened.
- Add tomato paste, Worcestershire sauce, and wine. Cook over low heat until smooth.
- Season to taste with salt and pepper.
- Press sauce through a sieve to strain. Set aside sauce. Discard solids.

Veal

4 large slices veal (1/4-1/3
  pound each)
1/4 cup flour
1/4 cup butter
4 thin slices prosciutto
4 slices Monterey Jack cheese
1/2 cup heavy cream

- To prepare veal, draw veal slices through flour to coat both sides.
- Sauté veal in butter until lightly browned.
- Place in a flat ovenproof dish. Cover each veal slice with prosciutto and cheese.
- Add cream to reserved sauce, stir, and pour over veal.
- Bake at 375° until sauce bubbles and cheese has melted.

Yield: 4 servings

Very elegant! Can make ahead of time and bake after your guests arrive!

Dilled Veal

¼ *cup sour cream*
½ *cup heavy cream*
2 *teaspoons dill weed*
1½ *pounds veal scallops*
3 *tablespoons butter or*
margarine
1 *tablespoon lemon juice*
1 *tablespoon white sherry*
1 *teaspoon salt*

- Combine sour cream, heavy cream, and dill weed. Cover and refrigerate at least 4 hours.
- Pound veal between 2 sheets of wax paper until thin.
- In a large skillet, sauté veal in butter until nicely browned.
- Pour lemon juice and sherry over veal and stir to blend.
- Remove veal to a heated platter. Keep warm in the oven.
- Stir cream mixture into pan juices; add salt. Heat and pour over veal.

Yield: 4 servings

Simple Veal Roast

1 (4 *pound) chunk veal leg*
1 *tablespoon dry mustard*
1 *tablespoon salt*
1 *teaspoon brown sugar*
1 *teaspoon sage*
3 *tablespoons vinegar*
4 *slices bacon*
1 (8 *ounce) package egg*
noodles
1 *can chicken broth*

- Preheat oven to 350°.
- Place veal leg in a large roasting pan, skin side up.
- Combine mustard, salt, sugar, sage, and vinegar. Mix well. Spread mixture over veal.
- Top with bacon slices.
- Roast veal for 20-30 minutes per pound, covered.
- Cook noodles in chicken broth and serve with veal.

Yield: 6-8 servings

Incredible!

Roasted Pork Loin with Boar's Head Inn Barbecue Sauce

Pork Loin

5 pounds trimmed boneless
   pork loin
5-6 cups apple cider
3-4 cloves garlic, minced
4-5 fresh rosemary sprigs
Salt and pepper to taste

- Marinate pork loin in apple cider, garlic, and rosemary for 3 days.
- Drain the marinated pork loin and pat dry. Season well with salt and pepper.
- Preheat oven to 425°.
- In a hot skillet, sear the pork on all sides.
- Roast pork loin until it reaches the desired level of doneness. Remove from oven and let stand covered for 20 minutes to recover.
- Heat prepared barbecue sauce.
- Slice the pork loin thinly and "shingle out" against a "pillow" of grits, if desired. Cover with the sauce and garnish with a rosemary sprig.
- Serve immediately.

Yield: 8 servings

Serve with grilled apples and sautéed fresh green beans.

Continued on next page

Boar's Head Inn Barbecue Sauce

1 cup chopped yellow onion
1 cup best quality ketchup
½ cup Worcestershire sauce
½ cup best quality red wine
  vinegar
¾-1 cup light brown sugar
1 teaspoon hot pepper sauce
1 tablespoon dry mustard
  (Coleman's is
  recommended)
¾ quart rich reduced beef
  stock
1 cup fresh apple cider
Salt and freshly cracked
  pepper

- Combine all ingredients except the stock and cider. Simmer until fairly thick. Skim often.
- Add the reduced stock and apple cider. Simmer gently until desired consistency. The chef suggests until it barely coats a spoon.
- Season with salt and pepper, if necessary.
- Strain and cool. It will keep for quite a few days if cooled down quickly.
- The flavor develops if allowed to set overnight.

Yield: 1½ quarts

Be careful not to burn the sauce. It is easy to do with all the sugar involved in this recipe. Also, the quality of this recipe depends greatly upon the richness of the stock/broth - don't skimp.

From The Boar's Head Inn & Sports Club, a beautiful country estate resort located in Charlottesville, Virginia in the picturesque foothills of the Blue Ridge Mountains. Thomas Jefferson's Monticello, James Monroe's Ash Lawn, and the Jefferson-designed University of Virginia are all nearby.

Pork Tenderloin with Cinnamon

4 tablespoons sugar
¼ teaspoon salt
4 tablespoons soy sauce
1½ teaspoons cinnamon
2 tablespoons sherry
1 teaspoon powdered ginger
2 teaspoons dry mustard
2 teaspoons lemon juice
2 pounds pork tenderloin

- Preheat oven to 325°.
- Place pork in roasting pan.
- Combine all remaining ingredients and pour over pork.
- Bake for 1 hour, basting frequently with sauce.

Yield: 4-6 servings

Serve on hamburger buns with Rosy Relish as a fantastic alternative to hamburgers or chili at your next informal party. Also a favorite on small rolls at your next cocktail party.

A favorite from **Virginia Seasons.**

Robert E. Lee's Pork Tenderloin

1 tablespoon butter
1 (2-3 pound) pork
  tenderloin, tied
Salt and pepper to taste
1 teaspoon sugar
2 cups cream
¼ cup wine, if desired
⅔ cup milk
2 teaspoons arrowroot
3 slices bacon, cooked crisp
  and crumbled

- Melt butter in a large pan. Add tenderloin; sprinkle with salt, pepper, and sugar. Brown meat on all sides.
- Add cream, wine, and milk. Simmer covered for 45 minutes.
- Remove pork from pan.
- Thicken gravy with arrowroot mixed with a small amount of water. Whisk with the addition of arrowroot to avoid lumps.
- Crumble bacon on top.
- Serve pork tenderloin sliced with gravy on top.

Yield: 6 servings

This recipe comes from Robert E. Lee, IV, a direct descendant of the beloved Civil War hero, General Robert E. Lee. General Lee is one of the famous Virginians prominently memorialized on Monument Avenue in Richmond.

Pork Chops with Orange-Raisin Sauce

6 thick-cut pork chops
1³/₄ cups water
³/₄ cup raisins
¹/₃ cup brown sugar
1¹/₄ tablespoons cornstarch
¹/₄ teaspoon cinnamon
¹/₄ teaspoon dry mustard
¹/₄ teaspoon ground cloves
¹/₄ teaspoon salt
2 tablespoons butter
1 tablespoon vinegar
¹/₄ cup orange juice

- Brown pork chops. Place in a large baking dish.
- Bring water to a rolling boil. Add raisins; cook for 5 minutes.
- Mix dry ingredients; add to raisins. Cook 10 minutes on medium-low heat.
- Stir in butter and vinegar.
- Add orange juice.
- Pour sauce over pork chops. Bake at 350° for 40 minutes.

Yield: 6 servings

After browning chops, slice to make a pocket and fill with your favorite stuffing. Add sauce and bake as directed above.

Gourmet Pork Chops

6-8 pork chops
Flour
Salt
3 tablespoons vegetable oil
1 can condensed cream of
  mushroom soup
¹/₂ cup water
³/₄ teaspoon ginger
1 teaspoon rosemary
Salt and pepper to taste
1 cup sour cream
1 (2.8 ounce) can French-
  fried onions

- Preheat oven to 350°.
- Dredge pork chops in a mixture of flour and salt.
- Heat oil in a large skillet. Brown pork chops lightly. Place chops in a shallow baking dish.
- Combine mushroom soup, water, ginger, rosemary, salt, pepper, and sour cream. Pour over chops.
- Sprinkle half the French-fried onions on top.
- Cover baking dish with foil. Bake for 50 minutes.
- Uncover dish, top with remaining fried onions, and bake 10 minutes more.

Yield: 6-8 servings

173

Apple-Glazed Pork Loin Chops

½ *cup ketchup*
¼ *cup tomato juice*
½ *cup finely chopped onion*
2 *tablespoons honey*
2 *tablespoons white vinegar*
1 *teaspoon dry mustard*
1½ *teaspoons Worcestershire*
  sauce
½ *cup applesauce*
1 *pound thinly sliced pork loin*
  chops

- Combine ketchup, tomato juice, onion, honey, vinegar, dry mustard, and Worcestershire sauce in a medium saucepan. Bring to a boil over medium heat. Reduce heat; simmer 5 minutes.
- Stir in applesauce. Set aside ½ cup of mixture, and cook remainder over low heat for 15 minutes.
- Place pork on a lightly greased broiler pan rack. Brush with half of the reserved ½ cup sauce.
- Broil pork 6 inches from heat (with oven door partially opened), 4-5 minutes.
- Turn and brush with remaining ¼ cup reserved sauce. Broil 4-5 minutes or until done.
- Transfer to a serving platter. Spoon remaining sauce over pork.

Yield: 4 servings

The chops could be grilled and brushed with the apple glaze.

Country Ham and Red Eye Gravy

*½ pound Roanoker Country
 Ham, wafer sliced or steaks*
⅓ cup water
*⅓ cup good freshly brewed
 coffee*

- Cook the country ham in an iron skillet until fat begins to brown. Remove ham from skillet and reserve on plate, leaving skillet on heat.
- Slowly add water and coffee to deglaze skillet. Be careful to pour the water slowly so the grease does not splatter and burn you.
- When mixture is hot, pour over ham or grits.
- Enjoy with The Roanoker Buttermilk Biscuits to sop up the Red Eye Gravy!

Yield: 2 servings

The Roanoker Restaurant, located on Colonial Avenue in Roanoke, Virginia, has been known for its Virginia Mountain Hospitality since 1941. This recipe for Country Ham and Red Eye Gravy is served there in true Southern style.

• • •

Roanoke is at the foot of the Shenandoah Valley and serves as the commercial and cultural center of western Virginia.

Senator John Warner's Roasted Chicken

1 (3 pound) Virginia roasting
   chicken
1 stalk celery, finely chopped
1 small onion, finely chopped
2 eggs
1 package herb-seasoned
   stuffing mix
Milk
Giblets
Flour to thicken gravy
Dash thyme
Dash onion salt
Dash basil
Salt and pepper to taste
1/2 teaspoon soy sauce

- Preheat oven to 350°.
- Thoroughly clean chicken. Rinse cavity well and dry with paper towels.
- Combine celery, onion, eggs, and stuffing mix. If stuffing mixture is too dry, add enough milk to bind the ingredients. Fill chicken's cavity with stuffing.
- Roast chicken, uncovered, for 1 hour; then reduce oven temperature to 300°. Continue to roast for 1 more hour, checking periodically.
- Prepare gravy while chicken is roasting. Boil giblets until tender, reserving giblet liquid. Chop giblets finely. Mix giblet liquid with flour; beat until smooth. Add a dash of thyme, onion salt, basil, salt, pepper, and soy sauce to taste. Heat until thickened.
- When chicken is ready for serving, pour gravy around, not over, chicken.

Yield: 6 servings

John Warner is the senior United States Senator from Virginia. He is an alumnus of Washington and Lee University and a former Secretary of the Navy.

Orange Chicken

²/₃ *cup plain bread crumbs*
²/₃ *cup Italian-style bread
crumbs*
¹/₄ *cup grated Parmesan cheese*
Freshly ground black pepper
*1 pound unsalted butter or
margarine, divided*
*12 boneless, skinless chicken
breast halves*
*1 cup white sherry (not
cooking sherry)*
*1 (10 ounce) jar orange
marmalade*

- In a large bowl, combine bread crumbs, the Parmesan cheese, and black pepper. Mix well.
- Melt half of the butter. While it is hot, dip each breast totally in it and then coat thoroughly in the bread crumb mixture.
- Place the breasts on a well-greased baking sheet or shallow baking pan. Refrigerate for at least 2 hours to set.
- Preheat oven to 350°.
- To prepare the coating, melt the remaining half of the butter in a medium saucepan. Bring the butter almost to a burning boil, then add the cup of white sherry all at once. Let this mixture reduce for a few minutes.
- Add the jar of marmalade and season with ground pepper to taste. Let this mixture cook on a slow boil for 10-15 minutes. Reduce heat to low and leave on very low heat.
- Place pan of chicken in the oven straight from the refrigerator. Bake for 45 minutes, basting with ⅓ of orange mixture every 15 minutes beginning after the first 15 minutes of baking time.
- After chicken has been basted the last time, return to oven (which has been turned off) to allow last baste to set, about 5 minutes.

Yield: 10-12 servings

Using nice, pink chicken, not orange-colored, will ensure freshness.

Delicious served with a rice dish!

Tex Mex Chicken and Rice

2 teaspoons vegetable oil
3 pounds chicken pieces,
 skinned
½ cup chopped onion
½ cup chopped green bell
 pepper
½ cup chopped red bell pepper
1 (15 ounce) can tomato sauce
¼ cup water
1 tablespoon instant chicken-
 flavored broth
1 tablespoon chili powder
2 teaspoons garlic
1 teaspoon paprika
¼ teaspoon ground cumin
2 tablespoons chopped
 jalapeño peppers
4-6 cups cooked rice

- Heat oil in a large skillet. Brown chicken in oil; remove from skillet. Set aside.
- Sauté onions and peppers until tender. Stir in remaining ingredients except rice. Add chicken. Bring to a boil, then reduce heat, cover and simmer for 30 minutes or until chicken is tender.
- Serve over rice.

Yield: 4-6 servings

Even better the next day.

Sautéed Chicken Breasts with Avocado

6 boneless, skinless chicken
 breast halves
1 pound mushrooms, sliced
½ cup butter or margarine,
 divided
¾ cup all-purpose flour
1 teaspoon salt
¼ teaspoon freshly ground
 pepper
2 ripe avocados, peeled and
 sliced
1 cup grated Monterey Jack
 cheese

- Pound breasts to flatten slightly. Set aside.
- In a skillet over medium heat, sauté mushrooms in ¼ cup butter. Remove mushrooms with a slotted spoon and set aside. Reserve juices in skillet.
- Combine flour, salt, and pepper in a small bowl. Coat chicken with flour mixture and shake off excess.
- In skillet with reserved juices, melt remaining butter. Sauté chicken breasts, about 3 minutes on each side.
- Place breasts on a broiler pan. Top with mushrooms, avocado slices, and cheese. Broil until cheese is melted.

Yield: 6 servings

Avocados will ripen if left in a dark place for a day or two. Do not refrigerate until fully ripened.

Chicken Breasts in Sour Cream

*6 boneless, skinless chicken
  breast halves*
*2 tablespoons butter or
  margarine*
Salt and pepper
¼ cup chopped green onion
1¼ cups water
*1 envelope dry gravy mix for
  chicken*
2 tablespoons sherry
1 tablespoon ketchup
½ cup sour cream
½ cup shredded Swiss cheese

- Pound chicken breasts to flatten slightly. Brown in butter 5-10 minutes. Season with salt and pepper. Remove from skillet; set aside.
- Sauté onion in skillet 3-4 minutes. Add water, gravy mix, sherry, and ketchup. Stir to blend.
- Heat mixture to boiling, stirring occasionally. Return chicken to skillet. Cover and simmer 10-15 minutes.
- Place chicken in a broiler-proof pan.
- Stir sour cream into sauce in skillet. Spoon over chicken and sprinkle with cheese.
- Brown lightly under broiler.

Yield: 4-6 servings

Can be prepared in less than thirty minutes. Prepare ahead of time for a dinner party, then broil it at the last minute.

When buying chicken on the bone, estimate ¾ pound per serving.

Chicken Breasts in Phyllo

1½ cups mayonnaise
1 cup chopped green onion
⅓ cup lemon juice
2 cloves garlic, minced
2 teaspoons dry tarragon
12 boneless, skinless chicken
  breast halves
Salt and pepper
24 sheets of phyllo dough
1⅓ cups butter, melted
½ cup freshly grated
  Parmesan cheese

- Preheat oven to 375°.
- Combine mayonnaise, green onion, lemon juice, garlic, and tarragon to make a sauce.
- Lightly sprinkle chicken breasts with salt and pepper.
- Place a sheet of phyllo on working surface. Quickly brush with melted butter (about 2 teaspoons). Place a second sheet on top of first. Brush with melted butter.
- Spread about 1½ tablespoons of sauce on each side of chicken breast (3 tablespoons in all). Place breast in one corner of buttered phyllo sheets. Fold corner over breast, then fold sides over and roll breast up in the sheets to form a package. Place in an ungreased baking dish. Repeat with remaining breasts and phyllo sheets.
- Brush packets with the rest of the butter. Sprinkle with Parmesan cheese. At this point, the dish may be tightly sealed and frozen. Thaw completely before baking.
- Bake for 20-25 minutes or until golden brown.

Yield: 12 servings

• • •

Winchester is the northern gateway to the Shenandoah Valley and is the oldest colonial city west of the Blue Ridge Mountains. The scenic Skyline Drive-Blue Ridge Parkway which has its northern terminus at Front Royal was built for leisurely travel through the mountains overlooking the valley.

Lemony Chicken

4 large chicken breast halves
2 lemons
¼ cup all-purpose flour
1 teaspoon paprika
2 tablespoons vegetable oil
2 tablespoons light brown
  sugar
1½ teaspoons salt
½ cup chicken broth

- Remove skin from chicken breasts. Pat chicken breast dry.
- Grate rind from one lemon; set aside. Squeeze juice from this lemon over chicken.
- Combine flour and paprika in a shallow dish. Turn each breast in flour to coat. Sauté chicken in oil until brown on all sides, approximately 10 minutes.
- Mix reserved lemon rind, brown sugar, and salt. Sprinkle over chicken. Add broth to chicken in skillet. Cook covered over low heat for 25 minutes.
- Cut second lemon into thin slices; arrange slices over chicken. Cook covered an additional 10 minutes or until fork tender.

Yield: 4 servings

Chicken Elegant

¼ cup butter
¼ cup all-purpose flour
2 cups diced cooked chicken
1 (10 ounce) package frozen
  chopped broccoli, cooked
½ cup grated Parmesan
  cheese, divided
¼ cup crumbled blue cheese
1 can condensed cream of
  chicken soup
½ teaspoon marjoram
1 cup sour cream
¼ cup buttered bread crumbs

- Preheat oven to 350°.
- In a large saucepan, melt butter. Add flour and cook 1-2 minutes.
- Gradually stir in chicken, broccoli, ¼ cup Parmesan cheese, blue cheese, soup, and marjoram. Heat mixture until just boiling.
- Remove from heat and add sour cream. Pour into a casserole dish.
- Combine remaining ¼ cup Parmesan cheese and buttered bread crumbs. Sprinkle over chicken casserole.
- Bake for 25-30 minutes or until brown and bubbly.

Yield: 4-6 servings

Chicken with Sun-Dried Tomatoes and Cream

4 boneless chicken breast
halves
3 tablespoons unsalted butter
½ teaspoon salt
¼ teaspoon pepper
1 large shallot, minced
⅔ cup half and half
½ cup dry white wine
⅛ teaspoon marjoram
¼ cup coarsely chopped sun-
dried tomatoes

- Pound chicken breast to about ¼-inch thickness or cut each unpounded chicken breast into 6 equal pieces on the diagonal.
- In a skillet over high heat, melt butter. Add chicken. Sprinkle with salt and pepper. Sauté, turning at least once, until cooked through, 4-5 minutes.
- Using a slotted spoon, remove chicken to a platter. Add the shallot to the skillet and sauté over medium heat until softened, about 1 minute.
- Add half and half, wine, marjoram, and sun-dried tomatoes to skillet. Cook over medium heat until warm and thickened, about 5 minutes. Return chicken to pan. Cook until heated through, about 5 more minutes.

Yield: 4 servings

• • •

The Middleburg area is the heart of Virginia's hunt country. It is well known for steeplechase races, fox hunts, antebellum mansions, and Early American antiques. Numerous Virginia vineyards can be found in this region.

Chicken Artichoke Casserole

*8 chicken breast halves,
cooked and cubed*
1 stick butter
6 tablespoons all-purpose flour
2 cups milk
Salt and pepper
*1½ cups grated Parmesan
cheese*
1 cup white wine
1½ cups chicken stock
*2 cups marinated artichoke
hearts, drained and sliced*

- Preheat oven to 350°.
- Place chicken in a large shallow baking dish.
- Melt butter in a medium saucepan. Add flour; mix well.
- Whisk in milk. Season with salt and pepper. Heat mixture until thickened.
- Add Parmesan cheese and wine to cream sauce. Stir in enough chicken stock to make the sauce thick and creamy.
- Gently fold in artichokes.
- Pour sauce over chicken. Cover and bake for 1 hour.

Yield: 8 servings

For a more colorful presentation, add ½ cup sautéed chopped green bell pepper and one (2 ounce) jar sliced pimientos.

May be made in advance. A perfect gift casserole.

Chicken Stir-Fry with Almonds

1 cup whole almonds
5 tablespoons peanut oil,
  divided
4 boneless, skinless chicken
  breast halves, sliced
1 (8 ounce) can sliced bamboo
  shoots, drained
1 (6 ounce) can sliced water
  chestnuts, drained
1 cup diagonally sliced carrots
½ red bell pepper, thinly sliced
½ cup chopped green onion
  (with tops)
½ cup chicken stock
2 teaspoons white liquor
  (vodka or gin)
1 teaspoon grated ginger root
1 teaspoon soy sauce
½ teaspoon cornstarch
Dash salt
Dash red pepper

- Preheat oven to 400°.
- Place almonds in a shallow pan and brown in oven, stirring often, 12-15 minutes. Chop half of the almonds; set aside.
- Heat oil in wok until it just begins to smoke. Add half the chicken; stir-fry until almost cooked, then remove from wok. Repeat with remaining chicken. Set chicken aside.
- Heat 2 tablespoons oil in wok. Stir in bamboo shoots, water chestnuts, carrots, and chopped almonds. Toss the mixture for 3 minutes.
- Add red bell pepper, green onion, chicken stock, liquor, ginger, and soy sauce. Heat for 1 minute.
- In a small bowl, mix cornstarch with 1 tablespoon water. Stir mixture slowly into wok.
- Add salt and pepper. Stir until liquid thickens, about 2 minutes.
- Turn onto a warmed serving platter and top with whole almonds.

Yield: 4-6 servings

Serve with noodles or steamed rice.

Spinach-Stuffed Cornish Hens

4 Cornish game hens
Salt and freshly ground
  pepper
4 tablespoons butter or
  margarine, divided
½ cup chopped onion
2 cloves garlic, finely chopped
1 cup coarsely chopped fresh
  mushrooms
1 (10 ounce) package frozen
  chopped spinach, thawed
  and squeezed dry
1 cup ricotta cheese
¼ cup sour cream
¼ teaspoon salt
¼ teaspoon pepper

- Preheat oven to 350°.
- Wash hens inside and out; pat dry. Season with salt and pepper.
- In a large frying pan, melt 2 table-spoons butter. Add onion and garlic; sauté until tender, about 2 minutes. Add mushrooms and cook until the liquid evaporates.
- Add spinach to mushroom mixture; cook for 1 minute. Remove from heat and let cool slightly.
- Stir in ricotta cheese, sour cream, salt, and pepper. Mix well.
- Loosely stuff hens with spinach/cheese mixture. Fold wings back and tie legs together. Place hens, breast side up, in a large shallow baking dish.
- Melt remaining 2 tablespoons butter and baste hens.
- Roast hens for 1 hour and 15 min-utes, basting frequently.

Yield: 4 servings

Serve with wild rice and Green Bean and Red Pepper Bundles.

An uncooked or cooked stuffed game hen, chicken, or turkey should never be refrigerated stuffed. The stuffing and poultry should be refrigerated in a separate container to avoid contamination.

Roasted Mustard Chive Game Hens

*6 tablespoons unsalted butter,
   room temperature*
¼ cup minced chives
*1½ tablespoons Dijon
   mustard*
*4 Cornish game hens, halved
   lengthwise*
Salt and pepper
Chopped chives for garnish

- Preheat oven to 450° with rack positioned in the center of the oven.
- Mix butter, minced chives, and mustard in a medium bowl.
- Use fingertips to loosen skin from breast portion of game hen halves. Spread 1 tablespoon chive butter over entire breast portion under the loosened skin of each game hen half. Lightly season hens with salt and pepper.
- Place game hens, skin side up, in a large baking pan. Roast until golden brown and juices run clear when thighs are pierced, about 30 minutes.
- Transfer hens to a serving platter. Garnish with chives and serve.

Yield: 4 servings

Cornish game hens, turkey, and young chickens are leaner than roasters and large hens.

Seafood & Fish

Nature's Way

Eastern Tidewater is divided into three parts: the Peninsula between the James and York Rivers; the Middle Peninsula between the York and Rappahannock; and the Northern Neck between the Rappahannock and Potomac. The rivers and tributaries supply seafood to East Coast cities as far as New York.

In the Chesapeake Bay, hanging like a Christmas stocking from Maryland, is Virginia's Eastern Shore, attached to Virginia Beach by the 17.5-mile Chesapeake Bay Bridge - Tunnel. The Eastern Shore is a 70-mile buffet abounding in delicacies along U.S. Route 13. Among them is the Hayman sweet potato, as homely as a potato could be. Its jacket is grayish white; its meat has a greenish cast. Only in flavor is the Hayman superior. Its syrupy juices make it a meal and a dessert in one. When it is baking, the aroma is almost maddening. A whiff of a Hayman would have stopped Odysseus in his tracks. To get by, he'd have had to put a clothes pin on his nose.

North Carolina ship captains of the Hayman family brought the fabled potatoes from the West Indies to the Carolina coast and it spread to Virginia.

A lovely sea-meadow is the site of the annual Chincoteague Seafood Festival on the first Wednesday in May. It offers everything from clam broth to steamed crabs. An annual oyster festival takes place at Chincoteague on October 8. On the mainland, the Urbanna Oyster Festival occurs the first weekend in November.

To overcome a decline of oysters in Virginia waters, scientists of the Virginia Institute of Marine Science began experimenting in 1989, working in hatcheries and laboratories to breed a better oyster. They were looking in selected brood stocks for oysters that grow rapidly and are less susceptible to disease and other vicissitudes, such as ravenous Walruses and Carpenters walking the beach.

In their natural habitat, growing atop reefs formed through the years, oysters escaped having to live on the muddy bottom. Food supplies were better and more easily obtained in the clearer waters above. The reefs were nature's way in lifting and preserving the oyster. But heavy over-harvesting during the past century destroyed the ancient reefs.

Man had to lend nature a hand. Scientists at VIMS devised ways to float the oyster off the bottom. They made round floats with a ring of plastic tubing supporting nets of wire. Watermen devised rigid artificial reefs. Others simply tied a bag of oysters to a dock and suspended it in water.

More than 40 entrepreneurs have raised several million oysters in the young, growing enterprise. All of us, including the Walrus and the Carpenter, are grateful to VIMS for saving the Oyster.

The Eastern Shore's thick, beguiling accent is the sort one would expect to hear when holding a seashell to the ear. A forthright sounding of the vowel "o" renders the pronoun "I" to full-bodied "Oy." On the Eastern Shore, "toime" and "toid" wait for no man. It is a "foin" land. The talk has been that way since their English ancestors set foot on the sand. Not even television can subdue the surf-like soothing sound, thank goodness.

The people are at one with nature. Guide Tom Reed, then 90, once explained: "Human nature's funny, wanting to kill anything that gets in its way. But you can't get rid of all of life's miseries. Now weeds are the farmer's best friend, but you try to convince one of that! Weeds cover the earth. The earth is alive just like we are, and a bare spot hurts. Nature covers it in no time. It hurts my feelings when I see men using weed killer on the roadsides. They're working against nature when they do it."

-Guy Friddell

Seafood Casserole

2 tablespoons butter
1 pound mushrooms, chopped
1 small onion, chopped
1 green bell pepper, chopped
1 cup chopped celery
1½ cups cooked wild rice
1¼ cups mayonnaise
½ cup sherry
2 teaspoons Worcestershire
  sauce
Salt and pepper to taste
2½ cups grated mild Cheddar
  cheese
1 pound cooked lobster meat
1½ pounds cooked shrimp
1½ pounds cooked crabmeat

- Preheat oven to 350°.
- Melt butter in a large sauté pan. Sauté mushrooms, onion, green pepper, and celery until slightly tender.
- Pour sautéed vegetables into a large bowl and add wild rice, mayonnaise, sherry, Worcestershire sauce, salt, pepper, and 2 cups Cheddar cheese.
- Fold in lobster, shrimp, and crabmeat.
- Pour mixture into a 3-quart casserole dish. Sprinkle top with remaining ½ cup Cheddar cheese.
- Bake for 45 minutes.

Yield: 12 servings

Omit lobster and increase the amount of shrimp and crabmeat to 2 pounds each, if desired.

Wonderful!

Grouper, Shrimp, and Scallops with Snow Peas, Tomatoes, and Tarragon Butter

¼ pound unsalted butter, softened and divided

3 tablespoons minced shallots

Salt and pepper to taste

6 tablespoons dry white wine

2 tablespoons chopped fresh tarragon

¾ pound snow peas, trimmed

2 pounds skinless grouper fillet

1 cup fish stock

2 tablespoons water

¼ pound large shrimp, peeled, deveined, and cut in half lengthwise

¾ pound sea scallops (side muscle removed), sliced ¼-inch thick

3 medium tomatoes, peeled, seeded, and chopped

- Heat 1 tablespoon butter in a non-stick sauté pan over medium heat. When hot, add the minced shallots. Season with salt and pepper and sauté for 1 minute.

- Add the wine, bring to a simmer, Adjust the heat and simmer until the pan is almost dry, about 15 minutes. Remove the pan from the heat, transfer the reduction to a stainless-steel bowl, and cool. When cool, combine with the remaining butter and chopped tarragon. Cover the tarragon butter with film wrap and keep at room temperature until ready to use.

- Blanch the snow peas in boiling salted water until tender but very crisp, 20-30 seconds. Drain the peas and transfer immediately to ice water. When the peas are cold, drain thoroughly, cover with film wrap, and refrigerate until needed.

- Slice the grouper into ¼-inch thick slices. Divide the grouper into 8 portions of 3 or 4 slices, with each slice partially overlapping another.

- Heat the fish stock to a boil in a 2½-quart saucepan over high heat. While waiting for the stock to come to a boil, place the grouper in a large non-stick sauté pan and season with salt and pepper.

- Place ½ tablespoon tarragon butter on each grouper portion. Gently pour the boiling stock into the pan around the grouper. Cover the pan with aluminum foil, place the pan over

Continued on next page

Grouper, Shrimp, and Scallops with Snow Peas, Tomatoes, and Tarragon Butter (continued)

medium heat, and allow the fish to cook for 6-7 minutes.

- While the grouper is cooking, heat the remaining tarragon butter and 2 tablespoons water in a large non-stick sauté pan over high heat. When hot, add the shrimp, scallops, and tomatoes. Season with salt and pepper and sauté for 2½ to 3 minutes. Add the snow peas, adjust the seasoning with salt and pepper, and sauté until the snow peas are hot, about 2 minutes.
- Portion the shrimp and scallop mixture onto each of 8 warm 10-inch soup/pasta plates. Place a grouper portion on top and serve immediately.

Yield: 8 servings

If fish stock is not available, substitute a lightly flavored chicken stock or use water.

An exquisite seafood entree from The Trellis in Williamsburg, Virginia. This recipe is reprinted courtesy of Fireside: Simon and Schuster Inc.

Seafood Gumbo

2 cups chopped onions
1½ cups chopped green bell peppers
1 cup chopped celery
2 whole bay leaves
2 teaspoons salt
½ teaspoon white pepper
½ teaspoon cayenne pepper
½ teaspoon black pepper
½ teaspoon dried thyme
½ teaspoon dried oregano
¾ cup vegetable oil
¾ cup all-purpose flour
1 tablespoon minced garlic
5½ cups chicken stock
1 pound sausage or polska kielbasa
1 cup okra
1 pound fresh shrimp, peeled and deveined
½ pint oysters, undrained
¾ pound crabmeat
3-4 cups cooked white rice

- Combine onions, bell peppers, and celery in a medium-sized bowl. Set aside.
- Combine ingredients for seasoning mix (bay leaves, salt, white pepper, cayenne pepper, black pepper, thyme, and oregano). Set aside.
- Heat oil in a large heavy skillet over high heat until it begins to smoke, about 5 minutes. Gradually add the flour, whisking constantly. Continue cooking, whisking constantly, until roux is dark brown, 2-4 minutes. Be careful not to scorch the roux.
- Immediately add half the vegetables and stir well. Continue stirring and cooking about 1 minute, then add remaining vegetables and cook 2 minutes longer.
- Stir in seasoning mix and cook 2 minutes, stirring frequently. Add the garlic; cook for 1 minute more. Remove from heat.
- Pour the chicken stock into a large Dutch oven and bring to a boil. Add roux mixture to boiling stock, stirring until dissolved. Bring mixture to a second boil, then add sausage and okra. Boil for 15 minutes. Reduce heat and simmer for 10 minutes.
- Stir in shrimp, undrained oysters, and crabmeat. Return to a boil over high heat, stirring occasionally. Remove from heat and skim any oil from the surface.
- Serve over cooked rice.

Yield: 6-8 servings

To make a modest amount of shrimp go further in this dish, slice large shrimp horizontally.

Shrimp Fantastic

¾ cup butter, divided
1 small onion, finely chopped
1 clove garlic, minced
1 teaspoon tarragon
¼ cup sherry
1 pound large fresh shrimp,
*   peeled and deveined*
Salt and pepper to taste
⅓ cup bread crumbs
Paprika

- Preheat oven to 350°.
- Melt ½ cup butter in a large skillet. Add onions, garlic, tarragon, and sherry. Simmer 5 minutes over medium heat.
- Melt remaining ¼ cup butter in same skillet. Add shrimp, cooking over low heat. Season with salt and pepper.
- Add bread crumbs when shrimp is almost done. Toss well.
- Transfer to a large casserole dish. Sprinkle with paprika.
- Bake for 10 minutes.

Yield: 4 servings

Also a superb appetizer!

Easy Company Scampi

2 cups butter
½ cup olive oil
2 tablespoons dried chopped
*   parsley*
1½ teaspoons dried basil
1 teaspoon dried oregano
2 cloves garlic, minced
Salt to taste
2 tablespoons lemon juice
1½ pounds fresh shrimp,
*   peeled and deveined*
1 (8 ounce) package spaghetti,
*   cooked and drained*
Grated Parmesan cheese

- Preheat oven to 450°.
- In a large shallow baking dish, melt butter in the oven. Add olive oil, parsley, basil, oregano, garlic, salt, and lemon juice. Mix well.
- Place shrimp in baking dish. Coat with butter mixture.
- Bake for 10 minutes or until shrimp turn pink.
- Place spaghetti on individual serving plates. Add shrimp and sauce. Top with grated Parmesan cheese.

Yield: 6 servings

Peel and devein fresh shrimp by slitting the shell of each shrimp down the back, then run an ice pick or a small sharp knife down the back of the tails and remove the black vein.

Barbecue Shrimp "New Orleans" Style

½ cup butter

1 cup olive oil

3 teaspoons finely minced garlic

4 whole bay leaves, finely crushed

1 teaspoon basil leaves

1 teaspoon oregano leaves

4 teaspoons finely crushed rosemary leaves

½ teaspoon salt

½ teaspoon cayenne pepper

⅓ cup paprika (regular paprika, not Hungarian)

¾ teaspoon black pepper

2 teaspoons lemon juice

1 pound large fresh shrimp in the shell

- In a large sauté pan, melt butter, then add oil; mix well. Add all remaining ingredients except the shrimp. Cook over medium heat, stirring constantly, until the sauce begins to boil. Reduce the heat to low and simmer 7-8 minutes, stirring frequently. Remove the pan from the heat and let it stand, uncovered, at room temperature for at least 30 minutes.

- Add the shrimp to the sauce, mix thoroughly, and put the pan back on the burner. Cook over medium heat 6-7 minutes, or just until the shrimp turn pink.

- Put the pan in a preheated 450° oven and bake for 10 minutes only.

- Serve with lots of the sauce poured over the shrimp and with an ample amount of French bread for soaking up the wonderful sauce.

Yield: 2 servings

Increase to 4 servings by using 2 pounds of shrimp and 1 cup butter. All other ingredients remain the same.

Shrimp Creole

1 tablespoon vegetable
   shortening
1 tablespoon all-purpose flour
2 medium-sized onions,
   chopped
2 cloves garlic, minced
1 green bell pepper, chopped
1 teaspoon coarsely chopped
   fresh parsley
1 (28 ounce) can crushed
   tomatoes
1/4 teaspoon red pepper
2 bay leaves
1/3 teaspoon celery seed
1/4 teaspoon thyme
Salt to taste
2 pounds fresh shrimp, peeled
   and deveined
2 teaspoons Worcestershire
   sauce
Cooked white rice
Chopped fresh parsley for
   garnish

- In a medium sauté pan, melt shortening over low heat. Blend in flour and cook until smooth and thickened.
- Add onion, garlic, bell pepper, and parsley. Cook until onion is golden.
- Add tomatoes and all seasonings except Worcestershire sauce. Cook for 30 minutes over low heat.
- Add shrimp and Worcestershire sauce. Continue cooking for an additional 30 minutes.
- Serve over hot rice garnished with chopped fresh parsley.

Yield: 4 servings

Add hot pepper sauce for extra punch!

Frogmore Stew

Salt
Old Bay Seasoning
¼ *pound smoked link sausage
    per serving, cut into 2-inch
    pieces*
¼ *pound new potatoes per
    serving*
*1-2 ears corn per serving,
    shucked and silked*
½ *pound fresh shrimp per
    serving*

- Bring a large amount of water to a rolling boil. Water volume should be about twice that of the other ingredients. Add ¼ cup salt per gallon of water and Old Bay Seasoning added liberally to taste.
- Add sausage and potatoes; boil for 8 minutes.
- Add corn; continue to boil for 8 minutes.
- Add shrimp and cook for 5 minutes. Do not overcook!
- Drain and serve in a large bowl or tub.

Yield: As many servings as desired

Raw cleaned crabs may also be added along with the corn.

York River Deviled Crab

1 pound crabmeat, well picked
1 teaspoon salt
¼ *teaspoon pepper*
2 eggs
2 tablespoons mayonnaise
*1 tablespoon prepared
    mustard*
4 tablespoons ketchup
*1 tablespoon Worcestershire
    sauce*
1 tablespoon chopped onion
*1 tablespoon chopped green
    bell pepper*
1 tablespoon chopped celery
1 teaspoon hot pepper sauce
3 slices bread, cubed
½ *stick butter or margarine,
    melted*

- Preheat oven to 350° .
- Combine all ingredients and put in a 1½-quart casserole dish or 6 crab shells.
- Bake for 30 minutes.

Yield: 6 servings

Tasty and easy!

Crab and Shrimp Casserole

1 pound fresh shrimp, peeled and deveined
¾ cup mayonnaise
¾ cup finely chopped celery
¼ cup finely chopped green bell pepper
1 medium-sized onion, finely chopped
1 tablespoon lemon juice
1 teaspoon Worcestershire sauce
1 teaspoon seasoned salt
½ teaspoon seafood seasoning
Few drops hot pepper sauce
8 ounces fresh crabmeat
¾ cup bread crumbs
3 tablespoons margarine, melted
Paprika and parsley for garnish

- Preheat oven to 350°.
- Combine shrimp with next nine ingredients.
- Gently fold in crabmeat so it does not fall apart too much.
- Place in a greased 1½-quart baking dish. Sprinkle bread crumbs on top. Drizzle with melted margarine. Sprinkle with paprika.
- Bake uncovered for 30-35 minutes. Garnish with fresh parsley before serving.

Yield: 4-6 servings

• • •

Virginia was named in honor of England's Elizabeth, the Virgin Queen, by Sir Walter Raleigh.

Crab Enchiladas with Salsa

2 tablespoons vegetable oil
12 corn tortillas
1¼ pounds fresh crabmeat
(3 cups)
1 cup sour cream, divided
1 (8 ounce) jar salsa, divided
½ red onion, minced
½ cup grated Monterey Jack
cheese
3 green onions, sliced (white
section only)
3 tablespoons chopped fresh
cilantro

- Preheat oven to 375°.
- Heat oil in a skillet over medium-high heat. Quickly heat tortillas one at a time in oil for 10 seconds on each side. Remove tortillas and drain on paper towels.
- Mix crabmeat with ½ cup sour cream, ½ cup salsa, and onion. Blend well and set aside.
- Spread a thin layer of salsa on the bottom of a 9"x13" baking dish.
- Place one tortilla flat on work surface. Put 2 heaping tablespoonsful of crab mixture down the middle. Roll up the tortilla and place seam side down in the baking dish. Repeat with all tortillas.
- Spread remaining salsa over top of the rolled tortillas.
- Combine cheese with remaining ½ cup sour cream. Place a dollop on each tortilla. Sprinkle with green onions.
- Bake 25 minutes. Garnish with chopped cilantro. Serve immediately.

Yield: 4-6 servings

Serve with thin avocado slices mixed with a jar of yellow corn relish.

Mussels Marinière

3 pounds mussels
2 tablespoons butter
¼ cup diced celery
¼ cup diced shallots
¼ cup diced carrots
¼ cup diced onions
1 small clove garlic, minced
½ cup fish stock
¼ cup vermouth
¼ cup white wine
1 cup heavy cream
2 sticks butter, diced
Salt, pepper, and lemon juice
*   to taste*
Fresh herbs to taste (thyme,
*   dill, oregano, parsley,*
*   garlic)*

- Scrub mussels carefully under cold running water, removing beards. Set aside.
- Heat butter in a large skillet. Sauté diced celery, shallots, carrots, onion, and garlic until tender.
- Add mussels to skillet. Pour in fish stock, vermouth, and white wine. Cover pan and steam mussels 7-8 minutes. Mussels will open when ready for eating. Discard unopened mussels.
- Remove mussels from pan and reduce liquid by ¾. Add cream to liquid and bring to a boil. Remove skillet from heat. Add diced butter, whisking continually, until butter is melted and mixture is frothy.
- Season with salt, pepper, lemon juice, and fresh herbs.
- Pour sauce over hot mussels. Serve in individual bowls.

Yield: 6 servings

Enjoy on a weekend afternoon with a bottle of white wine and toasted garlic bread.

Submerge an unpeeled lime, lemon, or orange in hot water for 15 minutes before squeezing to yield more juice.

Oyster Artichoke Casserole

40 oysters
5 tablespoons butter, divided
4 tablespoons all-purpose flour
2 bay leaves
¼ teaspoon thyme
2 cups coarsely chopped green
  onions
2 (14 ounce) cans artichoke
  hearts, quartered
Salt and pepper to taste
½ cup bread crumbs
½ cup grated Parmesan cheese
4 cups cooked rice

- Drain oysters overnight, reserving liquor.
- Melt 4 tablespoons butter in a small saucepan. Add flour and stir over medium heat until roux is smooth, bubbly, and golden. Set aside.
- Add water to oyster liquor to make 2 cups.
- Place oysters, oyster liquor, bay leaves, and thyme in a sauté pan. Bring liquor to a simmer. Poach oysters until edges begin to curl. Remove oysters to a 9-inch square casserole dish.
- Preheat oven to 350°.
- Continue to cook the liquor until it is reduced to about 1½ cups. Remove the bay leaves.
- Add the roux and blend thoroughly. Add green onions, artichokes, salt, and pepper. Remove the saucepan from heat and whisk in remaining butter. Spoon sauce over oysters.
- Combine bread crumbs and cheese. Sprinkle over oysters in casserole.
- Bake for 10 minutes or until topping is golden brown.
- Serve immediately over rice.

Yield: 4 servings

Fresh raw oysters are highly perishable and should be eaten as soon as possible. To shuck fresh oysters, open the shells carefully with an oyster knife and loosen the oyster from its lower shell.

Broiled Scallops in Spicy Lemon Butter

1 pound scallops
3-4 tablespoons butter, melted
1 tablespoon lemon juice
⅛ teaspoon paprika
⅛ teaspoon cayenne pepper
1 teaspoon minced parsley
½ lemon, sliced (for garnish)

- Preheat broiler.
- Rinse scallops and dry on a towel. Place scallops in a large shallow baking dish and top with butter, lemon juice, paprika, and cayenne pepper.
- Broil 3-5 inches from heat for 7-10 minutes.
- Remove from broiler and top with parsley. Garnish with lemon slices.

Yield: 4 servings

One pound of scallops usually yields 40 individual scallops. Cook scallops very quickly to avoid making them tough and tasteless.

Flounder Stuffed with Crabmeat

1 pound crabmeat
1 egg
¼ cup mayonnaise
½ teaspoon chopped parsley
Salt and pepper to taste
¼ cup fresh bread crumbs
12 flounder fillets
½ cup butter, melted
Dash paprika
Dash lemon juice

- Preheat oven to 350°.
- Combine crabmeat, egg, mayonnaise, parsley, salt, pepper, and bread crumbs. Mix well.
- Place one flounder fillet in the bottom of a buttered baking dish. Mound ⅙ of the crabmeat stuffing on top of the fillet. Place a second fillet over the stuffing and make a slit in the fillet just over the mound of stuffing. Repeat procedure with remaining fillets.
- Top each stuffed fillet with melted butter, paprika, and lemon juice.
- Bake for 20-25 minutes until tender and flaky.

Yield: 6 servings

To test the freshness of a fish, place it in cold water. A newly caught fish will float!

Lemony-Stuffed Flounder

⅔ *cup butter, divided*
⅓ *cup chopped celery*
2 *tablespoons chopped onion*
1 *cup herb-seasoned stuffing*
  mix
1 *tablespoon chopped parsley*
1 *tablespoon lemon juice*
1 *teaspoon grated lemon peel*
¼ *teaspoon salt*
¼ *teaspoon pepper*
4 *medium-sized flounder*
  fillets, cut in half
½ *teaspoon dill weed*

- Preheat oven to 350° .
- In a medium saucepan, melt ⅓ cup butter over medium heat. Add chopped celery and onion; sauté until tender. Add stuffing mix, parsley, lemon juice, lemon peel, salt, and pepper. Mix well and set aside.
- Place 4 fillet halves in an ungreased 9-inch square baking dish. Spread stuffing mixture equally on each fillet half. Top with remaining 4 fillets.
- Melt ⅓ cup butter in a small saucepan. Stir in dill weed. Pour dill butter over stuffed fillets.
- Bake near center of oven for 20-30 minutes.

Yield: 4 servings

Use frozen fish fillets that are well thawed.

Sole and cod are also suitable for this recipe.

Although most fish are low in fat content, white fish such as cod, haddock, scrod, and halibut are the least fatty. Tuna, bluefish, and catfish are moderately fatty, while salmon, swordfish, and mackerel are much fattier.

Orange Roughy with Herbed Orange Sauce

4 orange roughy fillets (1-1½
   pounds total)
Olive oil
Salt and freshly ground
   pepper
⅔ cup orange juice
2 tablespoons chopped fresh
   basil
2 tablespoons chopped fresh
   rosemary
2 tablespoons chopped fresh
   thyme
2 tablespoons chopped fresh
   parsley
¼ cup butter
1 tablespoon cornstarch,
   optional
1 tablespoon orange juice,
   optional

- Brush fish fillets with olive oil and sprinkle with salt and pepper to taste.
- Grill or broil fillets, turning once. Transfer fillets to warm plates when almost cooked in center. Fish will continue cooking while standing.
- In a medium saucepan, combine ⅔ cup orange juice and herbs. Bring to a boil; cook until reduced to about ½ cup liquid. Whisk in butter, bit by bit, until sauce is slightly thickened. Add cornstarch and 1 tablespoon orange juice to help thicken the sauce, if necessary. Season with salt.
- Spoon sauce over fish fillets and garnish with fresh herbs.

Yield: 4 servings

The herbed orange sauce is wonderful on grilled chicken.

Broiled Salmon-Herb Steaks

8 salmon steaks
¾ cup dry vermouth
¾ cup vegetable oil
1½ tablespoons lemon juice
¾ teaspoon salt
Dash pepper
¼ teaspoon thyme
¼ teaspoon marjoram
⅛ teaspoon sage
1 tablespoon parsley

- Place salmon steaks in a large shallow baking dish.
- Mix remaining ingredients and pour over salmon. Cover and let marinate 3-4 hours in refrigerator. Turn once.
- Preheat broiler.
- Remove fish from marinade and place on a greased broiler rack. Broil until brown on both sides, about 15 minutes total. Brush frequently with marinade.

Yield: 8 servings

Salmon Fillets with Herb Butter and Spinach

½ cup butter, softened
2 cloves garlic
3 shallots
½ cup fresh parsley
¼ cup fresh rosemary
¼ cup fresh thyme
⅛ teaspoon salt
Freshly ground pepper
6 (6-8 ounce) salmon fillets
  with skin
Vegetable oil
2½ pounds fresh spinach,
  rinsed, stemmed, and dried

Preheat oven to 450° .

• Combine butter, garlic, shallots, parsley, rosemary, thyme, salt, and pepper in a food processor. Mix well and set aside.

• Remove all bones from salmon. Sprinkle with salt and pepper to taste.

• Line a baking dish with foil and grease generously with oil.

• Oil fish skin and place each fillet, skin side down, in the lined baking dish.

• Bake on middle rack of oven for 5 minutes.

• Top each fillet with a generous tablespoonful of herb butter. Set aside remaining herb butter.

• Bake fish for an additional 9-10 minutes or until salmon flakes easily.

• Melt reserved herb butter in a large skillet over medium heat. Add spinach and sauté until wilted and hot, 3-4 minutes.

• To serve, arrange each salmon fillet in the center of a large plate with spinach surrounding it.

Yield: 6 servings

Very attractive!

Red Snapper on a Bed of Limes

½ cup whipped butter
2 tablespoons lemon juice
2 tablespoons minced parsley
2 tablespoons minced chives
2 tablespoons minced green
  onion
2-3 limes or lemons, cut into
  ¼-inch slices
1 pound red snapper fillets
½ teaspoon salt

- Preheat oven to 350°.
- Prepare lemon herb butter by combining butter, lemon juice, parsley, chives, and green onion. Blend well. Shape into a roll approximately 1½ inches in diameter. Wrap and freeze at least 30 minutes.
- Line a large shallow baking dish with a layer of lime or lemon slices. Arrange red snapper fillets snugly on top in a single layer. Sprinkle fillets lightly with salt. Top each fish fillet with two ½-inch thick slices of the lemon herb butter.
- Bake uncovered for 12-15 minutes depending on the thickness of the fish.

Yield: 4 servings

Lemon herb butter is excellent with any fish, but is essential to the success of this dish. Excellent!

Do not leave leftover fish on the lime or lemon slices. The bitter oil from the citrus peels will ruin the flavor of the snapper.

Broiled Snapper Delicacy

2 pounds snapper or other fish
  fillets (fresh or frozen)
⅓ cup frozen orange juice
  concentrate, thawed
½ cup butter or margarine,
  melted
1 tablespoon soy sauce
1 teaspoon salt, optional
Freshly ground pepper

- Preheat broiler.
- Cut fillet into serving-size portions.
- Place fillets skin side up on a greased pan.
- Combine remaining ingredients and spoon half of the mixture over fish. Broil 4-5 minutes. Turn and pour remaining mixture over fish. Broil an additional 4-5 minutes, until fish flakes.

Yield: 6 servings

A luscious dish!

Virginia Fare

Spanish Swordfish

2 tablespoons margarine
1 large Spanish onion, sliced
2 large green bell peppers,
   sliced
3 cloves garlic, minced
2 cups vermouth or fish stock
6 large tomatoes, peeled,
   seeded and sliced
2 tablespoons lemon juice
3 tablespoons olive oil
Salt and pepper to taste
4 swordfish steaks, skinned

- Preheat oven to 350°.
- Heat margarine in a large skillet; sauté onion, green pepper, and garlic until clear but not browned.
- Pour in vermouth or fish stock and cook until mixture is reduced by half. Add tomatoes, lemon juice, olive oil, salt, and pepper. Bring just to a boil.
- Place half of mixture in the bottom of a large casserole dish. Place swordfish steaks on top of mixture and cover with remaining vegetable mixture.
- Cover and bake for 15-20 minutes, basting every 7-8 minutes with vegetable juices.
- To serve, place fish on plates and spoon vegetables over and around the steaks.

Yield: 4 servings

Let cooking juices reduce until almost syrupy before spooning over fish.

Easy Gourmet Fish Fillets

4 fish fillets (catfish, flounder,
   or any white fish) or whole
   small spot or croaker
1 cup white wine
½ cup Marzetti's Veggie Dip
   or mayonnaise
Salt 'n Spice or Table Blend
   seasoning to taste

- Preheat oven to 350° .
- Place fillets in a single layer in an 8-inch square glass baking dish that has been sprayed with non-stick vegetable spray.
- Pour wine over fillets. Cover with Veggie Dip. Sprinkle with seasoning to taste.
- Cover with aluminum foil and bake 20-30 minutes until bubbly and fish is completely cooked.

Yield: 4 servings

Baked Swordfish with Dill Sauce

½ cup sour cream
½ cup plain yogurt
2 tablespoons mayonnaise
2 tablespoons minced fresh dill
1 teaspoon Dijon mustard
Dash hot pepper sauce
Salt and pepper to taste
4 swordfish steaks
Salt and white pepper to taste
1 teaspoon vegetable oil
1 teaspoon lemon juice
¼ teaspoon paprika
Fresh dill sprigs for garnish

- Prepare dill sauce by combining sour cream, yogurt, mayonnaise, dill, mustard, and hot pepper sauce. Add salt and pepper to taste. Blend well. Allow sauce to stand at least ½ hour to blend flavors. Sauce can be refrigerated up to 24 hours, but serve at room temperature.
- Preheat oven to 425°.
- Pat fish dry with a paper towel. Sprinkle lightly with salt and pepper.
- Combine oil and lemon juice; brush on both sides of steaks. Place steaks 1 inch apart in a lightly oiled baking dish.
- Bake just until fish flakes when tested with a fork, about 10 minutes per inch thickness measured at the thickest part of the steak.
- Transfer swordfish to warm plates. Spoon dill sauce over top. Sprinkle with paprika and garnish with dill sprigs.

Yield: 4 servings

Broiled White Fish with Fennel Butter

¼ cup butter, melted
3 tablespoons chopped fresh fennel
½ teaspoon salt
1 tablespoon fresh lemon juice
Freshly ground pepper
4 white fish fillets (about 1½ pounds)

- Preheat oven to 400°.
- Combine butter, fennel, salt, lemon juice, and pepper. Mix well.
- Place fish fillets in a large shallow baking dish. Brush with fennel butter.
- Bake 10 minutes or until fish is flaky.

Yield: 4 servings

Estimate ⅓ to ½ pound of boneless fish per serving.

Mountain Trout Cakes with Lemon-Butter Sauce

2 pounds trout fillets
3 large eggs, lightly beaten
3 tablespoons heavy cream
1 tablespoon Dijon mustard
2 teaspoons Old Bay seasoning
1 teaspoon Worcestershire
   sauce
1/4 teaspoon freshly ground
   black pepper
1/8 teaspoon ground red pepper
1/2 cup mayonnaise
3 tablespoons finely chopped
   green onions
2 tablespoons finely chopped
   fresh parsley
1 cup saltine cracker crumbs
1 cup fine dry bread crumbs
1/4 cup butter, divided
1/4 cup vegetable oil, divided
Fresh thyme sprigs for
   garnish
Lemon slices for garnish

- Preheat oven to 350°.
- Place trout fillets in a lightly greased 13"x9"x2" pan. Bake for 20-25 minutes or until fish flakes easily with a fork. Let fillets cool. Flake fish, carefully removing any bones. Set aside.
- In a large bowl, combine eggs, cream, mustard, Old Bay seasoning, Worcestershire sauce, black pepper, and red pepper. Beat with a fork until blended.
- In a small bowl, combine mayonnaise, green onions, and parsley; fold into egg mixture.
- Stir in trout and cracker crumbs. Cover and chill 1 hour.
- Shape mixture into 8 large or 16 small patties. Mixture will be somewhat sticky. Coat patties with bread crumbs.
- Heat 2 tablespoons butter and 2 tablespoons oil in a large skillet. Cook half the patties 3-4 minutes on each side or until golden. Drain on paper towels; keep warm. Repeat procedure.
- Serve with Lemon-Butter Sauce. Garnish with fresh thyme sprigs and lemon slices, if desired.

Yield: 6 servings

Continued on next page

Mountain Trout Cakes with Lemon-Butter Sauce (continued)

Lemon-Butter Sauce

1 cup dry white wine
2½ tablespoons grated lemon peel
½ cup fresh lemon juice
2 bay leaves
1 teaspoon black peppercorns
1 teaspoon white peppercorns
¼ cup heavy cream
1 pound unsalted butter, cubed

- In a small saucepan, combine wine, lemon peel, lemon juice, bay leaves, black peppercorns, and white peppercorns. Bring to a boil and cook, uncovered, 10-12 minutes or until liquid is reduced to one tablespoon.
- Stir in cream. Transfer mixture to the top of a double boiler. Place over hot, not boiling, water and add butter cubes one at a time, beating with a wire whisk until blended.
- Pour mixture through a wire mesh strainer.

Yield: 2 cups

An award-winning entree from The Daily News Leader in Staunton, Virginia.

Easy Baked Fish

Non-stick vegetable spray
¼ cup white wine
1 tablespoon lemon juice
4 white fish fillets (orange roughy, cod, perch)
1 tablespoon Greek or Creole seasoning
¼ cup bread crumbs
¼ cup Parmesan cheese

- Preheat oven to 400°.
- Spray a large baking dish with non-stick vegetable spray. Pour wine and lemon juice into the bottom of the baking dish.
- Place fish in liquid, turn to coat both sides.
- Sprinkle to lightly cover the tops of the fillets with seasoning, followed by the bread crumbs, and finally the Parmesan cheese.
- Bake uncovered 25-30 minutes until the fish flakes easily.

Yield: 4 servings

Very good, extremely easy!

Belle Aire Plantation Broiled Herb Fish

1 large bunch fresh lemon
balm or rinsed lettuce leaves
½ teaspoon fresh tarragon per
pound of fish
4 fish fillets
Mayonnaise, olive oil, or
butter
Lemon juice
Salt and pepper to taste
Paprika
Chopped fresh parsley
Fresh tarragon

- Preheat oven to 500°.
- Line a large shallow baking dish with fresh lemon balm or lettuce leaves. Sprinkle with fresh tarragon.
- Place fish fillets on top with skin side down. Brush fillets with mayonnaise, olive oil, or butter. Saturate fillets with lemon juice. Sprinkle with salt, pepper, paprika, chopped parsley, and additional fresh tarragon.
- Place baking dish in hot oven. Immediately turn oven to broil leaving the baking dish in the oven for 10-15 minutes, depending upon the thickness of the fillets.
- Turn oven off (or to 250°) and cover baking dish lightly with aluminum foil. Leave covered fish in the oven for an additional 10-15 minutes.

Yield: 4 servings

Belle Aire is a c. 1670 plantation home in Charles City County. One of the few surviving frame houses of that period, it features one of America's finest Jacobean stairways.It has been lovingly restored for occupancy by its 20th century owner, a charming Virginian who by reservation grants group tours and offers bed and breakfast.

Grilling

Run for the Run!

These days when TV dinners may be microwaved, how comforting, nevertheless, to know Virginians still catch, cook, and eat fare on which the nation was founded. Should hard times come, they can show us how to turn to the land.

During herring runs in April, when the delectable silvery fish are swimming up rivers and tributaries, crowding creeks and branches as they seek to spawn, cars parked on nearby roads seem as numerous as the fish. Lined along the banks, people dip nets to fetch their catch. Thus it has been since George Mason and George Washington lived on the Potomac near Alexandria. "When there was a herring run," said historian Helen Hill Miller, "everybody would drop everything and all would run after the run."

In Fredericksburg, during the run, the air seems more pellucid. Life itself is perceived with greater clarity. Older restaurants offer salt herring Saturday mornings as do staunch civic groups. In White Oak in March, the New Hope Methodist Church has a dinner open free to all. "All you have to do to be invited is show up," said Stafford County extension agent John Gray.

Salt herring is the centerpiece with fresh tomatoes, fried potatoes and onions, cantaloupe, corn cakes, and hot coffee. Offered a meal built around salt fish or sirloin steak, some would not hesitate to choose the fish, Gray said. "And one of 'em raises beef cattle." The feast is so plenteous as to recall one by the Sea of Galilee.

To make corn cakes, Anne Silver advised that you combine a cup of corn meal with a half cup of flour — two parts corn meal, one part flour — add a tablespoon of baking powder, an egg, salt, and some milk to produce a batter you ladle into a frying pan. "When my daughter comes from college, the first words out of her mouth are salt fish," she said.

To salt fish, some of which may be as long as eight inches, scale them, gutting them, cutting off the heads and tails. Wash them thoroughly and fill the belly cavities with salt. On the bottom of a 5-gallon plastic bucket, spread a quarter-inch layer of salt. Stack atop the salt a layer of herrings, belly up, side by side, and keep alternating layers of fish and salt until the bucket is filled. Make sure the lid is tight and put the bucket in a cool place. The roe, set aside during the packing, is tasty with scrambled eggs.

To cook a herring, split it along the backbone, wash it well in fresh water to remove the salt, changing the water at least four times over several hours. Bread the salt fish with corn meal and fry them in hot grease.

Another fine delicacy from Virginia's rivers and bays is the blue crab. Steamed and then cracked and picked and eaten over brown paper spread on broad tables, it is fit for royalty. On weekends, within a three-mile radius of Falmouth and Chatham, 20 roadside chefs steam crabs for sale, Gray said.

Washington and Mason were neighbors. Once, Washington asked him: "Mr. Mason, what services within the power of the people can I bestow on you?"

"Your services as President of the United States, Mr. Washington," Mason replied.

After which, surely, they had a breakfast of salt fish and corn cakes.

-Guy Friddell

Slow-Fire Chinese Steak

2 tablespoons hoisin sauce
2 tablespoons soy sauce
2 tablespoons medium-dry
  sherry or red wine
1 tablespoon plum sauce
2 green onions, sliced ⅛-inch
  thick
1 tablespoon minced fresh
  ginger
1 teaspoon minced garlic
1 boneless sirloin steak, cut 2
  inches thick (2¼ pounds)
Oil for brushing

- Combine hoisin sauce, soy sauce, sherry, plum sauce, green onions, ginger, and garlic in a medium bowl.
- Score the sirloin ¼" deep on both sides at 1-inch intervals with a sharp knife. Place the steak on a large platter and rub marinade into both sides. Cover and refrigerate for at least 2 hours or overnight.
- Remove steak from refrigerator 30 minutes before cooking.
- Scrub the grill clean and brush with oil.
- Place steak in the center of the grill and cover, leaving all the vents wide open. Cook for 5 minutes, then rotate 90° to achieve crisscross grill marks. Cover and grill for 5 minutes longer or until browned around the edges. If the steak is cooking too fast and beginning to char, move it to the side of the grill for the remainder of the cooking time.
- Turn steak over and repeat the grilling process on the other side for 13 minutes for medium-rare, rotating it once after 5 minutes.
- Remove the steak from the grill and let rest for at least 10 minutes.
- Slice steak thinly against the grain. Serve hot or at room temperature.

Yield: 4-6 servings

The ideal temperature for grilling is medium-high. At this temperature, you can comfortably hold your hand one inch above the coals for 4-5 seconds.

Grilled Chuck Roast or London Broil

1 (2-2½ pound) chuck roast or
  London broil
Instant meat tenderizer
¼ cup soy sauce
1 cup vegetable oil
1 tablespoon lemon juice
1 tablespoon Worcestershire
  sauce
1 teaspoon ginger
Juice of 1 clove of garlic

- Place meat in an oblong glass dish. Use meat tenderizer as directed on package.
- Mix all remaining ingredients. Pour marinade over meat. Cover and refrigerate overnight, turning meat at least once.
- Grill or broil 3 inches from heat, brushing with marinade, until done.

Yield: 4 servings

Soy Marinated Flank Steak

1 (2 pound) flank steak
1 medium-sized onion, sliced
6 tablespoons soy sauce
3 tablespoons olive oil
1 tablespoon vinegar
1 tablespoon sugar

- Score meat on both sides and place in a large plastic bag with onion slices.
- Combine soy sauce, olive oil, vinegar, and sugar. Pour into plastic bag with meat.
- Chill at least 8 hours, turning occasionally, so that all of the meat is saturated with marinade.
- Grill or broil meat to desired degree of doneness, brushing with marinade frequently.
- Slice meat diagonally.
- Heat remaining marinade and onion to a boil. Serve as sauce for steak.

Yield: 4 servings

To avoid contamination, always marinate meats in the refrigerator, not at room temperature.

Steakburgers with Blue Cheese Spread

2 pounds ground chuck
½ cup chopped fresh
  mushrooms
½ teaspoon soy sauce
1 teaspoon Worcestershire
  sauce
¼ teaspoon seasoned salt
¼ teaspoon pepper
2 egg whites, lightly beaten
4 tablespoons cream cheese
2 tablespoons finely chopped
  onions
5 tablespoons blue cheese
3 tablespoons plain yogurt
⅛ teaspoon white pepper

• Combine ground chuck, mushrooms, soy sauce, Worcestershire sauce, seasoned salt, pepper, and egg whites in a large bowl.
• Form patties and refrigerate 2 hours before grilling.
• Prepare blue cheese spread by combining cream cheese, onions, blue cheese, yogurt, and white pepper. Refrigerate until needed.
• Grill burgers to desired degree of doneness.
• Spread patties with blue cheese spread. Return to grill just long enough to heat cheese.

Yield: 8 servings

The blue cheese spread is spectacular served on steaks.

Bourbon and Soy Beef Marinade

1 cup Jack Daniels
½ cup brown sugar
½ cup soy sauce
1 (3-4 pound) beef tenderloin

• Combine all ingredients in a large plastic storage bag.
• Marinate tenderloin several hours or overnight, turning at least once.
• Grill tenderloin to desired degree of doneness. Slice and serve.

Yield: 6-8 servings

Karlbi (Korean Grill)

3-5 pounds beef or pork ribs (back or country-style)
4 green onions, sliced crosswise at a diagonal
10-12 cloves garlic, minced
3 tablespoons sesame oil
7 tablespoons soy sauce
Dash MSG, optional
1 teaspoon minced ginger
1½ tablespoons sugar
1 tablespoon roasted sesame seeds
Dash black pepper

- Cut ribs individually with ½-inch diagonal slashes on each side.
- Mix remaining ingredients; combine with meat. Mix together with gloved hands until meat is well coated.
- Marinate up to 72 hours. Barbecue on a slow grill, or bake in a 350° oven for 1 to 1½ hours until meat is completely cooked.

Yield: 6-8 servings

Tender beef or pork pieces can be skewered and grilled.

This is sensational for a casual barbecue for a crowd. Excellent with saffron rice and steamed vegetables.

Barbecue Spare Ribs

1 tablespoon sugar
¾ cup honey
3 tablespoons soy sauce
2 tablespoons vegetable oil
6 cloves garlic, minced
3 tablespoons sherry
3 tablespoons ketchup
1 large onion, chopped
2 pounds spare ribs

- Combine all ingredients. Cover and refrigerate.
- Allow ribs to marinate for 24 hours.
- Grill ribs until done.

Yield: 4 servings

• • •

Bath County, named for the English town of Bath, is the location of many natural springs. The waters at Warm Springs and Hot Springs bubble from the earth at 95° and are comparable to the finest natural springs of Europe. Since 1761, visitors have flocked to sample the restorative waters of the resort area.

Grilling

Smoked Mustard Glazed Ribs

2 tablespoons sugar
1 teaspoon salt
1 teaspoon paprika
1 teaspoon ground turmeric
4 pounds country-style pork
  ribs
Hickory chips
1/2 cup brown sugar, firmly
  packed
1/3 cup vinegar
1/4 cup prepared mustard
1/4 cup chopped onion
2 cloves garlic, minced
1/2 teaspoon celery seed
1 small onion, thinly sliced

- Combine sugar, salt, paprika, and turmeric in a small bowl.
- Thoroughly rub ribs with spice mixture.
- Cover and refrigerate ribs for 4 hours.
- One hour before cooking time, soak hickory chips in enough water to cover; drain well. Sprinkle slow coals with dampened hickory chips.
- Place ribs, bone side down, on grill; lower grill hood.
- Grill ribs over slow coals for 30 minutes. Turn meat and grill an additional 25-30 minutes.
- Sprinkle coals with dampened hickory chips every 20 minutes while cooking.
- Meanwhile, combine brown sugar, vinegar, prepared mustard, chopped onion, garlic, and celery seed in a small saucepan. Bring mixture to a boil, stirring until brown sugar dissolves.
- Brush sauce on both sides of grilled ribs. Continue to grill ribs, uncovered, 10-15 minutes or until ribs are done.
- Heat any remaining sauce in saucepan.
- Transfer ribs to a warm platter. Top ribs with additional sauce and garnish with sliced onions.

Yield: 6 servings

Great recipe for chicken, too!
Country-style ribs are the best cut to use with this recipe. They are very meaty and tender. The ribs taste wonderful even without using the hickory chips on the grill.

217

Grilled Pork Chops with Raspberry Sauce

1 pound pork chops
⅛ teaspoon cayenne pepper or
  to taste
1 tablespoon ketchup
⅓ cup raspberry preserves
2 tablespoons red wine
  vinegar
½ teaspoon horseradish
Dash white pepper
½ teaspoon soy sauce
½ teaspoon hot pepper sauce
1 clove garlic, minced
Fresh raspberries for garnish

- Rub pork chops very lightly with cayenne pepper. Let sit for 15 minutes.
- Combine all other ingredients except fresh raspberries in a medium saucepan. Bring to a boil, then reduce to a simmer. Simmer 10-15 minutes.
- Grill or broil chops according to thickness.
- Serve chops on individual serving plates with warm sauce spooned over the top and sprinkled with fresh raspberries.

Yield: 4 servings

Bourbon Basted Pork Chops

1 lemon
3 tablespoons butter
½ cup soy sauce
1 tablespoon minced onion
⅛ teaspoon salt
⅛ teaspoon pepper
¼ teaspoon hot pepper sauce
2 tablespoons bourbon
4 pork chops, cut 1 inch thick

- Cut lemon in half. Squeeze juice from both halves into a small saucepan and drop peels in. Add butter, soy sauce, onions, salt, pepper, hot pepper sauce, and bourbon. Boil for 5 minutes.
- Grill pork chops 7-10 minutes on each side, basting often with sauce.
- Serve chops with remaining bourbon sauce.

Yield: 4 servings

After grilling, while grill is still warm, use a metal brush to remove any residue. Be careful not to damage the special coatings that may protect the grill.

Honey Glazed Grilled Pork Loin

¼ cup brown sugar, firmly
  packed
⅓ cup honey
1½ teaspoons sesame oil
1 pork loin roast

- Combine brown sugar, honey, and sesame oil in a medium saucepan. Cook over medium heat until brown sugar dissolves.
- Spray grill with non-stick vegetable spray. Place pork loin on grill.
- Brush pork loin with honey glaze frequently.
- Cook 20-25 minutes or until meat thermometer reaches 160°, turning twice.

Yield: 4-6 servings

Pork Tenderloin Kabobs

½ cup sherry
1 cup soy sauce
2 teaspoons ground ginger
2 cloves garlic, minced
1 medium-sized onion,
  chopped
1 tablespoon sugar
1½ pounds pork tenderloin,
  cut into 2-inch pieces
Vegetables for kabobs (green
  pepper pieces, cherry
  tomatoes, whole mushrooms,
  onion pieces)

- Combine sherry, soy sauce, ginger, garlic, onion, and sugar to make marinade.
- Pour marinade over pork tenderloin. Marinate 1-2 hours or overnight.
- Cut vegetables into bite-size pieces.
- Alternate pork and vegetables on skewers.
- Grill over slow coals.

Yield: 4-6 servings

Barbecued Spring Leg of Lamb

*1 (6 pound) leg of lamb,
  boned and butterflied*
1 teaspoon cracked pepper
4 cloves garlic, sliced
*½ teaspoon dried tarragon or
  rosemary*
*2 tablespoons red wine
  vinegar*
½ cup red wine
½ cup olive oil
2 bay leaves
2 teaspoons salt

- Rub pepper, garlic, and tarragon on lamb.
- Mix remaining ingredients. Pour over lamb and marinate for 24-36 hours using only a glass or plastic container.
- Over hot coals, grill lamb on all sides to seal in juices.
- Remove meat from grill until coals cool to medium-high heat.
- Return lamb to grill. Cover and cook, turning occasionally, about 30 minutes or until done.
- Slice across grain.

Yield: 12 servings

Grilled Lamb Chops

½ cup white wine vinegar
½ cup olive oil
½ cup soy sauce
4 cloves garlic, crushed
⅛ teaspoon pepper
*4 lamb loin chops (about 1
  pound)*

- Combine vinegar, oil, soy sauce, garlic, and pepper in a shallow container or heavy-duty sealable plastic bag.
- Add lamb chops. Cover or seal. Chill 8 hours, turning occasionally.
- Remove chops from marinade.
- Grill, covered, over medium coals 5-6 minutes on each side or to desired degree of doneness, basting frequently with the marinade.

Yield: 4 servings
Easy and tasty!

Minty Lamb Chops

1/3 cup chopped fresh mint
3 cloves garlic, crushed
1 1/2 cups white sherry
2 pounds lamb chops,
   trimmed of fat and cut 1
   inch thick
Fresh mint for garnish

• Combine mint, garlic, and sherry. Pour over lamb chops, covering all sides.
• Refrigerate and marinate overnight, turning chops occasionally.
• Grill over hot coals, basting with marinade frequently, until meat is cooked, approximately 7-10 minutes per side.
• Garnish with mint and serve.

Yield: 3-4 servings

Rosemary Grilled Lamb Chops

1/4 cup vegetable oil
1/4 cup dry white wine
2 tablespoons lemon juice
1/2 teaspoon rosemary
1/2 green bell pepper, thinly
   sliced
3-4 green onions, chopped
1 clove garlic, minced
1 tablespoon chopped fresh
   parsley
1/4 teaspoon crushed red pepper
   flakes
Seasoned salt
4 lamb loin chops, cut 1 inch
   thick

• Combine all ingredients except lamb. Mix well.
• Place lamb in a shallow dish. Pour marinade over lamb. Cover and refrigerate for 8 hours, turning often.
• Grill 7-10 minutes per side.

Yield: 4 servings

Basil-Rosemary Marinated Chicken

³/₄ cup dry white wine
¹/₄ cup orange juice
2 tablespoons fresh lemon
* juice*
1 tablespoon chopped fresh
* basil*
1 tablespoon vegetable oil
1 tablespoon cracked
* peppercorns*
1 sprig fresh rosemary or 1
* teaspoon dried rosemary,*
* crumbled*
2 small bay leaves
4 boneless chicken breast
* halves*

- Combine all ingredients except chicken. Mix well.
- Pour marinade over chicken and marinate in refrigerator for 8 hours.
- Grill over medium-high heat, turning occasionally, until chicken is thoroughly cooked.

  Yield: 4 servings

Basil Butter Grilled Chicken

1 tablespoon coarsely ground
* pepper*
4 boneless, skinless chicken
* breast halves*
¹/₄ cup butter, melted
¹/₄ cup chopped fresh basil
¹/₄ cup butter, softened
2 tablespoons minced fresh
* basil*
1 tablespoon grated Parmesan
* cheese*
¹/₄ teaspoon garlic powder
¹/₈ teaspoon salt
¹/₈ teaspoon pepper
Fresh basil sprigs for garnish

- Divide and press pepper onto chicken breasts.
- Combine melted butter with chopped basil. Stir well. Brush chicken lightly with butter mixture.
- Combine softened butter, minced basil, Parmesan cheese, and seasonings in a small bowl. Beat with an electric mixer at low speed until mixture is smooth and well blended. Transfer to a small serving bowl; set aside.
- Grill chicken, basting frequently with melted butter mixture.
- Serve chicken with basil butter mixture. Garnish with fresh basil.

  Yield: 4 servings

Grilled Cantonese Chicken

1 cup soy sauce
2 (6 ounce) jars strained
apricots (baby food)
½ cup apricot preserves
2 tablespoons ground ginger
1 teaspoon crushed garlic
4 pounds chicken breasts

- Mix all ingredients. Marinate 12-24 hours. Do not shorten the marinating time...the results will reflect it!
- Grill or broil chicken approximately 8 minutes per side.

Yield: 10-12 servings

If halving the recipe, go ahead and make a full batch of marinade and save half in the refrigerator for another time.

Skewered Chicken Wrapped in Prosciutto

4 skinless, boneless chicken
breast halves
12 thin slices prosciutto, cut in
half
1 loaf Italian bread, cut into
1-inch cubes
Extra virgin olive oil for
brushing

- Cut each chicken breast half into six pieces.
- Wrap a half slice of prosciutto around each piece of chicken.
- Skewer chicken and bread cubes alternately beginning and ending with bread cubes. Brush liberally with olive oil.
- Grill or broil until chicken is firm to the touch and a little springy. Brush with olive oil during grilling, if desired.

Yield: 4 servings

Substitute thinly sliced Smithfield ham for prosciutto, if desired.

Wrapping the chicken in prosciutto seasons the chicken and keeps it moist and tender during grilling.

Grilled Soft-shelled Crab Sandwiches

⅓ cup vegetable oil
2 cloves garlic, sliced
1 teaspoon Old Bay seasoning
Salt and pepper to taste
8 soft-shelled crabs
1 stick unsalted butter,
* softened*
2 tablespoons lemon juice
1 tablespoon minced shallot
1 tablespoon minced fresh
* parsley*
8 split English muffins,
* flattened with a rolling pin*

- Combine vegetable oil, garlic, Old Bay, salt, and pepper. Marinate crabs in oil mixture overnight.
- Prepare herb butter by combining butter, lemon juice, shallot, and parsley.
- Grill crabs 3-5 minutes on each side.
- Grill English muffins. Spread with herb butter.
- Serve by placing grilled crabs between English muffin halves.

Yield: 8 servings

Shrimp and Tomatoes on a Skewer

½ cup Italian salad dressing
2 cloves garlic, minced
½ teaspoon hot pepper sauce
1 tablespoon chopped parsley
1 pound large shrimp, peeled
* with tails remaining*
1 pint cherry tomatoes

- Whisk Italian dressing, garlic, hot pepper sauce, and parsley until well blended. Pour over shrimp. Marinate for 30 minutes to 1 hour.
- Thread shrimp and tomatoes on skewers.
- Grill or broil for 6 minutes, turning after 3 minutes.

Yield: 2-3 servings

Serve with Stunning Pasta Salad.

Grilled Shrimp Seasoned with Chili Peppers

3-4 pounds large shrimp,
* peeled and deveined*
1 stick margarine, melted
½ cup mayonnaise
4 tablespoons lemon juice
1 teaspoon dried crushed red
* chili peppers*
4 cloves garlic, minced

- Combine all ingredients in a large bowl. Marinate for 1 hour in the refrigerator.
- Skewer shrimp and grill uncovered on a greased grill for 1-2 minutes on each side until shrimp are pink and curling.
- Serve immediately as an entree or appetizer.

Yield: 6-8 entree servings, 30-40 appetizer servings

Delicious summer fare!

Spicy Hot Grilled Scallops

3 tablespoons olive oil
3 cloves garlic, minced
1½ teaspoons ground cumin
½ teaspoon chili powder
½ teaspoon salt
Dash cayenne pepper
Juice of 1 lime
1 pound scallops
12-16 cherry tomatoes

- Whisk first seven ingredients until well blended. Pour over scallops in a glass pan or dish; marinate for 30 minutes to 1 hour.
- Thread scallops and tomatoes on skewers.
- Grill or broil until thoroughly cooked, 5-7 minutes.
- Serve over rice.

Yield: 4 servings

Wonderful mix of spices!

To prevent food from sticking to the grill as it cooks, spray the grid with non-stick vegetable spray before lighting the coals.

Barbecued Swordfish Steaks

1 onion, chopped
2 tablespoons brown sugar
1 tablespoon prepared
*   mustard*
½ clove garlic, minced
½ cup butter
½ green bell pepper, chopped
1 tablespoon Worcestershire
*   sauce*
½ cup tomato sauce
Dash hot pepper sauce
2 pounds swordfish steaks

- Combine all ingredients except swordfish. Boil for 15-20 minutes.
- Grill swordfish 8-10 minutes per side, basting frequently with sauce.

Yield: 6 servings

Delicious Marinated Swordfish

¼ cup soy sauce
¼ cup dry sherry
¼ cup minced green onions
2 tablespoons vegetable oil
2 tablespoons red wine
*   vinegar*
1 tablespoon sugar
1 teaspoon minced garlic
½ teaspoon dry mustard
½ teaspoon ginger
1½ pounds swordfish steaks

- Combine all ingredients except swordfish steaks. Blend well.
- Place swordfish in a shallow dish. Pour marinade over fish. Marinate at room temperature for 1 hour.
- Grill 8-10 minutes per side.

Yield: 4 servings

Marinade can also be used with tuna or shark.

• • •

Surrounded by the Chesapeake Bay, the Potomac River, and the Rappahannock River, Virginia's Northern Neck is a peaceful haven for boaters and fishermen. The relaxed atmosphere of the area is enhanced by outstanding dining opportunities, recreation, and early national history.

Grilled Tuna with Lemon, Tomato, and Garlic Herb Sauce

3 tomatoes, peeled, seeded, and chopped
½ cup extra virgin olive oil
3 tablespoons fresh lemon juice
3 cloves garlic, minced
Salt to taste
1 cup fresh herb of choice (parsley, tarragon, chive, basil)
4 (6-8 ounce) tuna steaks
1 tablespoon extra virgin olive oil

• Prepare sauce 1-2 hours ahead of time by combining tomatoes, ½ cup olive oil, lemon juice, garlic, salt, and herbs. Let stand 1-2 hours so flavors can develop.

• Allow tuna to get to room temperature. Brush with 1 tablespoon olive oil. Grill over coals that have passed their peak heat, until fish is no longer pink inside, about 4 minutes per side. Cook carefully to avoid drying out the tuna.

• Serve tuna topped with sauce.

Yield: 4 servings

Sesame Tuna Marinade

3 tablespoons sesame oil
½ cup vegetable oil
¼ cup rice wine vinegar
2 tablespoons vermouth
1 tablespoon brown sugar
¼ cup soy sauce
3 cloves garlic, minced
2 tablespoons ginger
4 tuna steaks
¼ cup butter, softened
2 teaspoons dry mustard

• Combine sesame oil, vegetable oil, vinegar, vermouth, brown sugar, soy sauce, garlic, and ginger. Mix well.

• Pour marinade over tuna steaks. Marinate in the refrigerator for 6-8 hours.

• Grill tuna for 8-10 minutes, turning once.

• Combine butter and mustard. Spread over tuna before serving.

Yield: 4 servings

Marinate foods in glass, ceramic, or stainless steel containers. Do not use aluminum since the acidity in the marinade will damage your container.

Tuna with Mustard Butter

4-6 large pieces of tuna steak
White wine Worcestershire
  sauce
1 stick butter, softened
5 tablespoons Dijon mustard
3 tablespoons prepared
  horseradish
Salt and pepper to taste

- Marinate the tuna steaks in Worcestershire sauce for 6 hours or overnight.
- Combine butter, mustard, horseradish, salt, and pepper to make mustard butter. Mix well.
- Grill tuna steaks approximately 10 minutes, spreading mustard butter on each side.
- Use remaining mustard butter at table to spread on tuna if desired.

Yield: 4-6 servings

So easy, yet so good!

Grilled Fruit with Butter Glaze

2 cups of fruit (banana, fresh
  pineapple, cantaloupe,
  papaya, strawberries, honey
  dew, peaches)
¼ cup butter, melted
2 tablespoons brown sugar

- Cut fruit into large chunks. Place on skewers.
- Combine butter and brown sugar. Brush over fruit pieces.
- Grill over low coals until lightly caramelized, about 5 minutes. Turn skewers frequently while grilling.

Yield: 4 servings

Grilled Artichokes

2 fresh artichokes
1 lemon
3 cloves garlic, coarsely
  chopped
4 tablespoons olive oil
Salt and pepper to taste
½ cup water

- Trim off stems and spiny tips of the artichoke leaves. Slice the artichokes in half lengthwise. Rinse well under running water.
- Scrape out the choke (small center leaves) leaving a "bowl".
- Using half a lemon for each artichoke, squeeze lemon juice all over the cut side.
- Using heavy-duty aluminum foil, make thick baking cups large enough to hold each artichoke with extra foil to fold over the top.
- Place one artichoke half, cut side up, in each foil cup. Sprinkle with garlic. Drizzle a tablespoon of olive oil over each one. Season with salt and pepper. Pour 2 teaspoons of water into each cup.
- Fold top edges over to completely cover the artichoke.
- Grill over medium-hot coals with vents closed 1 hour or until tender.

Yield: 4 servings

Grilled Corn On The Cob with Herb Butter

6 tablespoons butter
1 tablespoon minced fresh
  garlic
1 tablespoon white vinegar
Several dashes hot pepper
  sauce
1/4 teaspoon cayenne pepper
1 tablespoon fresh chopped
  thyme
Salt to taste
4 whole, unhusked ears of
  corn

- Melt butter in a small saucepan over low heat. Whisk in garlic, vinegar, hot pepper sauce, cayenne pepper, thyme, and salt.
- Gently pull the corn husk away from the ears, leaving them connected at the base. Remove silk. Brush ears liberally with butter baste mixture. Pull husks back up around ears.
- Grill over medium-hot coals for 10-12 minutes. Remove husks, brush again with butter baste, and serve.

Yield: 4 servings

To easily remove the silk from ears of corn, rub a dampened paper towel or cloth along the cob from end to end.

Grilled Red Onion Slices

3-4 medium-sized red onions,
  peeled and cut into 1/2-inch
  thick slices
1/4 cup extra virgin olive oil
Salt and freshly ground
  pepper to taste

- Combine all ingredients in a small bowl.
- Grill onion slices until tender, turning frequently, 2-3 minutes.

Yield: 6 servings

Grilled Whole Heads of Garlic

8 whole garlic heads
½ cup olive oil
Several sprigs of fresh
* rosemary*
Salt and pepper to taste

- Peel away some of the papery layers from the garlic heads, particularly from around the top cloves, being careful not to break off the cloves.
- Slice off the tops of the cloves.
- Using heavy-duty aluminum foil, form 8 cups large enough to hold each garlic head. Place heads in cups. Drizzle with olive oil, allowing oil to run down between cloves and into the bottom of the cup.
- Sprinkle with rosemary, salt, and pepper.
- Place foil cups on a covered grill away from the hottest coals. Cook 1 hour. Baste with additional olive oil once or twice while grilling.
- The garlic is done when brown and soft.

Yield: 4 servings

Use as a spread on Italian bread or grilled meat.

Grilled Potatoes and Onions

4 teaspoons butter or
* margarine*
2 large baking potatoes, diced
1 large onion, diced
1 green bell pepper, diced
* (optional)*
Butter
Seasoned salt and pepper to
* taste*

- Cover four squares of aluminum foil with butter. Place vegetables on foil. Dot with additional butter. Sprinkle with seasoned salt and pepper to taste. Close foil to make packets.
- Grill, turning once, until potatoes are tender, approximately 30 minutes.

Yield: 4 servings

231

Salmon Marinade

½ cup white wine
¼ cup vegetable oil
⅓ cup soy sauce
2 teaspoons ginger
Pepper to taste
Juice of ½ lemon
1 tablespoon honey
2 tablespoons parsley
3 cloves garlic, minced

- Combine all ingredients in a blender.
- Marinate salmon overnight or use as basting sauce while grilling.

Yield: 1⅓ cups

Mango and Avocado Salsa

1 large mango, peeled and
    diced
¼ cup diced green bell pepper
¼ cup diced red bell pepper
1 very small red onion,
    chopped
2 tablespoons white wine
    vinegar
1½ tablespoons olive oil
1½ tablespoons chopped fresh
    cilantro
1 teaspoon minced fresh chives
Dash hot pepper sauce
1 large avocado, peeled and
    diced
Salt and pepper to taste

- Mix mango, peppers, onion, vinegar, oil, cilantro, chives, and hot pepper sauce gently in a large bowl. Cover and chill for up to 3 hours.
- Add avocado to salsa mixture and stir gently to combine. Season with salt and pepper to taste.

Yield: 4-6 servings

Wonderful as a topping for grilled fish or chicken. Can also be served with tortilla chips.

Grilling

Pat's Oriental Marinade for Two

¼ cup orange juice
¼ cup soy sauce
2 tablespoons ketchup
½ teaspoon pepper
½ teaspoon oregano
2 tablespoons chopped parsley
1 tablespoon lemon juice
1 teaspoon minced garlic
2 tablespoons canola oil

- Combine all ingredients.
- Marinate your favorite fish for at least 20 minutes or red meat for at least 8 hours.

Yield: 1 cup

Barbecue Sauce

3 beef bouillon cubes
3 cups hot water
6 tablespoons red wine vinegar
⅔ cup brown sugar, firmly packed
⅔ cup Worcestershire sauce
1½ teaspoons garlic juice
1 tablespoon liquid smoke
1 tablespoon black pepper
½ teaspoon cayenne pepper
1½ teaspoons dry mustard
1 tablespoon grated onion or onion juice
3 (6 ounce) cans tomato paste
3 bay leaves

- Combine all ingredients in order listed in a large saucepan. Cover and simmer for 2 hours, stirring occasionally.
- Refrigerate until ready to use.

Yield: 6 cups

Serve with pork or chicken. Keeps in the refrigerator for months. Makes a wonderful homemade gift item!

Betty's Barbecue Sauce for Chicken

7 ounces vegetable oil
7 ounces cider vinegar
1 tablespoon salt
¼ teaspoon pepper
2 teaspoons poultry seasoning
2 ounces water
1 large egg

- Combine all ingredients and use as marinade for chicken.
- When grilling chicken, baste frequently with marinade.

Yield: 2 cups

Cajun Rub

1 tablespoon salt
1½ teaspoons garlic powder
1½ teaspoons onion powder
1½ teaspoons paprika
1½ teaspoons dried thyme
1 teaspoon dried oregano
1 teaspoon ground red pepper
¾ teaspoon freshly ground black pepper
½ teaspoon ground bay leaves
½ teaspoon chili powder

- Combine all ingredients. Store in an airtight container.
- Sprinkle on seafood, chicken, or beef before grilling or roasting.

Yield: ⅓ cup

Dried Herb Rub

1 tablespoon dried thyme
1 tablespoon dried oregano
1½ teaspoons dried basil
1½ teaspoons dried parsley flakes
1½ teaspoons poultry seasoning
1 teaspoon dried marjoram
1 teaspoon dried rosemary
1 teaspoon dried tarragon
½ teaspoon salt
⅛ teaspoon pepper

- Combine all ingredients. Store in an airtight container.
- Sprinkle on fish, poultry, or pork before grilling.

Yield: ½ cup

Rubs are a highly concentrated blend of herbs and spices used to flavor the exterior of the meat as it grills. If you are in a hurry and don't have time to marinate, but want extra flavor, try a rub instead!

Desserts

Pilgrimage

When Virginians speak of the Valley of Virginia, they could be referring to any one of the four valleys - Shenandoah, Fincastle, Dublin, Abingdon - that make up the Great Valley. Its trough lies between the Blue Ridge and the Alleghenies west of Staunton. In the fall, when leaves are turning, folk long to go on pilgrimages to the Skyline Drive and Blue Ridge Parkway, squiggling along 322 mountainous miles as if poured from a cake-decorating cone.

Some Virginians feel a spiritual uplift as they marvel at the mountainsides ablaze in shades of red, orange, yellow, bronze, purple, with an occasional green and lonesome pine. From a distance, the motley raiment, as with camouflage, is to render a most substantial mountain into a wavery, vari-hued veil that could be parted with a hand. Watching from the Peaks of Otter as the sun rose on just such a scene, the acerbic John Randolph of Roanoke was so moved that he commanded his servant to kneel and join him in prayer.

On the way home from so soulful an experience, Virginians stop on the road for soul food - a bushel of peaches or apples and, mayhap, a jug of apple cider. Since 1981, they can purchase "sparkling cider," a non-alcoholic carbonated beverage, tingly and bubbling when poured into the glass. It is worthy of being sipped from a slipper.

A Richmonder, Ben Lacy III, who had worked in orchards from childhood, organized the Linden Beverage Co. with a dozen family members in Linden. He named it Alpenglow, a phenomenon seen in the mountains at sunrise or sunset when the refracted rays bathe the land in a rosy, hazy glow. He first heard of it from his father, Dr. Benjamin R. Lacy Jr., former president in Richmond of the Union Theological Seminary. Dr. Lacy had enjoyed the sight during trips to the Alps and a beverage similar to the one his son created.

In 15 years Virginia has developed a fine wine industry. Greatest concentrations of vineyards are in Albemarle County and in the Valley at Markham, Middleburg and Winchester. There is one in Danville and in Williamsburg.

Highly respected wine critic James Raper of Zuni rates Virginia as fifth among two dozen wine-producing states. "Virginia is producing some very, very fine white wines," he said. "From almost the first bottles, we sent out excellent Chardonnay. Exciting developments are under way with the white wines. The red wines are coming along nicely, but lagging in quality compared to that of the white wines. Wonderful people are busy with wines. Some are working in other jobs as well. They just love wine and they buy some land and vines and start. There are major producers, but many are family owned in which husband and wife spend long hours in the vineyards and wineries. You have to admire them."

A global economy is nothing new to the apple industry. When Queen Victoria tasted the Albemarle Pippin, she declared that there would be no duty on it. Now, Clayton Griffin, director of the Virginia Apple Board reports that a way is being cleared for shipment of apples to Mexico. Already, they go to Europe and South America.

The most exciting news is the focus on flavor and taste in developing new varieties, said Griffin. One such is the Ginger Gold, now sold by Tom Bomar's Mountain Cove Orchard. It was discovered after Hurricane Camille swept away, in August 1969, orchards owned by Clyde and Ginger Harvey of Lovingston. From that survivor, they bred Ginger Gold. It is being planted around the world. Ginger Gold is a cross between Victoria's Albemarle Pippin and the Golden Delicious.

-Guy Friddell

Virginia Diner Southern Peanut Pie

3 eggs
½ cup granulated sugar
1½ cups dark corn syrup
¼ cup butter, melted
¼ teaspoon salt
½ teaspoon vanilla extract
1½ cups chopped roasted peanuts
1 9-inch deep dish pie shell, unbaked

- Preheat oven to 375°.
- Beat eggs until foamy. Add sugar, corn syrup, butter, salt, and vanilla; continue to beat until thoroughly blended.
- Stir in peanuts. Pour into unbaked pie shell.
- Bake for 50-55 minutes.
- Serve warm or cold. May be garnished with whipped cream or ice cream.

Yield: 6 servings

In the heart of Virginia peanut country, halfway between Richmond and Norfolk on Route 460, The Virginia Diner, in Wakefield, Virginia, has been known since 1929 for its Southern cooking and delicious gourmet peanuts. It is a favorite dining place for travelers heading to and from the beach.

Mucky Duck Homemade Key Lime Pie

1 (8 ounce) can sweetened
  condensed milk
7 tablespoons bottled lime
  juice
3 large egg whites
1 prepared 9-inch graham
  cracker crust
Whipped cream for garnish

- Mix the condensed milk with the lime juice in a large mixing bowl.
- In another bowl, whip the egg whites until you find you can almost turn the bowl over without the beaten egg whites falling out.
- Add the egg whites to the bowl of condensed milk and lime juice. Mix slowly with a whisk so as not to deflate the whipped whites.
- Pour mixture into the pie crust and freeze.
- Serve sliced and topped with whipped cream.

Yield: 6-8 servings

Submitted by a good friend to all Junior Leagues...Mr. Willard Scott, weatherman for NBC's Today Show. He travels extensively throughout the United States, but is proud to claim Virginia as his home and favorite state. This heavenly dessert is from **Willard Scott's All-American Cookbook.**

Extra Easy Chocolate Chess Pie

2 (1 ounce) squares
  unsweetened baking
  chocolate
1 stick butter
2 eggs
1 cup sugar
1 tablespoon vanilla extract
1 9-inch pie shell, unbaked
Frozen whipped topping

- Preheat oven to 375°.
- Melt chocolate and butter in a small saucepan or in the microwave; set aside.
- Beat eggs and sugar until fluffy.
- Combine chocolate and sugar mixtures. Stir in vanilla. Pour into pie shell.
- Bake for 25 minutes.
- Serve with frozen whipped topping.

Yield: 8 servings

Fabulous! A chocolate lover's dream...quick, easy, and very rich!

Mother's Chocolate Pie

1 9-inch pie shell, unbaked
3 (1 ounce) squares
  unsweetened baking
  chocolate
2 tablespoons butter or
  margarine
1/2 teaspoon salt
6 tablespoons all-purpose flour
1 3/4 cups milk
2 eggs
3/4 cup sugar
1 teaspoon vanilla extract
Lightly sweetened whipped
  cream for topping

- Preheat oven to 350°.
- Bake pie shell for 10-12 minutes; set aside.
- Melt chocolate and butter in a double boiler. Stir in salt. Remove from heat. Add flour and mix thoroughly.
- Add milk, stirring constantly until smooth. Return to heat. Allow mixture to thicken.
- Add eggs and sugar. Cook just until sugar melts. Remove from heat and stir in vanilla. Pour mixture into pie shell. Cool.
- Top with whipped cream.

Yield: 8 servings

The contributor noted that "when this was served on special occasions, my father asked us to dim the lights and refrain from talking" so as to fully appreciate this chocolate delight!

Bourbon Chocolate Pecan Pie

¼ cup butter
1 cup sugar
3 eggs, beaten
¾ cup light corn syrup
¼ teaspoon salt
1 teaspoon vanilla extract
½ cup semi-sweet chocolate
  morsels
½ cup chopped pecans
2 tablespoons bourbon
1 9-inch pie shell, unbaked

- Preheat oven to 375°.
- Cream butter. Add sugar gradually. Add beaten eggs, syrup, salt, and vanilla.
- Stir in chocolate morsels, nuts, and bourbon until well mixed.
- Pour into an unbaked pie shell.
- Bake for 50 minutes or until the center has set. You can never overcook this, but the crust may turn too brown if cooked too long.
- Rewarm to serve with vanilla ice cream or whipped cream.

Yield: 8 servings

This is the one and only chocolate pecan pie recipe worth having!

Cool White Chocolate Pecan Pie

1 9-inch pie shell, unbaked
2 tablespoons butter
2 cups chopped pecans
1 cup chopped white chocolate
  baking bar
¼ cup milk
2 cups heavy cream
½ cup sugar
1 tablespoon vanilla extract
Grated chocolate or chocolate
  syrup, optional

- Preheat oven to 450°.
- Bake pie shell 9-11 minutes until brown. Cool completely.
- Melt butter in a 10-inch skillet over medium heat. Stir in pecans. Cook until golden brown. Cool completely, approximately 1 hour.
- Melt chocolate or vanilla chips and milk in a small saucepan over low heat. Cool completely.
- Beat cream in a large mixing bowl until stiff. Add sugar, vanilla, melted mixture, and pecans. Mix well.
- Fold mixture into pie shell. Refrigerate at least 4 hours.
- Garnish with grated chocolate or chocolate syrup, if desired.

Yield: 10-12 servings

Perfect cool dessert for a warm summer night.

Coconut Cream Pie

1 cup sugar
¼ teaspoon salt
¼ cup cornstarch
3 cups milk
4 eggs, separated
9 ounces frozen coconut,
    divided
2 tablespoons butter
2 teaspoons vanilla extract
4 tablespoons sugar
1 9-inch pie shell, baked

- Preheat oven to 300°.
- Combine 1 cup sugar, salt, and cornstarch. In a double boiler, scald milk. Slowly pour over sugar mixture.
- Beat egg yolks. Pour milk mixture over beaten egg yolks. Return to double boiler and cook until thick, stirring constantly.
- Remove double boiler from heat. Add coconut (reserving ¼ cup), butter, and vanilla. Cool.
- Pour coconut mixture into baked pie shell.
- Beat egg whites until stiff, add 4 tablespoons sugar, and spread meringue over pie, sealing with crust. Sprinkle remaining coconut on top.
- Bake until meringue peaks are brown.

Yield: 8 servings

Japanese Pie

1½ sticks margarine, softened
1¾ cups sugar
4 eggs, lightly beaten
2 tablespoons vinegar
1 cup pecan pieces
1 cup raisins
1 cup coconut
2 9-inch pie crusts, unbaked

- Preheat oven to 350°.
- Cream margarine and sugar. Add eggs.
- Stir in vinegar. Add pecans, raisins, and coconut.
- Pour into 2 pie crusts.
- Bake for 30-40 minutes.

Yield: 12 servings

Add ½ cup chocolate chips and / or use rum-soaked raisins for a variation.

Another treat from **Virginia Seasons.**

241

Cranberry Apple Pie

2 cups coarsely chopped
   cranberries
3 cups pared, sliced apples
1¼ cups sugar
1 tablespoon all-purpose flour
½ teaspoon cinnamon
Dash allspice
Dash salt
2 9-inch pie crusts, unbaked
2 tablespoons butter
Milk for brushing

- Preheat oven to 400°.
- Combine cranberries and apples.
- Mix sugar, flour, and spices. Add to cranberries and apples.
- Line a 9-inch pie plate with one pastry. Pour in the fruit mixture. Dot with 2 tablespoons butter.
- Make a lattice with second pastry for top of pie. Brush with milk.
- Bake 40-45 minutes or until apples are tender and crust is golden.

Yield: 8 servings

Cranberry Apple Pie is a favorite of acclaimed film and stage actress Sissy Spacek. She and her family have made their country home in Albemarle County for many years.

French Apple Pie

6 cups sliced apples
½ cup sugar, or less
   depending on variety of
   apples used
1 teaspoon cinnamon
2 tablespoons all-purpose flour
1 9-inch pie shell, unbaked
½ cup butter
½ cup brown sugar
1 cup all-purpose flour

- Preheat oven to 425°.
- Combine apples, sugar, cinnamon, and 2 tablespoons flour. Pour into unbaked pie shell.
- With pastry blender, mix butter, brown sugar, and 1 cup flour until crumbly. Sprinkle over apple mixture and pat down with your hands.
- Bake for 15 minutes. Lower temperature to 350° and bake an additional 30 minutes. Watch that pie does not brown too quickly.

Yield: 8 servings

A traditional autumn favorite!

Cream Cheese Peach Pie

1 9-inch pie shell, unbaked
4 cups peeled, sliced peaches,
    divided
1 cup sugar
3 tablespoons cornstarch
1 tablespoon lemon juice
1 tablespoon butter
1 (3 ounce) package cream
    cheese, softened
Whipped cream for garnish

- Bake pie shell at 350° for 9-11 minutes until brown. Set aside to cool.
- Crush 2 cups peaches in a saucepan. Add sugar, cornstarch, lemon juice, and butter. Cook over low heat until thickened. Cool.
- Spread cream cheese in pie shell. Top with remaining 2 cups of peaches. Pour cooked peach mixture over the sliced peaches.
- Refrigerate or serve immediately garnished with whipped cream.

Yield: 8 servings

Nana's Apple Crow's Nest with Brown Sugar Sauce

4 medium-sized tart apples
1¼ teaspoons cinnamon
Sugar for sprinkling
1 cup all-purpose flour
2 teaspoons baking powder
¼ teaspoon salt
¼ cup sugar
3 tablespoons vegetable
    shortening
1 egg, well beaten
¼ cup milk
2½ tablespoons butter
1 cup brown sugar
2 tablespoons cornstarch
1 cup boiling water

- Preheat oven to 400°.
- Slice apples and place in a greased Pyrex loaf pan. Sprinkle with cinnamon and some sugar to your taste.
- Combine flour, baking powder, salt, and ¼ cup sugar. Cut in shortening with 2 knives or a pastry blender. Add egg and enough milk to make a soft dough.
- Spread dough over apples.
- Bake for 25 minutes or until the apples are tender. Cover with foil if the top gets too brown or lower the oven temperature after 12-15 minutes.
- For sauce, combine butter, brown sugar, and cornstarch. Pour in boiling water and stir until thick and smooth. Pour sauce over baked apple dish.

Yield: 8 servings

Wonderful on a cold winter night!

Strawberry Cream Tart

Crust
½ cup margarine
⅓ cup sugar
1¼ cups all-purpose flour

Filling
1 (8 ounce) package cream cheese, softened
⅓ cup sugar
¼ teaspoon almond extract or ½ teaspoon vanilla extract
1 cup heavy cream
4 cups fresh strawberries
½ cup chocolate chips, optional
1 tablespoon vegetable shortening or corn oil, optional

- Preheat oven to 375°.
- Prepare crust by beating margarine and ⅓ cup sugar until fluffy. Add flour. Mix well.
- Press crust mixture into bottom and up sides of a 9-inch tart pan with a removable bottom.
- Bake for 12-14 minutes until lightly browned. Cool.
- Prepare filling by beating the cream cheese until fluffy. Add ⅓ cup sugar and extract. Blend well.
- Fold in heavy cream.
- Spoon mixture into the tart shell.
- Cut the stem ends off the strawberries to give each a flat bottom.
- Place strawberries pointed side up over the cream cheese mixture in the tart shell.
- If desired, melt chocolate chips with shortening. Drizzle over berries.
- Chill until set. Remove metal tart ring when ready to serve.

Yield: 10-12 servings

An elegant dessert that takes a minimum amount of time to prepare. Impressive with strawberries arranged in concentric circles.

Chocolate Bread Pudding

4 slices white or wheat bread
1½ ounces unsweetened
  baking chocolate
1½ cups milk
1 cup sugar
2 tablespoons butter
2 eggs
½ cup milk
¼ teaspoon salt
1 teaspoon vanilla extract

- Preheat oven to 350°.
- Cut the bread slices into quarters and place the pieces in the bottom of a greased baking dish in 2 layers.
- In a double boiler over simmering water, combine chocolate, 1½ cups milk, and sugar. Stir until chocolate is melted. Add butter and let it melt.
- Beat the eggs until fluffy. Add ½ cup milk, salt, and vanilla.
- Add the egg mixture to the chocolate mixture. Stirring constantly, pour over the bread pieces in the baking dish. Let it stand for 15-20 minutes.
- Bake for 45 minutes or until set.

Yield: 6 servings

A chocolate variation on a traditional Southern dish.

Royal Romance

1 cup all-purpose flour, sifted
½ cup butter, softened
2 tablespoons sugar
2 eggs
1 teaspoon vanilla extract
2 tablespoons all-purpose flour
1 teaspoon baking powder
1½ cups brown sugar
1 cup chopped pecans
1 cup shredded coconut
Juice of 1 lemon
Zest of 1 lemon
1 cup confectioners' sugar

- Preheat oven to 350°.
- Combine 1 cup flour, butter, and 2 tablespoons sugar. Mix well.
- Press dough into a foil-lined 9-inch square baking dish.
- Bake for 15 minutes.
- Combine eggs, vanilla, 2 tablespoons flour, baking powder, and brown sugar. Fold in pecans and coconut. Spread mixture over the hot crust.
- Bake for 30 minutes. Let cool completely.
- Prepare glaze by combining lemon juice, lemon zest, and powdered sugar. Stir until smooth. Drizzle over dessert.
- Cut into squares to serve.

Yield: 2 dozen squares

A wonderful Elizabethan-era dessert, perfect for the holiday season.

Raspberries and Sour Cream

¾ cup sour cream
1½ cups vanilla ice cream, softened
¼ cup rum, Chambourd, or liqueur of choice
1 pint fresh raspberries

- Combine the sour cream and the softened ice cream. Add rum and stir well. Refrigerate at least 20 minutes, or until serving time.
- Divide raspberries among 4 large goblets. Pour sauce over berries just before serving.

Yield: 4 servings

White Chocolate Charlotte Russe

1 envelope unflavored gelatin
²/₃ cup cold water
1 (10 ounce) package white
chocolate baking pieces
2 eggs, separated
¼ cup sugar
1 teaspoon vanilla extract
2 tablespoons sugar
2 cups heavy cream, whipped
20 ladyfingers, split
lengthwise
2 tablespoons Amaretto or
Kirsch, if desired
2 quarts fresh strawberries

- Sprinkle gelatin over cold water in the top of a double boiler. Bring water to a boil. Cook, stirring constantly, until gelatin dissolves.
- Add white chocolate pieces, stirring constantly until melted. Cool slightly.
- Beat egg yolks in a large bowl with an electric mixer at medium speed until thick and lemon colored. Gradually add ¼ cup sugar, beating well.
- Stir in gelatin mixture and vanilla.
- Beat egg whites (at room temperature) until foamy. Gradually add 2 tablespoons sugar. Beat until stiff peaks form.
- Gently fold egg whites and whipped cream into yolk mixture.
- Line a 3-quart bowl with split ladyfingers. Brush with liqueur. Pour in filling. Cover and chill at least 8 hours.
- Garnish with fresh strawberries and serve with Raspberry-Strawberry Sauce.

Yield: 8-10 servings

Raspberry-Strawberry Sauce

1 (10 ounce) package frozen
raspberries, thawed
1 (10 ounce) package frozen
strawberries, thawed
3 tablespoons cornstarch
2 teaspoons sugar
3 tablespoons lemon juice
3 tablespoons Kirsch

- Drain raspberries and strawberries, reserving juice. Put berries through a food mill or sieve and discard seeds.
- Combine juice, fruit puree, and enough water to make 2 cups of the mixture.
- Combine juice mixture, cornstarch, and sugar in a saucepan. Stir until blended. Cook over low heat, stirring constantly, until mixture is smooth and thickened.
- Stir in lemon juice and Kirsch. Cool.

Yield: 2 cups

Frozen Lemon Torte with Raspberry Sauce

1 bag Pepperidge Farm
Lemon Crunch cookies
6 tablespoons butter, melted
Non-stick vegetable spray
4 egg whites
1 cup sugar
4 egg yolks
½ cup fresh lemon juice
1½ tablespoons grated lemon
peel
1½ cups heavy cream,
whipped
1 (10 ounce) box frozen
raspberries
1-2 tablespoons Grand
Marnier or other orange
liqueur

- Crush cookies into a powder in food processor. Mix with melted butter. Press into the bottom of a 9-inch springform pan that has been sprayed with non-stick vegetable spray.
- Beat egg whites until foamy. While still beating, gradually add sugar until stiff peaks form. Set aside.
- Beat egg yolks until thick. Add lemon juice and lemon peel. Fold in egg whites first, then the whipped cream. Pour mixture into crust and freeze overnight.
- Before serving, prepare raspberry sauce by pureeing frozen raspberries in food processor. Add Grand Marnier to taste.
- Remove torte from pan, cut into wedges, and serve with raspberry sauce.

Yield: 10-12 servings

Light dessert for a special luncheon or following a heavy dinner.

Raspberry Fluff

6 large egg yolks
7 tablespoons sugar
½ cup good quality sweet
 Marsala wine (or to taste)
1¾ cups heavy cream
1 pint raspberries (reserve 12
 berries for garnish)

- In a large mixing bowl, beat the egg yolks and sugar until thick and pale. Add the Marsala and put into the top of a double boiler.
- Beat mixture with a wire whisk over water at a medium boil. Cook until thick enough to hold a small mound when the whisk is withdrawn.
- Cool in the refrigerator.
- Whip the cream and gently fold in the raspberries. Carefully fold the raspberry/whipped cream mixture into the Marsala/egg mixture. Chill.
- Garnish with the remaining raspberries before serving.

Yield: 6-8 servings

An excellent light dessert.

Sherbet Delight

3 pints lemon sherbet
⅓ cup Crème de Menthe or
 Crème de Menthe syrup
1 quart fresh strawberries or
 raspberries
Confectioners' sugar

- Soften sherbet slightly. Beat in Crème de Menthe with an electric mixer.
- Freeze overnight in a six-ring mold.
- Unmold. Fill center cavity of the molded sherbet with fruit and dust with confectioner's sugar.

Yield: 8-10 servings

Refreshing to the palate and to the eye!

New Wave Custard

1 pint heavy cream
1 vanilla bean, split in half and scraped
3 ounces granulated sugar
Pinch salt
4 egg yolks
2 ounces turbinado sugar

- Preheat oven to 250°.
- Heat the cream and vanilla bean in a heavy saucepan. Bring to a boil.
- Add the granulated sugar and salt to the cream mixture.
- Beat the egg yolks in a stainless steel bowl with a whisk. Slowly add the cream mixture to the egg yolks to equalize the temperature so as not to scramble the eggs.
- Return the mixture to the saucepan and heat slowly for 30 seconds or so while stirring constantly with a wooden spoon until the mixture is slightly thickened.
- Pass the mixture through a fine sieve and ladle it into four 5-ounce shallow molds or dishes. They do not need to be ovenproof.
- Set the dishes in a large shallow pan and put into the slow oven. Fill the pan with water up to the level of the custard. Bake for 45 minutes, checking often to assure that they do not color on top.
- Remove from oven and cool completely, at least 2 hours.
- Sprinkle the turbinado sugar on top and caramelize by placing under a broiler.

Yield: 4 servings

This dessert is featured at The Frog and The Redneck restaurant located in the historic Shockoe Slip area of Richmond. Shockoe was built in the 1730s as a trading post. The area was burned to the ground during the Civil War and rebuilt following the war. The historic warehouses and grain exchanges have been renovated and now house galleries, shops, and restaurants.

Fudge Sundae Bars

27 *Oreo cookies*
½ *stick butter, melted*
½ *gallon vanilla ice cream,*
softened
1 *cup chopped pecans*
½ *stick butter*
1 *(12 ounce) can evaporated*
milk
2 *cups confectioners' sugar*
⅔ *cup semi-sweet chocolate*
chips

- Chop cookies in a blender or food processor until they are fine crumbs. Add ½ stick melted butter. Mix well. Press mixture into a 9"x13" baking dish.
- Spread softened ice cream over cookie crumbs. Sprinkle pecans over the ice cream. Freeze while preparing sauce.
- Combine ½ stick butter, evaporated milk, confectioners' sugar, and chocolate chips in a large saucepan. Bring to a boil. Reduce heat to low and simmer for 10 minutes. Allow mixture to cool. Spread over ice cream.
- Freeze for several hours or until firmly set.

Yield: 12-15 servings
Ideal for a summer party!

Chocolate Almond Velvet

⅓ *cup chocolate syrup*
⅓ *cup sweetened condensed*
milk
¼ *teaspoon vanilla extract*
1 *cup heavy cream, whipped*
¼ *cup toasted slivered*
almonds

- Combine chocolate syrup, condensed milk, and vanilla. Chill well.
- Fold whipped cream into chocolate mixture.
- Spoon into sherbet dishes. Sprinkle with almonds.
- Freeze 3-4 hours or until firm.

Yield: 4 servings

To increase the volume of whipped cream, chill the bowl and beaters before whipping.

Excellent Cheesecake

1 cup graham cracker crumbs
4 tablespoons butter, melted
*3 (8 ounce) packages cream
  cheese, softened*
1 cup sugar
*3 large eggs, room
  temperature*
1 teaspoon vanilla extract
1/2 teaspoon almond extract
*1 1/2 cups sour cream, room
  temperature*

- Preheat oven to 350°.
- Lightly butter a 9-inch springform pan.
- Combine graham cracker crumbs and melted butter in a medium mixing bowl. Press mixture evenly onto the bottom of the pan.
- Beat cream cheese in a large bowl with an electric mixer until smooth. Beat in sugar and eggs. Add vanilla extract, almond extract, and sour cream. Combine well.
- Pour mixture onto the graham cracker crust.
- Bake for 45-50 minutes until cheese-cake is puffed and firm to touch. Remove from oven. Run knife around inside edge of cheesecake to loosen.
- Cool completely and chill for several hours or overnight before serving.

Yield: 8 servings

*Try adding crushed fruit toppings
such as pineapple or strawberries
for beautiful presentation and a
delicious alternative.*

Do not overbake!

Chocolate Marble Cheesecake

1²/₃ *cups chocolate cookie*
crumbs
¹/₃ *cup margarine, melted*
5 (8 ounce) packages cream
cheese, softened
1¹/₂ *cups sugar*
3 eggs
3 teaspoons vanilla extract
6 ounces semi-sweet chocolate
chips, melted

- Preheat oven to 350°.
- Combine chocolate cookie crumbs and margarine, mixing well. Press mixture into the bottom and slightly up the sides of a 9-inch springform pan.
- Bake for 5 minutes. Remove from oven and cool.
- Beat cream cheese with an electric mixer at high speed until fluffy. Add sugar gradually, mixing well. Add eggs one at a time, mixing well after each addition. Stir in vanilla extract.
- Divide mixture in half. Add melted chocolate to half of cream cheese mixture, stir to blend well.
- Pour half of plain mixture into chocolate crust; top with half of chocolate mixture. Repeat layers.
- Gently swirl batter with a knife to achieve marble effect.
- Bake for 40 minutes, then turn off the oven and open oven door. Leave cheesecake in cooling oven for 45 minutes. Remove from oven and let cool on a wire rack.
- Chill at least 8 hours or overnight before serving.

Yield: 10 servings

A substantial dessert; great for coffees!

Praline Cheesecake

1 cup graham cracker crumbs
3 tablespoons sugar
3 tablespoons margarine,
melted
3 (8 ounce) packages cream
cheese, softened
1¼ cups dark brown sugar
2 tablespoons all-purpose flour
3 eggs
1½ teaspoons vanilla extract
½ cup chopped pecans
Maple syrup for topping
Additional chopped pecans for
topping, approximately ⅛
cup

- Preheat oven to 350°.
- Mix graham cracker crumbs, sugar, and melted margarine; press into the bottom of a 9-inch springform pan.
- Bake for 10 minutes.
- Mix cream cheese, brown sugar, and flour with an electric mixer at medium speed until well blended. Add eggs one at a time, beating well after each addition. Add vanilla and nuts; mix well.
- Pour cream cheese mixture into crust.
- Bake 50-55 minutes.
- Cool and loosen from rim of pan. Chill in pan overnight.
- Remove from pan to serve. Brush the top of the cheesecake with real maple syrup and sprinkle with additional chopped pecans.

Yield: 10-12 servings

Surprise your family with this non-traditional Thanksgiving Day dessert!

Blue Ribbon Jam Cake

1 cup butter or margarine
2 scant cups sugar
3 eggs, beaten
4 cups sifted all-purpose flour
¼ cup cocoa powder
1 teaspoon salt
2 teaspoons baking powder
1 teaspoon baking soda
2 teaspoons cinnamon
2 teaspoons allspice
2 teaspoons nutmeg
1 teaspoon cloves
2 scant cups buttermilk
1 cup raisins
2 cups blackberry jam
1 cup pecans or walnuts

- Preheat oven to 350°.
- Cream butter and sugar. Add eggs.
- Sift dry ingredients with spices. Alternately add sifted dry ingredients with buttermilk.
- Add raisins, jam, and nuts; mix well.
- Pour into 3 greased and floured 9-inch cake pans.
- Bake for 30-35 minutes. Remove from oven and cool.
- Ice with Caramel Frosting.

Yield: 24 servings

Caramel Frosting

4 cups light brown sugar
1 cup butter
1 cup heavy cream
2 teaspoons vanilla

- Combine brown sugar, butter, and cream in a medium saucepan.
- Stir over medium heat until dissolved.
- Boil to soft ball stage (238° using a candy thermometer).
- Remove from heat and beat with electric mixer until cool. Add vanilla.
- Spread on cake.

Yield: 4 cups

An exquisite frosting! Excellent on other cakes as well.

To prevent a cake from sticking to its serving plate or doily, lightly dust the surface with confectioners' sugar.

Crème de Menthe Cake

1 cup sugar
2 sticks plus 6 tablespoons butter, softened, divided
4 eggs
1 cup all-purpose flour
½ teaspoon salt
1 (16 ounce) can chocolate syrup
1 teaspoon vanilla extract
2 cups confectioners' sugar
4 tablespoons green Crème de Menthe
1 (6 ounce) package semi-sweet chocolate chips

- Preheat oven to 350°.
- Cream sugar with 1 stick butter. Add eggs, flour, salt, chocolate syrup, and vanilla. Mix well.
- Pour mixture into a greased and floured 9"x13" baking dish.
- Bake for 25-30 minutes. Cool.
- Combine 2 cups confectioners' sugar, 1 stick butter, and Crème de Menthe. Stir until smooth. Spread over cooled cake.
- Melt chocolate chips and 6 table-spoons butter. Stir until smooth. Cool slightly and spread on top of Crème de Menthe layer.

Yield: 30 servings

Butter is a necessity for this recipe. Do not substitute margarine.

Chocolate Coffee Rum Cake

3 cups all-purpose flour
1½ teaspoons baking soda
¾ teaspoon salt
1 (12 ounce) package semi-sweet chocolate chips
3 sticks unsalted butter, cut into pieces
⅓ cup dark rum
2 cups strong brewed coffee
2¼ cups granulated sugar
3 large eggs, lightly beaten
1½ teaspoons vanilla extract
Confectioners' sugar for dusting

- Preheat oven to 300°.
- Grease and generously flour a 4½-inch deep (12 cup) Bundt pan.
- Combine flour, baking soda, and salt.
- In a double boiler, slowly melt chocolate and butter, stirring until smooth. Remove chocolate from heat and place in a large mixing bowl. Stir in rum, coffee, and granulated sugar.
- With an electric mixer, beat in flour mixture, ½ cup at a time, scraping down side of bowl, and beat in eggs and vanilla until batter is combined well.
- Pour batter into prepared pan.
- Bake cake in the middle of the oven until tester comes out clean, about 1 hour and 50 minutes.
- Let cake cool completely in pan on a rack, then turn it out onto a plate.
- Dust cake with confectioners' sugar and serve with halved strawberries, raspberries, or vanilla ice cream.

Yield: 12-16 servings

Can be made 3 days in advance. Wrap well and chill to keep even longer.

This is very, very moist! Absolutely fabulous!

Killer Chocolate Cake

½ cup butter, softened
2 cups light brown sugar
3 (1 ounce) squares
unsweetened baking
chocolate, melted
3 eggs
1½ teaspoons vanilla extract
2 teaspoons baking soda
½ teaspoon salt
2 cups cake flour
¾ cup sour cream
1 cup strong brewed coffee
⅓ cup Kahlúa
½ (4 ounce) jar raspberry
preserves

- Preheat oven to 350°.
- Cream butter and brown sugar. Add melted chocolate.
- Add eggs, one at a time, beating after each addition. Add vanilla, baking soda, and salt.
- Slowly add cake flour and sour cream alternately.
- Mix in coffee and Kahlúa.
- Pour into two 9-inch cake pans that have been sprayed with non-stick vegetable spray.
- Bake for 35-40 minutes. Remove from oven and let cool completely.
- Place 1 cake layer on a plate. Spread with raspberry preserves. Top with second layer. Frost cake with Mocha Icing.

Yield: 12 servings

Mocha Icing

½ cup butter, softened
1 egg
2 teaspoons cocoa powder
3 tablespoons strong brewed
coffee
½ tablespoon vanilla extract
1 (16 ounce) box
confectioners' sugar

- Cream butter. Add egg, cocoa, coffee, and vanilla.
- Gradually add sugar. Beat until fluffy.
- Ice cake.

Yield: 2 cups

Superior flavor! Serve with after-dinner coffee.

To prevent cake layers from sticking to the pan when dumping, place the pans on a wet towel as soon as the cake is removed from the oven.

Cream Cheese Pound Cake

3 cups sugar
3 sticks margarine
1 (8 ounce) package cream
cheese, softened
1 (3 ounce) package cream
cheese, softened
6 eggs
3 cups cake flour
2 teaspoons vanilla extract
1 teaspoon almond extract
1 teaspoon imitation butter
flavoring
1 teaspoon lemon juice
Confectioners' sugar

- Preheat oven to 325°.
- Grease and flour a 10-inch Bundt pan.
- Combine sugar, margarine, and cream cheese in a large bowl with an electric mixer.
- Blend in 2 eggs with 1 cup cake flour at a time until all eggs and flour are added.
- Add vanilla extract, almond extract, imitation butter flavoring, and lemon juice.
- Bake for 1 hour and 15 minutes or until toothpick comes out clean.
- Cool 15 minutes, then remove from pan.
- Cool completely and dust with confectioners' sugar.

Yield: 12-16 servings

Lemon Curd

4 eggs
Pinch salt
2 cups sugar
½ cup lemon juice
½ cup butter, softened
2 tablespoons grated lemon
peel

- Beat eggs in a large mixing bowl. Stir in salt.
- Add sugar, lemon juice, butter, and lemon peel. Combine well.
- Cook mixture in a double boiler over simmering water for 30 minutes or until thick and smooth, stirring occasionally.
- Cool and store in refrigerator until ready to serve.

Yield: 2 cups

To loosen cake layers that have been left in the pan too long, place the pan in a 350-degree oven for 2 minutes. Dump cake immediately after removing from the oven.

Most Moist Carrot Cake

2 cups sugar
4 eggs
1½ cups vegetable oil
2 cups all-purpose flour
2 teaspoons baking soda
2½ teaspoons cinnamon
2-3 carrots, grated
¾ cup crushed pineapple,
drained

- Preheat oven to 325°.
- Cream sugar and eggs. Add oil; mix well.
- Sift together flour, baking soda, and cinnamon. Add dry ingredients to batter.
- Fold in carrots and pineapple.
- Grease and flour three 9-inch cake pans. Pour batter into cake pans.
- Bake for 35 minutes. Cool completely before frosting with Easy Cream Cheese Icing.

Yield: 8-10 servings

Easy Cream Cheese Icing

1 (8 ounce) package cream
cheese, softened
⅓ cup butter, softened
1 (16 ounce) box
confectioners' sugar
2 teaspoons vanilla extract
½ cup nuts, optional

- Cream the cream cheese and butter. Add confectioners' sugar and vanilla; mix very well.
- Frost cake with icing. Decorate top and sides of cake with nuts, stir them into the icing, or omit them, as desired.

Yield: 2 cups
Your guests will love this!

Italian Coconut Cream Cake

2 cups granulated sugar
5 eggs, separated
½ cup butter
½ cup vegetable shortening
2 cups all-purpose flour
1 teaspoon baking soda
1 cup buttermilk
2 cups coconut
1 teaspoon vanilla extract
½ cup chopped pecans

- Preheat oven to 350°.
- Cream the sugar, egg yolks, butter, and shortening. Add flour, baking soda, buttermilk, coconut, vanilla, and pecans. Mix well.
- Beat the egg whites until stiff and fold into the batter.
- Grease and flour three 8-inch cake pans. Pour the batter into the cake pans.
- Bake for 30-35 minutes or until done. Remove from pans and cool completely.
- Frost with Buttery Cream Cheese Frosting.

Yield: 12 servings

A wonderfully rich, moist cake you'll make over and over again!

Buttery Cream Cheese Frosting

1 (8 ounce) package cream cheese, softened
6 tablespoons butter, softened
2 cups confectioners' sugar, sifted
1 teaspoon vanilla extract

- Combine all ingredients; beat well.
- Spread over cooled cake.

Yield: 2 cups

Easy Brownies

2 *(1 ounce) squares*
unsweetened baking
chocolate
1 *stick butter*
1 *cup sugar*
2 *eggs, beaten*
½ *cup all-purpose flour*
Pinch salt
1 *teaspoon vanilla*
½ *cup chopped pecans*

- Preheat oven to 325°.
- Melt chocolate and butter in a medium saucepan over low heat. Add sugar while still hot. Mix well and cool.
- Add beaten eggs, flour, salt, vanilla, and pecans. Mix well.
- Pour mixture into a greased 6½"x10" baking dish and bake for 25-30 minutes.

Yield: 1 dozen

Substitute ½ cup white chocolate chips for the pecans.

Katie Couric, anchorperson and journalist for NBC's Today Show, sent us this recipe. She is a native Virginian and graduate of the University of Virginia. Despite a demanding career based in New York City, she enjoys weekend retreats with her family at their home in Virginia.

Chocolate Mint Brownies

1 cup sugar
½ cup butter, softened
4 eggs
1 cup all-purpose flour
½ teaspoon salt
1 (16 ounce) can chocolate
   syrup
1 teaspoon vanilla extract
2 cups confectioners' sugar
½ cup butter, softened
4 tablespoons green Crème de
   Menthe
1 (6 ounce) package semi-
   sweet chocolate chips
6 tablespoons butter

- Preheat oven to 350°.
- Cream sugar and ½ cup butter. Add eggs, flour, salt, chocolate syrup, and vanilla.
- Pour batter into a greased and floured 9"x13" baking dish.
- Bake for 30 minutes. Cool completely.
- Combine confectioners' sugar, ½ cup butter, and Crème de Menthe. Stir until smooth. Spread on cooled cake. Refrigerate until topping is set.
- In a double boiler or in the microwave, melt chocolate chips and 6 tablespoons butter. Stir until smooth. Cool slightly and spread on cake. Let set in refrigerator.
- Cut into small squares to serve.

Yield: 3-4 dozen

One of the best from **Virginia Seasons.**

Melt-A-Ways

First layer

1 ounce unsweetened baking
   chocolate
½ cup butter or margarine
¼ cup sugar
1 egg, beaten
1 teaspoon vanilla extract
2 cups graham cracker
   crumbs
1 cup coconut
½ cup chopped pecans

- In a medium-sized saucepan, melt chocolate and butter over low heat. Stir in sugar until it is dissolved.
- Add beaten egg slowly and stir until well blended.
- Add remaining ingredients and mix well.
- Press mixture into 9-inch square glass pan. Refrigerate until well chilled.

Second layer

1¼ cups butter or margarine,
   softened
2 cups sifted confectioners'
   sugar
2 tablespoons heavy cream
1 teaspoon vanilla extract

- Beat all ingredients with an electric mixer at high speed for 10 minutes. The mixture will increase in volume and become very light and fluffy.
- Spread over first layer and refrigerate.

Third layer

2 ounces unsweetened baking
   chocolate
2½ tablespoons butter or
   margarine

- Melt chocolate and butter over very low heat, stirring constantly.
- Spread over the second layer. Refrigerate at least 30 minutes or until ready to serve.
- Cut into 1-inch squares using a knife that has been dipped in hot water.

Yield: 5-6 dozen

This is a triple-layer, refrigerated dessert that is delicious, very rich, and easy to make.

Oatmeal Fudge Bars

Fudge mixture

1 (12 ounce) package semi-
  sweet chocolate chips
3 tablespoons margarine
1 (14 ounce) can sweetened
  condensed milk
2 teaspoons vanilla extract

Cookie mixture

1 cup margarine
2 cups brown sugar
2 eggs
1 teaspoon vanilla extract
2½ cups all-purpose flour
1 teaspoon baking soda
1 teaspoon salt
3 cups old fashioned rolled
  oats
¼ cup chopped nuts

- In a small saucepan, melt chocolate chips and margarine in condensed milk over low heat. Add vanilla; set aside.

- Preheat oven to 350°.
- In a large mixing bowl, cream margarine and brown sugar. Add eggs and vanilla to creamed mixture, beat well.
- Add all remaining ingredients and mix until well blended.
- Press ⅔ of the cookie mixture in a 9"x13" baking dish or pan. Spread with fudge mixture. Sprinkle remaining ⅓ of cookie mixture over the fudge.
- Bake for 20-25 minutes.
- Cool completely. Cut into squares.

Yield: 3-4 dozen

• • •

Native Americans had inhabited the area that is now Arlington for over nine thousand years before Captain John Smith sailed up the Potomac River in 1608. The city is now Washington's closest suburb.

Peanut Butter Cup Bars

2 sticks butter

1 cup creamy-style peanut
butter

1³/₄ cups confectioners' sugar

2¹/₂ cups graham cracker
crumbs

1 (12 ounce) package semi-
sweet chocolate chips, melted

- In a medium saucepan, melt butter over low heat. Add peanut butter, confectioners' sugar, and graham cracker crumbs. Mix well.
- Spread in a 9"x13" baking dish or pan.
- Spread melted chocolate chips over graham cracker mixture.
- Refrigerate until hard.
- Let stand at room temperature for 20 minutes before cutting.

Yield: 3 dozen

Kids love these!

Rice Krispies Chocolate Peanut Butter Bars

³/₄ cup sugar

³/₄ cup light corn syrup

¹/₂ teaspoon salt

1 teaspoon vanilla extract

1 cup peanut butter

4¹/₂ cups Rice Krispies

8 ounces semi-sweet chocolate
chips

8 ounces butterscotch chips

2-3 tablespoons milk

- Bring sugar and corn syrup to a boil. Remove from heat and add salt, vanilla, and peanut butter. Mix well.
- Stir in Rice Krispies. Mix well.
- Grease hands and pack mixture into a greased 9"x13" baking dish or pan.
- Combine chocolate and butterscotch chips with a small amount of milk in a medium saucepan, stirring constantly until melted. Pour over Rice Krispies mixture. Let cool 20-30 minutes.
- Cut into bars.

Yield: 3 dozen

Kids can help make these!

Glazed Pecan Bars

Cake

¾ cup vegetable oil
¼ cup honey
1 cup sugar
1 egg
2 cups all-purpose flour
½ teaspoon salt
1 teaspoon baking soda
1 teaspoon cinnamon
1 cup chopped pecans

- Preheat oven to 325°.
- Combine all cake ingredients and mix well. Dough will be very stiff.
- Press dough into a 9"x13" baking dish or pan.
- Bake 25 minutes.

Glaze

1 cup sifted confectioners'
  sugar
1 teaspoon vanilla extract
1 tablespoon mayonnaise
1 tablespoon water
1 teaspoon almond or lemon
  extract, optional

- Combine all ingredients for glaze. Mix until smooth.
- Spread glaze while cake is still hot.
- Cool. Cut into 1½-inch squares.

Yield: 3 dozen

Great flavor for the fall season.

Virginia Fare

Nell's Lemon Coconut Squares

1½ cups all-purpose flour, sifted
½ cup light brown sugar
½ cup butter, melted
2 eggs
1 cup brown sugar
1½ cups coconut flakes
2 tablespoons all-purpose flour
½ teaspoon baking powder
½ teaspoon vanilla extract
½ teaspoon salt

- Preheat oven to 275°.
- Combine first 3 ingredients. Pat mixture into a greased 9"x13" baking dish or pan.
- Bake for 10 minutes.
- Combine remaining ingredients and spread on top of crust.
- Bake at 350° for 20 minutes.

Icing

½ (16 ounce) box confectioners' sugar
Juice of 1 lemon
½ teaspoon vanilla extract
½ teaspoon butter, melted
1 teaspoon milk (or more if needed to spread)
Pinch salt

- Combine all icing ingredients in a small bowl. Stir until smooth.
- Spread over lemon coconut cake while still warm.
- Cut into squares.

Yield: 1 dozen

Lime instead of lemon...equally delicious!

Butter Cookies

1 cup butter, softened
½ cup plus 1½ tablespoons sugar
1¾ cups all-purpose flour
1 teaspoon vanilla extract
Sugar for rolling

- Preheat oven to 300°.
- Cream butter and sugar. Add flour and vanilla. Stir until blended.
- Roll dough into balls at least ¾" in diameter. Roll in sugar and flatten with the bottom of a glass dipped in sugar each time.
- Bake for 17-20 minutes until edges are lightly browned.

Yield: 3 dozen

Perfect with sorbet, sherbet, or ice cream.

Low-Fat Chocolate Chip Cookies

2 sticks low-fat, no cholesterol margarine
2/3 cup sugar
1 1/3 cups brown sugar, firmly packed
1/2 cup egg substitute (equivalent to 2 eggs)
2 teaspoons vanilla extract
2 2/3 cups all-purpose flour
1/2 teaspoon sea salt
1 (12 ounce) package semi-sweet chocolate chips
1/2 cup chopped walnuts

- Preheat oven to 400°.
- Cream margarine, sugar, and brown sugar. Add eggs and vanilla; stir well.
- Combine flour and salt; add to creamed mixture.
- Stir in chocolate chips and nuts.
- Bake on an ungreased baking sheet for 6-8 minutes. Remove to a cooling rack.

Yield: 5-6 dozen

Lace Oatmeal Cookies

1 1/4 cups old-fashioned rolled oats
3/4 cup sugar
1 stick butter, softened
3 tablespoons all-purpose flour
1/4 teaspoon salt
1/2 teaspoon vanilla extract
1 egg
1/4 teaspoon baking powder

- Preheat oven to 300°.
- Combine all ingredients. Mix well.
- Cover baking sheet with foil, shiny side up.
- Drop cookie mixture by the teaspoonful onto the foil.
- Bake for 15 minutes. Let cool completely on foil. Place in the freezer if in a hurry. Peel off cookies.
- Store in an airtight container with wax paper between cookie layers to prevent cookies from sticking together.

Yield: 3 dozen

Do not make these sweet cookies on a humid day. They will get very sticky.

Ranger Cookies

1 cup vegetable shortening
1 cup sugar
1 cup brown sugar
2 eggs or equivalent amount
   of egg substitute
1 teaspoon vanilla extract
1 teaspoon almond extract
2 cups sifted all-purpose flour
1 teaspoon baking soda
1 teaspoon baking powder
2 cups old-fashioned rolled
   oats
2 cups crispy rice cereal
1 cup chopped nuts

- Preheat oven to 350°.
- Cream shortening and sugar. Add the remaining ingredients and mix well.
- Drop by the teaspoonful onto an ungreased baking sheet.
- Bake for 10 minutes.

Yield: 2 dozen

A good chewy cookie!

Chocolate Chip Macaroons

6 eggs
2¼ cups sugar
1 cup all-purpose flour
¾ teaspoon baking powder
⅜ teaspoon salt
1 teaspoon vanilla extract
3 tablespoons butter, melted
32 ounces coconut
1 (12 ounce) package chocolate
   chips

- Beat eggs and sugar for 5 minutes.
- Add dry ingredients to egg/sugar mixture; blend well. Add vanilla and butter.
- Stir in chocolate chips and coconut. Let stand in refrigerator for 20 minutes.
- Preheat oven to 375°
- Pack cookie dough into 1-inch balls.
- Bake for 10-12 minutes on a greased baking sheet or until bottoms are golden brown.

Yield: 6 dozen

Can be made without the chocolate chips for a delightful coconut cookie.

Make smaller for party fare! Don't forget to decrease the baking time.

A special treat from Incredible Edibles in Richmond, Virginia.

Chocolate Butter Pecan Toffee

1 cup butter
1 cup sugar
3 tablespoons water
3 tablespoons corn syrup
6 plain chocolate bars
¾ to 1 cup ground pecans,
walnuts, or almonds

- Combine butter, sugar, water, and corn syrup in a heavy skillet. Heat slowly until candy thermometer reads 300° (hard ball in cold water).
- Pour onto a greased flat baking sheet or marble slab to harden.
- Melt half the chocolate and spread over hardened mixture. Sprinkle with half the nuts. Allow chocolate to cool and harden. Turn toffee over and repeat.
- Break into pieces.

Yield: 12 candy pieces

Makes a great gift!

Peanut Butter Fudgies

2 cups sugar
1 stick butter or margarine
½ cup milk
4 tablespoons cocoa
2½ cups quick oats
½ cup chunky peanut butter
2 teaspoons vanilla extract

- Combine sugar, butter, milk, and cocoa in a medium saucepan. Bring to a full boil and let boil 1½ minutes. Timing is critical...do not overboil!
- Remove from heat and stir in oats, peanut butter, and vanilla.
- Drop by the tablespoonful on wax paper. Cool on glass or marble surface, if available.
- Store in an airtight container.

Yield: 5 dozen

• • •

Southside Virginia is a quiet land of tobacco and cotton farms, beautiful lakes for bass fishing and other outdoor recreation, and friendly residents. Anchored by Danville and Martinsville, the area is known for its thriving textile industry and for the production of fine furniture. Visitors to Danville enjoy viewing turn of the century mansions along Millionaire's Row.

Chocolate Peanut Butter Candy

*1 (16 ounce) box
confectioners' sugar*
½ cup butter
Dash salt
1 teaspoon vanilla extract
Milk
*Confectioners' sugar for
dusting*
Creamy peanut butter
*5-6 (1 ounce) squares semi-
sweet baking chocolate*
Paraffin

- Combine confectioners' sugar, butter, salt, and vanilla. Add enough milk to bind the ingredients into a ball. The candy must be dry enough to be rolled out.
- Dust a sheet of wax paper with confectioners' sugar.
- Roll out ⅓ of the candy onto the wax paper. Spread with a thin layer of peanut butter.
- Melt chocolate. Add 5 slivers of paraffin for every 3 squares of chocolate used. The paraffin is added to make the chocolate hard when it cools. Spread a thin layer of chocolate mixture over the layer of peanut butter.
- Roll lengthwise like a jelly roll and seal the ends.
- Spread a fresh sheet of wax paper on a baking sheet and transfer the roll. "Shape up" to round the roll. Spread chocolate mixture over roll. Repeat this process to make 2 more rolls using remaining candy.
- Refrigerate the rolls to harden. Once hard, turn the rolls over and cover the undersides with chocolate. Refrigerate to harden.
- Slice thinly.

Yield: 4 dozen candy pieces

A holiday tradition that makes a lovely gift.

Chocolate that has been exposed to air will begin to lighten in color. The chocolate is not stale and is still good for cooking.

Chocolate Spiders

1½ cups semi-sweet chocolate chips
1 (5 ounce) can chow mein noodles
1 cup salted peanuts

- Melt chocolate chips in a double boiler. Add noodles and peanuts; stir well.
- Drop mixture by the teaspoonful onto greased baking sheets.
- Refrigerate 8 hours or overnight.

Yield: 3 dozen

Use butterscotch chips instead of chocolate chips as a variation.

A fun Halloween treat that your children can make!

Kiddie Chow

1 (8 ounce) box Golden Graham cereal
1 (5 ounce) box golden raisins
1 (5 ounce) can mixed nuts and cashews
1 (12 ounce) bag semi-sweet chocolate chips
1 (12 ounce) jar creamy peanut butter
¼ cup butter
1 teaspoon vanilla
1 pound confectioners' sugar

- In a large bowl, mix together cereal, raisins, and nuts.
- Melt chocolate chips, peanut butter, butter, and vanilla over low heat or in the microwave.
- Cool slightly, then place melted mixture, cereal, raisins, and nuts in a large container with a lid or a small unscented garbage bag. Shake to mix.
- Add confectioners' sugar, shake to coat.
- Store in an airtight container.

Yield: 20-30 servings

Omit nuts and raisins if Kiddie Chow is for very young children.

Great for kids!

Recipe Contributors

The Cookbook Committee expresses its appreciation to League members and friends who gave unselfishly of their time and talents to make this book possible. We would like to thank the following people who contributed recipes to this book. We regret that many recipes could not be included due to duplication or lack of space. A special thanks to our families and friends for being so patient and supportive throughout the production of Virginia Fare.

Johanna Abbe	Cheryl Christoffers	Page Frischkorn
Willoughby Adams	Dwayne Clemmons	Barbara Fritzman
Jeannie Alcott	Carol Colby	Elizabeth Garber
Amelie Allen	Mary Helen Collins	Joy Garrett
Jody Allen	Tamlyn Comer	Kathy Gasperini
Terry Allen	Gale Cooper	Summa Gayle
Sarah Anders	Carroll Cottrell	Dorothy Gentil
Betsy Anderson	Nancy Cox	Gordon Gibson
Carolyn Anderson	Susan Creasey	Grace Ginn
Evelyn Anderson	Peggy Crowley	Melanie Gorsline
Tracy Anderson	Sondra Cruickshanks	Emmett Graybill
Ellen Armstrong	Beth Daly	Elizabeth Gualdoni
Sally Ayers	Eleanor Darden	Missy Gullquist
Lorna Aylor	Rosemary Davenport	Joan Haithcock
Candi Baird	Amy Davidson	Lee Hall
Kitty Bayliss	Marilyn Davis	Bettie Hallberg
Cynthia Bays	Meg Deacon	Lindsay Halsey
Melissa Beacom	Cammy Dennis	Janice Hamilton
Lori Beebe	Janet Dennis	Alice Hansbarger
Mary Alice Beeghly	Paula Dennison	Karen Harper
Candace Blades	Alice Dixon	Dorothy Hart
Frances Blanchard	Linda Douglas	Cathy Hatcher
Laura Bland	Katy Draper	Sally Hawthorne
Rebecca Blieden	Susan Dull	Brooke Hearn
Amy Bridge	Wesley Dunn	Alice Hickman
Frances Bridge	Julie Durkee	Cathy High
Elisabeth Brown	Audrey Eggleston	Kathy Hoover
Suzanne Brown	Morton Eggleston	Kenzie Hubard
Sally Buck	Darrin Ellis-May	Leilani Hughes
Anne Burnett	Jane Fain	Cora Huitt
Gail Burton	Mary Farley	Rita Hummell
Margie Cain	Pamela Farrar	Debbie Hungerford
Michele Calkins	Catherine Ferris	Paige Ingram
Cammy Carleton	Sharon Fitzgerald	Anne Watson Irvin
Ann Carpenter	Connie Fitzsimmons	Teri Iverson
Pam Cavedo	Sally Flinn	Lally Jennings
Nancy Cheely	Justin Frackelton	Elaine Johns

Recipe Contributors

Hendry Jones
Ruth Jimmie Jones
Kathy Keeler
Kathy Keller
Emily Kendig
Kate Kerns
Mike Kerr
Laurie Kershner
Tyler Kilpatrick
Mimi Kline
Katherine Knopf
Patti Koehler
Carol Kozak
Frances Kusterer
Sharon LaRoe
Laura Lee
Valerie Lemmie
R.J. Loderick
Terry Long
Kathy Louthan
Bebe Luck
Irene Luck
Margaret Lundvall
Alice Lynch
Meri Major
Gini Mallory
Lisa Manchester
Lyn Kyle Manson
Wendy Marino
Judy Marsella-
   Gonzales
Blair Martin
Hilary Martin
Pam Masters
Ann Mason
Betty Mauck
Louise Mauck
Andrea McDaniel
Shelly McDowell
Anne McVey
Harry Mercer
Margaret Mikel
Josephine Miller

Lu Moller
Patsy Morrissette
Nancy Moses
Gay Moss
Alice Mountjay
Anita Moynihan
Sally Moxley
Karen Murphy
Laura Murray
Brenda Myla
Kim O'Shea
Becca Ott
Mary Pace
Sherryll Anne Pace
Laura Partee
Ann Bray Pastore
Cindy Peaseley
Connie Pettit
Carrie Pickard
Karen Ponton
Julia Poppell
Lynne Porfiri
Sherry Porter
Mary Porterfield
Lesley Powell
Lila Putney
Jennifer Randolph
Katherine Randolph
Karen Rascoe
Sarah Reeves
Cindy Rhodes
Jacquelin Riggs
Cheryl Ann Rilee
Dorothea Robertson
Camilla Rohrbach
Carolyn Russ
Ruth Sams
Mary Kay Samp
Elizabeth Schaut
Diana Seaman
Janie Sellers
Connie Shannon
Lucy Shelley

Laura Shuford
Mary Shuford
Torrey Shuford
Anne Smith
Debbie Smith
Julie Smith
Sally Snead
Penny Southwick
Frances Spear
Susan Sperry
Julie Stepp
Parker Sternbergh
Anne Sullivan
Marty Tabor
Betty-Anne Teter
Kim Thomas
Stella Thompson
Janet Trivette
Cathy Tullidge
Connie Tuttle
Gayle Vest
Jeanie Vertner
Laura Lee Viergever
Jennifer von Coelln
Nancy von Coelln
Julie Vosmik
Kelly Waddell
Lucy Wallace
Sara Wallace
Melan Waugh
Julie Watson
Gwen Weeks
Cabell West
Sandra
   Westmoreland
Mary-Elliott Wheeler
Cynthia Whited
Lorie Williams
Kimberly Williamson
Laura Wilson
Weezie Wiltshire
Lucie Yudkin

Index

Index

Index

Index

Virginia Fare
Junior League of Richmond
205 West Franklin Street
Richmond, Virginia 23220
(804) 782-1022

Please send _____ copies of **Virginia Fare** @ $19.95 each _____
Postage and handling @ $ 4.00 each _____
Virginia residents add sales tax @ $ .90 each _____
TOTAL _____

Name _____

Address _____

City _____ State _____ Zip _____

Make checks payable to **JLR Cookbooks**

Virginia Fare
Junior League of Richmond
205 West Franklin Street
Richmond, Virginia 23220
(804) 782-1022

Please send _____ copies of **Virginia Fare** @ $19.95 each _____
Postage and handling @ $ 4.00 each _____
Virginia residents add sales tax @ $ .90 each _____
TOTAL _____

Name _____

Address _____

City _____ State _____ Zip _____

Make checks payable to **JLR Cookbooks**

Virginia Fare
Junior League of Richmond
205 West Franklin Street
Richmond, Virginia 23220
(804) 782-1022

Please send _____ copies of **Virginia Fare** @ $19.95 each _____
Postage and handling @ $ 4.00 each _____
Virginia residents add sales tax @ $ .90 each _____
TOTAL _____

Name _____

Address _____

City _____ State _____ Zip _____

Make checks payable to **JLR Cookbooks**